Scribbles of A Struggling Handmaid

CATHOLIC POETRY for CONVERSION

THOMAS V. YANOTI MTS

TABLE OF CONTENTS:

FOR THOSE WHO HAVE MOST EXEMPLIFIED OUR LORD'S UNCONDITIONAL LOVE IN MY LIFE-MARIA, MARISSA, MARTY, AND JUAN-I DEDICATE THIS BOOK. +

"LIFE IS TO LIVE AND LIFE IS TO GIVE AND TALENTS ARE TO USE FOR GOOD IF YOU CHOOSE. DO NOT PRAY FOR EASY LIVES. PRAY TO BE STRONGER. DO NOT PRAY FOR TASKS EQUAL TO YOUR POWERS. PRAY FOR POWERS EQUAL TO YOUR TASKS-THEN THE DOING OF YOUR WORK SHALL BE NO MIRACLE BUT YOU SHALL BE A MIRACLE. EVERY DAY YOU SHALL WONDER AT YOURSELF…AT THE RICHNESS OF LIFE WHICH HAS COME TO YOU BY THE GRACE OF GOD. BUT EVERYONE NEEDS SOMEONE-KNOWING THAT SOMEWHERE SOMEONE IS THINKING OF YOU. +
FATHER SOLANUS CASEY O.F.M. CAP

"COME TO ME, ALL WHO LABOR AND ARE HEAVY LADEN, AND I WILL GIVE YOU REST. TAKE MY YOKE UPON YOU, AND LEARN FROM ME; FOR I AM GENTLE AND LOWLY IN HEART, AND YOU WILL FIND REST FOR YOUR SOULS. FOR MY YOKE IS EASY, AND MY BURDEN IS LIGHT."
MATTHEW 11; 28-30
THE HOLY BIBLE
REVISED STANDARD VERSION/SECOND CATHOLIC EDITION
IGNATIUS PRESS

GOD THE FATHER

"JESUS REVEALED THAT GOD IS FATHER IN AN UNHEARD OF SENSE: HE IS FATHER NOT ONLY IN BEING CREATOR; HE IS ETERNALLY FATHER IN RELATION TO HIS ONLY SON, WHO IS ETERNALLY SON ONLY IN RELATION TO HIS FATHER: 'NO ONE KNOWS THE SON EXCEPT THE FATHER, AND NO ONE KNOWS THE FATHER EXCEPT THE SON AND ANY ONE TO WHOM THE SON CHOOSES TO REVEAL HIM.'"
CATECHISM OF THE CATHOLIC CHURCH 240
MATTHEW 11:27

"TOO LATE HAVE I LOVED YOU, O BEAUTY SO ANCIENT AND SO NEW."
ST AUGUSTINE OF HIPPO

+THE LORD IS ALMIGHTY,
OMNIPOTENT, IN SILENCE AND IN ACTION.

LIFE, AND LIFE'S END, FLOW FROM HIS HAND-
IN JUSTICE AND MERCY, MYSTERY AND SURPRISE.

ONLY IN REVELATION, FAITH, AND REASON
CAN ONE PIERCE HIS CLOUD, DIMLY.

YET, THE PURE OF HEART
EXPERIENCES HIS LOVE…
ABUNDANTLY. +

+THE POOR MAN'S PATER NOSTER

HOLY FATHER, HEAVENLY HOPE,
REIGN SUPREME IN MY LIFE,
TRANSFORM THIS DUST INTO CHRIST,
NOURISH ME DAILY IN YOUR BELOVED SON,
TREAT ME NOT AS I DESERVE,
IN MERCY MAKE MERCY OF ME,
GRACE ME TO CONQUER THE TEMPTER,
SAVE ME FROM SIN,
FOR YOU ARE MY KING,
YOU ARE MY GLORY,
AND YOU ARE MY POWER,
IN FAITH AND HOPE AND LOVE,
FOUND ESPECIALLY IN THE PRECIOUS BODY AND BLOOD
OF JESUS CHRIST OUR LORD. +

+THE SMALL AND RELUCTANT JONAH IN ME
ACCEPTS THE PROMPTINGS OF THE HOLY SPIRIT OF GOD
AND TRAVERSES THE GREAT AND ARID LAND OF MY SOUL,
PROCLAIMING THE IMPENDING JUDGMENT OF THE LORD,
AND THE SUITABLE TIME FOR REPENTANCE-
BEING THESE FORTY DAYS.

AND GREAT AND SMALL,
FROM THE KING OF MY MIND
AND THE QUEEN OF MY WILL
DOWN TO THE PEASANTS OF MY LITTLE TOES,
I PROCLAIM A FAST
FOR BOTH MAN AND BEAST
IN MY SPIRIT AND MY FLESH,
A RENUNCIATION OF VICE
IN MY PRAYER AND MY ALMSGIVING,
PLACING ALL MY HOPE
IN THE ABUNDANT MERCY
OF A JUST AND LOVING FATHER. +

+PRAISE BE TO GOD FOR EVERY PRAYER HEARD!
PRAISE BE TO GOD FOR EVERY YES, AND EVERY NO,
IN PERFECT TIME!
PRAISE BE TO GOD FOR EVERY MASS IN THE ANGEL'S SIGHT.
PRAISE BE TO GOD FOR EVERY EUCHARIST IN THE SAINTS DELIGHT.
THANKSGIVING FOR DIVINE MERCY!
THANKSGIVING FOR YOUR BELOVED SON!
ALL PRAYER SEEKING GRACE IS DELIVERED IN STRENGTH. ALLELUIA!

ATTACKED FROM EVERY SIDE, PINNED IN BECAUSE OF FAITH,
MY HOPE ABOUNDS AS I CONTINUE TO FLOURISH IN YOUR
UNCONQUERABLE LOVE.
FOR YOUR MIGHTY ARMS, STRETCHED OUT ON THE CROSS OF YOUR
BELOVED SON, ARE STRONG ENOUGH TO OVERCOME ALL EVIL.
I, THEREFORE, PLACE MY TRUST IN THE FATHER OF COMPASSION, IN
THE SUFFERING OF HIS SON, IN THE SPIRIT OF HIS RISEN LOVE. +

+ASK...
LOVE WILL DELIVER.
SEARCH...
TRUTH WILL SELF-REVEAL.
KNOCK...
AND *THE WAY* WILL OPEN.

FOR FRIENDS
-EVEN FOES-
GIVE UPON PERSISTENT REQUEST.
HOW MUCH MORE IS THE CHARITY OF GOD!

THIS IS WHY-IN ASKING,
SEARCHING,
AND KNOCKING-
WE MUST LOVE OUR NEIGHBOR AS OURSELF,
MOTIVATED SOLELY AND PURELY
FOR THE LOVE OF GOD-
FOR WE PRAY TO THE CREATOR AND THE REDEEMOR OF ALL,
HE WHO IS UNCONDITIONAL AND EVERLASTING LOVE. +

+TO THE DISMAY OF MANY WORLDLY JUDGES,
THE EVIL MAN DOES NOT PERISH.
FOR THE EVIL MAN IS LOVED BY GOD,
NOT FOR HIS EVIL, BUT FOR THE GOOD GOD DESIRES FOR HIS SOUL.
HIS SENTENCE OF DEATH IS STAYED FOR A DAY
IN THE DIVINE AND MERCIFUL PATIENCE OF GOD.
LIKEWISE,
TO THE DISMAY OF PIOUS AND PRUDISH PERFECTIONISTS,
THE GOOD MAN PERISHES IN MORTAL SIN.
FOR SIN, MORTAL SIN, IS FREELY CHOSEN,
AND GOD LOVES MAN TOO MUCH
TO DISRESPECT HIS FREEDOM..
BUT HIS SENTENCE OF DEATH, SELF IMPOSED,
CARRIES NO IMMUNITY TO THE REDEEMING LOVE OF GOD-
IN PERSISTENT, DETERMINED, AND DIVINELY GRACED REPENTANCE
UNTO RECONCILIATION AND ETERNAL LIFE. +

+GROWTH IS FOUND IN NEARNESS TO GOD.
NEARNESS TO GOD IS FOUND IN THE SPIRIT OF HIS LOVE.
THIS LOVE IS THE LOVE SHARED BETWEEN FATHER AND SON.

THE FATHER LOVES ALL MANKIND IN THE WORD OF HIS SON.
THE WORD, HIS SON, ETERNAL MERCY INCARNATE,
CAME DOWN FROM HEAVEN TO SUFFER AND DIE AS MAN,
SO THAT MAN MAY RISE IN GOD.

RISEN IN GOD,
MAN RECEIVES GOD
AND IS BROUGHT TO GOD
IN THE PERPETUAL SACRIFICE OF THE SAVIOR OF MAN-
IN THE BREAD AND WINE,
TURNED BODY AND BLOOD,
IN THE SPIRIT OF THE LOVE
BETWEEN GOD THE FATHER
AND GOD, THE SON OF MAN. +

+AS FAR BACK AS I CAN *SEE*,
IN THE FAITH OF MY FAMILIES *TREE*,
THE DOUBT AND DESPAIR OF MY FATHERS,   RHYME
ARE THE SAME TROUBLES BESETTING *ME*!
WITH GOLD AND FIRE AND PRIDE AND *ZEAL*,
MY FATHERS WORSHIPPED A BEAST *UNREAL*.
IN THE SMOKE AND DELIRIUM OF THE PAGANS PRANCING WILD,
MY FATHERS FORGOT *THE FATHER*,
AND CRUCIFIED THE GOLDEN CHILD!
REMEMBERING NOT THE EXODUS AND THE CROSS,
THEY FELL IN A DEMONS TRANCE, AND A FOG OF SINFUL DROSS.
NOW I STAND REDEEMED IN BLOOD.
YET, STILL I SIN, FALLEN IN MUD.
OH PRAY FOR ME FOREGONE FATHERS,
FROM THE FIRES OF PURGATIVE LOVE,
HELP ME REMEMBER THE GLORY OF MY SAVIOR,
HELP ME REJOIN MY FAMILY ABOVE. +

+MY SHEPHERD IS FOREVER MY LORD.

MY SOUL AND MY SPIRIT ARE IN HIS GOOD HANDS.
I AM EVER VIGILANT IN FAITH AND IN HOPE OF HIS LOVE.

FOR HIS GLORY AND MY SALVATION,
HE LEADS ME ON THE SANCTIFIED WAY.

IN DARKNESS HE GUIDES ME
BY PURGATIVE FIRE!

IN BREAD AND WINE HE FEEDS ME.
IN OIL AND SPIRIT HE ANOINTS ME.
IN BLESSED PRAYER AND HOLY SACRAMENT,
I AM PART OF THE BODY OF HIS SON,
THE SPIRIT FILLED BODY WHICH WILL NEVER DIE.

AND FOR THIS,
I OFFER HIM PRAISE AND THANKSGIVING. +

+THROUGH THE MAN FROM UR,
CAME GOD'S PROMISE OF ETERNAL FIDELITY.
THROUGH FIRE IN HALVED HEIFER, HALVED GOAT, HALVED RAM,
TURTLE DOVE AND PIDGEON,
GOD SACRAMENTALLY SET
HIS FAMILY COVENANTWITH HIS PEOPLE FOREVER.

THROUGH ABRAHAM,
GOD REVEALED HIMSELF AS THE FAITHFUL GOD
OF LOVING COVENANT.

AND NOW AND FOREVER MORE,
HE REVEALS THE PROMISED LAND
FOR THOSE WHO REALIZE IN FAITH
THE SACRAMENT OF FIRE IN THE LAMB OF GOD-
THE LAMB WHO FULFILLS GOD'S PROMISE
IN THE NEW AND ETERNAL COVENANT OF LOVE. +

+IN THE SODOM AND GOMORRAH OF OUR VICE,
GOD SPEAKS THE CLEAR MESSAGE
OF REPENTANCE AND CONVERSION.

REND OUR FILTHY GARMENTS, WE MUST!

DESTROY OUR HAUGHTINESS,
OUR HARDNESS OF HEART,
IN MERCY WE PRAY!

TURN TO GOODNESS,
TO JUSTICE,
TO CHARITY,
IN THE POOR AND THE WEAK AND THE OUTCAST;
TURN TO THE GOOD,
BE REFORMED IN GOODNESS,
FOR GOODNESS ALONE
SHALL LAST FOREVER IN THE PRESENCE OF GOD.

FOR THE LIFE OF GOD
IS THE EVERLASTING TASTE OF HIS SWEETNESS...
AND IN TURNING FROM GOD,
THE BITTERNESS OF DEATH
SHALL ENSLAVE US IN UNENDING SORROW. +

+THE WINDS OF CHANGE-
TURBULANT AND UNCERTAIN.

THE QUAKING OF DISASTER-
GUT WRENCHING AND SORROWFUL.

THE FIRE OF PURGATION-
LONELY, AGONIZING, AND DRY.

THE GENTLE BREEZE OF THE *FATHER'S* MERCY-
FAITH FILLED, HOPE FORTIFYING, AND LOVE STRENGTHENING. +

+WHAT SHALL I GRASP?
TO FAITH AND HOPE IN WHAT SEEMS TO BE AN INVISIBLE GOD?

OR SHOULD I GRASP THE TOOLS AND TOYS AND TITLES AND
TITILATIONS WHICH I CAN KNOCK LIKE WOOD?

OH, FAITH AND HOPE ARE SO PRECIOUS,
YET THEY CANNOT BE ACHIEVED!

THE TEMPORAL TANGIBLES TICKLE MY FANCY FOR A TIME,
BUT NEVER FULFILL THE GNAWING ANXIETY IN ME.

THE INVISIBLE, IF I JUST LET GO,
GIVES ME A DEEP, FULL, REFRESHING PEACE AND JOY
THAT REVEALS TRUTH AND LIFE FOR ME.

THE VISIBLE FADES, OR FALLS APART.
THE INVISIBLE NEVER CHANGES!
THE VISIBILE STRUGGLES TO LOVE ME.
THE INVISIBLE CLAIMS ME AS HIS OWN, HIS BELOVED!
THE VISIBLE ENSNARES ME AND WOUNDS ME.

THE INVISIBLE FORGIVES ME,
GRACES ME WITH FAITH AND HOPE AND LOVE!
I SHALL GRASP NEITHER!
FOR THE INVISIBLE GRASPS ME! +

+**THE** EYE OF THE FATHER IS ON THE MAN OF FAITH,
THE WOMAN OF HOPE; FAITH AND HOPE IN GOD ALONE.
FOR GOD'S EYE SEARCHES HEARTS AND MINDS AND SOULS
TO FIND MAN'S PASSION AND DRIVING FORCE.
FOR GOD SEEKS TO INFUSE ALL MEN
WITH FAITH, HOPE, AND CHARITY.
YET, ONLY THE MAN AND WOMAN WHO FEAR THE LORD
AND RELY ON HIS BREAD FOR LIFE
CAN TRULY CRY: "ABBA, FATHER,"
AND IN DOING SO, RECEIVE HIS LIFE IN SANCTIFYING GRACE. +

+REVELATION
DEPICTS THE ACTS OF GOD.

THESE DIVINE INTRUSIONS
TRANSCEND
PURELY PHILOSOPHICAL, METHODOLIGICAL, AND PRAGMATIC
SCHEMES.
IN ORDER FOR MAN TO COMPREHEND GOD
-OBLIQUELY-
GOD SPEAKS TO MAN
TRUTHFULLY
ARTISTICALLY
POETICALLY
ROMANTICALLY
PLAINLY
-AND YES-
PHILOSOPHICALLY
PRAGMATICALLY
AND THEOLOGICALLY.
BUT MOST OF ALL LOVINGLY. +

+GOD SPEAKS THROUGH GRACE, SILENCE, DISTURBANCE, AND PAIN.
WE CANNOT CHOOSE WHICH AVENUE HE PURSUES.
WE CAN ONLY CHOOSE TO LISTEN, OR TO TURN AWAY. +

+GOD IS LOVE-MAN HATES.
GOD IS LOVE-MAN TIRES.
GOD IS LOVE-MAN IS DISTRACTED.
GOD IS LOVE-MAN SINS.
GOD IS LOVE-MAN IS CONFUSED.
GOD IS LOVE-MAN IS FORGETFUL.
GOD IS LOVE-MAN IS FICKLE.
GOD IS LOVE-MAN IS MANIPULATIVE.
GOD IS LOVE-MAN IS NEEDY.
GOD IS LOVE-MAN NEEDS LOVE.
GOD IS LOVE, IN GOD MAN BECOMES LOVE. +

+MY PRAYER IS BUT A SELFISH MOAN,
A BEGRUDGING GROAN, THE CRY OF A BABY FOR MILK.

FORTUNATELY,
YOU ARE A LOVING FATHER,
NEVER HOLDING MY LACK OF MATURITY AGAINST ME.

RATHER, EVERY CRY IS ANSWERED WITH WHAT I TRULY NEED.

AND IN THE PROCESS,
MY TEARS AND FEARS
ARE EDUCATED IN THE SCHOOL OF TRUE,
FAITHFUL,
AND UNCOMPROMISING PROVIDENTIAL LOVE. +

+TRULY GRACED
IS THE GRACED SAINT,
PERFECTED FOR GOD'S PURPOSE,
IN GOD'S PROVIDENTIAL WILL.

YET EQUALLY GRACED
IS THE STRUGGLING PILGRIM,
PERFECTED IN FAILURE AND HUMILIATION,
REWARDED IN MEEKNESS AND WISDOM,
FOR GOD'S PURPOSE,
IN GOD'S BENEVOLENT WILL.

FOR SUFFERING AND EVIL
ARE BUT CLOWNS IN THE CIRCUS OF THE DEVIL-
INSTANCES OF GRACE AND MERCY,
WHERE GOD OVERCOMES THE FOOL,
RECREATING MAN AND WOMAN
IN THE ETERNAL WISDOM OF LOVE. +

+HUSH! CENTER YOURSELF-CEASE YOUR MOVEMENT-
BREATHE, FOCUS, REMEMBER...
"...EVERYTHING IS POSSIBLE WITH GOD." +

+JUSTIFICATION IS NEVER WON
 IN GOOD DEEDS.

FOR GOOD DEEDS MAY FLOW FROM A HEART
FULL OF INSECURITY AND FEAR.

JUSTIFICATION
IS ALWAYS WON
IN HUMBLE SELF REFLECTION.

JUSTIFICATION
IS GRACED REPENTANCE...
AND THE GIFT OF QUICKNESS,
WHICH SPURS THE SOUL
-IN FAITH-
TO SEEK THE ONLY SOURCE OF LIFE
IN MERCY HIMSELF,
GOD, THE FATHER ALMIGHTY. +

+WHAT DO I TRULY OWN?
WHAT, IN DEATH, CAN MY SOUL GRASP?
IN THE GROUND,
AFTER THE WORMS,
IN THE PURGATIVE FIRE,
WHAT WILL I TRULY OWN?

I SENSE THE NAKEDNESS OF MY SPIRIT ESSENCE,
THE VULNERABILITY OF MY SOUL,
THE REALITY OF MY BEING,
WHO I TRULY AM IN MY CHOICES
-*A SINNER*-
IN THE TRANSCENDENT SIGHT OF THE ALMIGHTY GOD.

MAY I CARRY WITH ME
ONLY FAITH AND HOPE
IN THE ABUNDANT LOVING MERCY OF THE LORD. +

+EXILE
IS A TERRIBLE THING!
LIBERATION
IS THE THOUGHT WHICH FUELS HOPE.
BUT BABYLON
NEEDS CHARISMATIC CONVERSION,
FOUND IN EVANGELIZATION…
THE EVANGELIZATION OF LIVING FAITH!

AND EXODUS
IS A WONDERFUL THING!
BUT THE REMNANTOF ISRAEL
-RETURNING IN RANK-
SWOLLEN
WITH NEW CONVERTS,
THIS IS THE LORD'S DESIRE! +

+GOD IS ALWAYS WORKING
IN THE IN-BETWEENS OF OUR LIFE.
IN BETWEEN
TRANSGRESSIONS AGAINST US AND FORGIVENESS GIVEN,
IN BETWEEN TEMPTATION AND A PRAYER FOR STRENGTH,
IN BETWEEN POTENTIAL DISCORD AND AN ACT OF CHARITY,
IN BETWEEN THE BEATEN MAN AND THE PASSING SAMARITAN,
IN BETWEEN THE GARDEN TORMENT AND THE FREELY CHOSEN YES,
IN BETWEEN THE REPENTANT AND MOCKING THIEF,
IN BETWEEN GOOD FRIDAY AND EASTER SUNDAY.

AND ALWAYS IN BETWEEN OUR LAST BREATH
AND THE MYSTERY OF WHAT IS TO COME!
FOR THIS IS THE IN BETWEEN OF GRACED AND MERCIFUL LOVE. +

+I OWN NOTHING AND GOD OWNS ME.
MY INVENTIONS ARE FRIVILOUS. ALL IS *HIS* HANDIWORK-EX NIHILO.
THE PRESENCE OF GOD IS NOT MY PRIVILEDGE, BUT HIS GIFT!
FOR NO MAN, NO MATTER HIS EFFORTOR HIS STRENGTH EARNS GOD.
FOR STRENGTH IS IN *ONE!* AND THE MEN *HE* STRENGTHENS, MANY! +

+TO FIND *THE WAY* TO HEAVEN
IS TO PERCEIVE REPENTANCE AS A GIFT
FROM THE FATHER IN HEAVEN.

TO REST SECURELY IN CHRIST,
IS BUT TO SEEK HIM EARNESTLY.

TO DISCOVER DISCIPLESHIP
IS TO BE LED BY THE SPIRIT,
STEP BY STEP BY STEP.

TO FIND ONES PURPOSE
IS TO SEEK FOR LIFE,
WORK FOR SALVATION,
AND LIVE FOR RESURRECTION.

FOR THE ALMIGHTY FATHER
IS FOUND IN THE LOVE OF THE SON,
THROUGH THE GRACE AND THE MERCY
AND THE SUMMONS OF THE HOLY SPIRIT,
IN THE CHURCH FOR THE WORLD-TODAY. +

+HEAVEN WILL BE SPENT PLUMBING THE DEPTHS
AND SOARING THE HEIGHTS
AND MEASURING THE BREADTH
OF GOD'S IMMEASURABLE LOVE.

LIKE CHILDREN JOYFULLY WRESTLING WITH THEIR ABBA,
WE WILL TACKLE, TICKLE, TUG, AND GIGGLE
WITH MYSTERY UPON MYSTERY REVEALED.

ALL THAT IS GOOD IN GOD
WILL BE OUR POOL
WHERE WE WILL SWIM
IN THE INTIMACY AND THE KNOWLEDGE
OF LOVE UNENDING. +

+ARMAGEDDON,
END OF DAYS,
THE APOCALYPSE,
TALES OF TERROR AND HARBINGERS OF FEAR;
YET, WE SHALL WALK IN COURAGE,
IN THE FACE OF FEAR AND UNCERTAINTY,
IN FAITH AND IN HOPE
OF LOVE'S CERTAIN VICTORY
IN THE PASSION, DEATH, AND RESURRECTION OF CHRIST JESUS.

AS THE WORLD PASSES AWAY,
NARY A CITIZEN OF THE NEW JERUSALEM SHALL PERISH!

FOR ALL UNHOLY WARS,
ALL MALISCIOUS KINGDOMS,
ALL VAIN PRINCIPALITIES,
ALL EVIL POWERS,
SHALL FALL TO THE SPIRIT OF LOVE,
LOVE WHICH RESIDES IN THE HEART OF THE GREAT *I AM*,
THE ALMIGHTY WARRIOR OF LOVE!   +

+FEAR NOT THE HANDS OF THE EXECUTIONER!
FOR NO MAN HAS CREATED THE PROCESS OF BIRTH.
AT BEST, MAN PARTICIPATES-AT WORST, HE MANIPULATES.

FEAR NOT THE HANDS OF THE EXECUTIONER!
FOR NO MAN HAS FULLY GRASPED THE REALITY OF DEATH.
AT BEST MAN RESPECTS IT-AT WORST, HE SUPPLIES ITS MEANS.

FEAR NOT THE HANDS OF THE EXECUTIONER!
FOR NO MAN HAS CONQUERED DEATH BY HIS OWN WILL.
AT BEST, HE BELIEVES, AND IS RISEN!
AT WORST, HE DESPAIRS,
AND CHOOSES ETERNAL SOLITUDE,
SEPARATE FROM THE FATHER OF ALL LIFE! +

+GREATNESS IS GOD!
POWER IS HIS LOVE.
SPLENDOUR IS HIS COMPASSION!
LENGTH OF DAYS IS THE GIFT OF HIS SON!
GLORY IS FOUND IN HIS SPIRIT ALONE!

HEAVEN AND EARTH
AND ALL IN BETWEEN
ARE HIS,
FOR HIS PURPOSE,
HIS MERCY,
HIS LOVE.

SOVERIEGN KING,
ALPHA AND OMEGA,
CREATOR,
REDEEMER,
ALL IN ALL. +

+THE GOD OF ABRAHAM, ISAAC, AND JACOB
IS THE GOD OF THE DECEASED, THE EARTHLY PILGRIM,
AND THE YET TO BE BORN.

HE IS THE GOD OF THE PAST, THE PRESENT, AND THE FUTURE.
HE IS THE GOD OF FORGIVENESS, OF HOPE, AND OF RESURRECTION.
HE IS THE GOD OF CREATION, REDEMPTION, AND ETERNAL LIFE.
HE IS THE GOD OF OUR LIFE, OUR DEATH, AND OUR JUDGMENT.
HE IS JUSTICE AND JUDGMENTFOR THOSE HELLBENT IN DEFIENCE.
BUT HE IS MERCY,
SWEET MERCY,
IN TRUE REPENTANCE,
-FOR THOSE WHO TRULY DESIRE LIFE-
WHICH COMES FROM HIS OWN BLESSED GRACE,
FLOWING FROM THE INFINITE FONT OF MERCY,
IN THE PRECIOUS BLOOD COMING FROM THE SIDE OF HIS SON
IN HIS UNCONDITIONAL LOVE FOR ALL. +

+GOD OF MY FATHER,
AND OF MY FATHER'S FATHER,
BY MY FATHER IN LIEU OF YOUR SON'S WORTHY PASSION,
WHICH GRACES REPENTANCE IN ME.

OH GLORIOUS FATHER IN HEAVEN,
MAY YOUR SPIRIT AND THE BODY AND BLOOD OF YOUR SON,
COARSING THROUGH MY VEINS,
LEAD ME TO HOLINESS, SOLELY, FOR THE GLORY OF YOUR NAME.

YOUR KINGDOM, OUR LIVES!
YOUR THRONE, OUR HEARTS!
UNFATHOMABLE HOLINESS,
REVEALED BY THE FACE OF YOUR MERCY,
FORGIVE ME OF MY POVERTY,
INSTILL IN ME YOUR RICHES,
AND BLESS ME
WITH A SMALL PART
OF THE MESSIANIC SPIRIT AND THE BEATIFIC LIFE. +

+AS CREATURE, I BLESS THE CREATOR!
AS FINITE, I BLESS THE INFINITE!
UNDER ANGELS PROTECTION, I BLESS THE PROTECTOR!
IN HOPE OF HEAVEN, I BLESS THE HOLY ONE!
IN MYSTERY, I BLESS THE ALL KNOWING!
IN FAITH AND WEAKNESS, I BLESS THE ALMIGHTY!
IN THANKSGIVING AND PRAISE, I BLESS HE WHO IS LOVE!

ENJOY THE CATHEDRAL,
THE GOLD, SILVER, AND FINELY HEWN STONE.
BUT NEVER FORGET *THE ONE* YOU COME TO WORSHIP.
FOR A DAY WILL COME WHEN THE CATHEDRAL WILL BE NO MORE.

BUT THE TEMPLE OF THE LORD,
-THE BODY OF HIS SON IN THE SPIRIT OF HIS LOVE-
THIS IS THE ETERNAL GLORY OF GOD,
THE SAINTS *MARCHED* HOME IN RESURRECTION AND LIFE. +

+WHAT I STRUGGLE WITH IS MUCH STRONGER THAN ME.
BUT IN ALL THE FORCES DESPERATE TO DO ME HARM,
ALL KNEEL IN FEAR IN THE AWESOME PRESENCE OF GOD.

FOR EVERYTHING DESTRUCTIVE,
PREDATOR IN ONE SEASON,
IS PREY IN THE NEXT.

FOR ALL LASTING POWER PRESIDES IN GOD!

AND ALL POWER ABUSED
APART FROM CHARITY
DISSIPATES AND DISAPPEARS AS EMPTINESS,
REPLACED IN THE FULLNESS OF ETERNAL REALITY
WHICH IS THE LOVE OF THE ALMIGHTY FATHER
FOR HIS BELOVED SON
IN THE SPIRIT WHICH CONQUERS ALL EVIL. +

+SEED OF ADAM, FRUIT OF EVE,
PRAISE THE LORD!

SONS AND DAUGHTERS OF ABRAHAM, ISAAC AND JACOB,
PRAISE THE LORD!

PROPHETS, PRIESTS, AND KINGS IN CHRIST,
PRAISE THE LORD!

APOSTLES AND DISCIPLES OF JESUS,
PRAISE THE LORD!

SAINTS, AND SINNERS REPENTANT,
PRAISE THE LORD!

ARDENT BELEIVERS AND THOSE OF FIRST SPARK,
PRAISE THE LORD!

PRAISE THE LORD OF LOVE AND LIFE! +

+YOUR *WAY* IS A FOREIGN ROAD,
YOUR PATHS PAIN AND SUFFERING.
CORNER ME IN TRUTH, CHASTISE ME, SAVE ME-
DESPITE MY OWN DESIRE!

FOR YOUR GOODNESS DRIVES ME TO HIDE IN FEAR.
YOUR LOVE SHAKES MY SECURITY TO THE CORE.
FOR YOUR GUIDANCE AND INSTRUCTION SEEM LOST
IN MY PRIDE AND MY VANITY.
YOUR COMMANDMENTS,
ONLY REMINDING ME OF THE HEAT OF HELL.

FOR THE REVERANCE OF GOD
IS THE BEGINNING OF WISDOM;
BUT MY IGNORANCE ATTESTS TO AN *UNHOLY* FEAR. +

+GENTLE IS THE BREEZE IN THE GARDEN OF PRAISE.
FOR HE WHO TILLS THE GROUND RESTORES THE SOIL.
PLANTER AND PRUNER, HE SAVES THE DELICATE AND VULNERABLE.
NOT A FLOWER, NOR A SEED ESCAPES HIS LOVING CONCERN.
FOR THE GARDEN OF ALL,
THIS GARDEN OF HIS,
GROWS HIS BELOVED DELIGHT!
AND EVERY FLOWER
WHICH BENDS TOWARDS HIS LIGHT
SHALL RECEIVE LIVING WATER FOR ALL DAYS. +

+SADNESS BECAME THE FACE OF THE FATHER AS HE WITNESSED THE
FOLLY OF THE DECEPTION OF EVE, AND THE WEAKNESS OF ADAM,
AND THE TOTAL COLLAPSE OF THE FIRST COMMUNION OF LOVE...
AS HUSBAND AND WIFE POINTED FINGERS OF BLAME, SHAMEFULLY,
NON COMPASSIONATELY, IN THE FIRST DIVORCE OF SPIRIT IN THE
GARDEN MEANT FOR LOVE...BUT CONFIDENCE FILLED THE HEART OF
THE FATHER IN BANISHING THE SERPENT, AND ANNOUNCING THE
COMING OF VICTORY IN THE WOMAN AND HER BELOVED CHILD...JOY
FOR THE WORLD...IN THE FALLING OF THE FIRST ADAM AND THE
BIRTH OF THE SECOND ADAM IN THE MERCY AND WISDOM OF GOD. +

+TO BE LED BY GOD,
I HAVE TO BE ALIVE TO HIS PRESENCE.
TO BE ALIVE TO HIS PRESENCE,
I HAVE TO BE HELD IN SANCTIFYING GRACE.
TO BE HELD IN HIS LOVING ARMS,
IN THE SANCTIFYING GRACE OF HIS SPIRIT,
I MUST DIE TO SIN IN CRUCIFORM REPENTANCE.
IN ORDER TO DIE TO SIN
IN CRUCIFORM REPENTANCE,
I MUST ACCEPT HIS SON AS MY LORD AND MY SAVIOR.
TO ACCEPT HIS SON
AS MY LORD AND MY SAVIOR,
I MUST DENOUNCE MYSELF,
DENOUNCING MY SIN,
WHILE ACCEPTING *HIS* PASCHAL WAY. +

+THIS UNIVERSE IS EITHER AN INDIFFERENT BEAST
OR THE PURGATIVE POWER OF GOD.

FOR WINTER COLD AND CHILLING WINDS
AND DEEP DARK OCEAN AND COLD CRUEL MAN
CAN EITHER SIGNIFY THE BARRONNESS OF CHANCE-
OR FULLNESS IN THE PREPARATION OF PURPOSE.

FIVE SENSES UNITE
WITH FAITH OR DESPAIR
WITH PERSEVERANCE OR SURRENDER
WITH OBEDIENCE OR REBELLION
TO INTERPRET
"THE SIGNS OF THE TIMES"
 AND THE MEANING OF IT ALL
IN THE SIGNATURE OF CREATION
WRITTEN POETICALLY IN LOVING PROVIDENCE-
OR DASHED IN A CRASH OF MINDLESS MATTER. +

GOD THE SON

"ABOVE ALL, LOVE IS GREATER THAN SIN, THAN WEAKNESS, THAN THE 'FUTILITY OF CREATION;' IT IS STRONGER THAN DEATH; IT IS A LOVE ALWAYS READY TO RAISE UP AND FORGIVE, ALWAYS READY TO GO TO MEET THE PRODIGAL SON, ALWAYS LOOKING FOR 'THE REVEALING OF THE SONS OF GOD,' WHO ARE CALLED 'TO THE GLORY THAT IS TO BE REVEALED.' THIS REVELATION OF LOVE IS ALSO DESCRIBED AS MERCY; AND IN MAN'S HISTORY THIS REVELATION OF LOVE AND MERCY HAS TAKEN A FORM AND A NAME: THAT OF JESUS CHRIST."
POPE JOHN PAUL II
REDEMPTOR HOMINIS

OH MY JESUS, FORGIVE US OUR SINS, SAVE US FROM THE FIRES OF HELL, LEAD ALL SOULS TO HEAVEN, ESPECIALLY THOSE IN MOST NEED OF THY MERCY.
THE FATIMA PRAYER

+WHEN THE FIGHT SEEMS FAR TOO TOUGH
AND THE ENEMY SEEMS TOO GREAT IN NUMBER...
FEAR NOT!

STAND FIRM IN CHRIST!
KEEP STILL IN SPIRIT AND FAITH!
FOR GOD, THE WARRIOR,
WILL WIN REDEMPTION AND PEACE AND JOY
FOR THIS LIFE'S DESERT SOJOURNER
IN THE FIRM STAND OF HUMBLE REPENTANCE
AND THE STILLNESS FOUND IN THE SPIRIT OF FAITH FILLED HOPE
IN THE LOVE POURED FORTH ON THE CROSS,
THE LOVE OF BODY AND BLOOD, SOUL AND DIVINITY,
WILLING TO DIE SO WE MAY LIVE,
ABLE TO CONQUER IN THE HUMILITY OF SEEMING DEFEAT,
SO THAT WE MAY RISE ABOVE SEEMING DESTITUTION
IN THE VICTORY OF AGAPE STRUGGLE
FOUGHT TO THE END. +

+IN TOUGH TIMES,
WHEN THE WHEAT IS SPARSE
FROM A GROUND HARD AND DRY,
ALL WE CAN DO IS PRAY FOR OUR DAILY BREAD.

FOR YESTERDAY WE WERE FED,
AND TOMORROW IS BUT A MYSTERY
YET TO BE ENCOUNTERED.

BUT TODAY IS A DAY IN WHICH FAITH AND HOPE AND TRUST
PROVIDE FOR STRENGTH AND PATIENCE
IN THE PROVIDENCE AND THE MERCY OF THE LORD
-HE WHO PROVIDES FOR WHAT WE TRULY NEED
WHEN WE TRULY NEED IT-
FROM THE ABSOLUTE TRUTH OF HIS MOST GENEROUS
AND MOST LOVING SACRED HEART. +

+THE LAW AND ITS ORDINANCES, THE PROPHETS AND THEIR INSIGHT,
ARE SUMMED UP IN THE LIFE OF CHRIST-
WHICH IS LOVE THROUGH SUFFERING,
FELT AS MERCY...FOR THE UNDESERVED SOUL. +

+PRAISE SPRINGS FORTH
FROM A SOUL SAVED FROM DAMNATION.

THANKSGIVING BURSTS FORTH
FROM A HEART FREED FROM SLAVERY.

FAITH AND HOPE DISPLAY THEMSELVES
-RESPLENDENTLY-
FROM A CHILD
OF THE GOD
WHO FEEDS THEM ON THE BREAD OF LIFE.

LOVE IS THE ARTIST WHO CREATES OUT OF LOVE
AND IN RETURN IS LOVED BY HIS MASTERPEICE...
MADE IN THE IMAGE OF THE CHRIST,
HE WHO IS HIS WORD,
HIS SON,
AND HIS VERY LIVING IMAGE. +

+THOSE WHO TURN FROM GOD
CHOOSE THE DECEPTIVE BEAUTY OF THE GOLDEN CALF
OVER THE SUBLIME GRACE OF THE GOD OBSCURED
IN THE WEAKNESS OF HIS BODY.

FOR NO MAN WOULD TURN FROM PURE GOODNESS
TO UTTER EMPTINESS
UNLESS HE WERE DECEIVED,
SEDUCED, AND BLINDED
IN HIS OWN SINFUL WEAKNESS
AND THE TREACHERY OF A DEVILISH WORLD.

COMPASSION DEMANDS A CLEAN MIRROR AND A LONG GAZE!

ONLY IN SELF-ACKNOWLEDGMENT
OF OUR OWN SIN
AND AN HONEST AND FEARFUL OFFERING OF PRAISE
TO THE ONE HOLY AND MERCIFUL GOD
MAY WE MEET OUR FALLEN BRETHREN
ON THE PASCHAL PATH OF DIVINE MERCY,
FOUND ONLY IN JESUS CHRIST. +

+GOD GAVE US HIS LAW;
WE CHOSE A BEAST OF GOLD.

A BLESSED MEDIATOR
SPRANG UP FROM AMONGST HIS PEOPLE;
WE FORGOT HIS PRESENCE.

HE MET THE LORD OF HEAVEN
FOR THE LAW OF OUR LIFE;
WE DANCED AND CHANTED
LIKE A WILD PACK OF PAGANS.

A *DIVINE* MEDIATOR
SPRANG UP FROM AMONGST HIS PEOPLE;
WE HARDLY NOTICED HIS *PRESENCE*.

HE PAID THE PRICE FOR OUR SIN
IN SUFFERING AND IN DEATH-
AND WE ARE FREED TO STRUGGLE
ON THE PILGRIMAGE OF FAITH.

WE HAVE BEEN LIBERATED,
EMPOWERED IN THE SPIRIT,
FED ON THE BREAD OF ANGELS,
IN THE VERY LIFE OF CHRIST,
THE VERY FREEDOM OF DIGNIFIED HUMANITY:
TO CHOOSE BETWEEN DEATH IN SIN
OR LIFE IN THE GRACE OF FAITH, HOPE AND LOVE. +

+*I* HAVE WORSHIPPED THE GOD OF LIES AND PLEASURES...
REJECTING THE GOD OF TRUTH AND REALITY!
I HAVE FREELY CHOSEN TO FORGET MERCY UPON MERCY
FOR SIN UPON SIN,
ONLY TO DWELL ON THE INCONVENIENCE OF PAIN AND SUFFERING,
CAUSED BY THE CONSEQUENCES OF MY OWN ACTS.
MY LIFE, MY VERY BREATH, MY HOPE AND MY JOY,
ARE ALL GRACED, ALL GIFTS,
IN THE SPIRIT OF UNDESERVED AND DIVINE HEROISM-
THAT OF MY LORD AND MY CHRIST, THE SON OF THE LIVING GOD,
DIVINE MERCY HIMSELF, JESUS. +

+GOD-
THAT FUNNY THREE LETTER WORD,
SO OFTEN ABUSED, SO OFTEN MISUNDERSTOOD.
SO PERFECTLY REVEALED IN THE GOD-MAN,
JESUS OF NAZARETH.

GOD,
YOU WHO I DON'T KNOW IN ESSENCE,
I KNOW THROUGH CHRIST!

FOR CHRIST
IS YOUR FACE
AND YOUR VOICE
AND YOUR MIND
AND YOUR HEART
AND YOUR SOUL
AND YOUR LOVE.

CHRIST JESUS IS YOUR MERCY…
AND MY LIFE!   +

+REVELATION
IS THE COSMIC BURST OF JUSTICE!

SALVATION HISTORY
REVEALS THE ALMIGHTY AND HOLY ONE
WHOSE ANGER MELTS MOUNTAINS;
YET WHOSE MERCY REVEALS HIS SACRED HEART.

CHRIST JESUS
REVEALS THE HEIGHTOF HIS HOLINESS
AND THE DEPTH OF HIS MERCY
AND WIDTH AND BREADTH OF HIS COMPASSION
-WITNESSED IN HIS PASSION-
WHERE MERCY REVEALS LOVE
AS THE ULTIMATE POWER
AND THE ULTIMATE FORCE
IN ALL OF THE UNIVERSE…
GOD *AGAPE!*   +

+WE WORSHIP,
NOT AT THE HEAD,
BUT AT THE FOOT OF THE HOLY ONE.

FOR HE IS THE CRUCIFIED,
AND WE ARE BLESSED TO KISS HIS FEET!

OUR PRAYER,
RISES FROM THE DEPTHS!
INCARNATE,
HE ELEVATES OUR NEEDS.
IN THE SPIRIT,
HE CARRIES THEM TO THE MOUNTAINTOP
OF THE FATHER'S GLORY. +

+WITH LAZARUS IN THE TOMB,
MARTHA CHALLENGED THE LORD
FROM THE RIGIDNESS OF HER FAITH.   (JOHN 11:19-27)

AS CHRIST REMINDED HER OF GOD'S FAITHFULNESS,
SHE REMINDED HIM OF BLESSED DOGMA.

THEN THE FATHER IN HEAVEN
HELD TIME IN CHECK,
AND ETERNITY ENTERED THE HEART AND SOUL
OF MARTHA'S AWARENESS.

FOR CHRIST REVEALED *HIMSELF* AS BLESSED DOGMA ALIVE!

TRANSFORMED FOREVER, SHE SAID:
"I BELIEVE THAT YOU ARE THE CHRIST, THE SON OF GOD,
THE ONE WHO WAS TO COME INTO THIS WORLD." +

+WHY DO WE TURN TO DEATH, AND RUN FROM LIFE HIMSELF?
WHY DO WE DENY THE VERY DIGNITY OF HUMANITY?
"YAHWEH'S PORTION...HIS PEOPLE..."
WHY DO WE REFUSE THE GOD OF LIGHT IN REVELATION-
REFUSING THE GOD OF MERCY, THE FATHER OF BEAUTY HIMSELF?
COULD IT BE THE CROSS? DO WE NOT BELIEVE HE IS RISEN? WHY? +

+IN THE DAY CLOUD AND THE NIGHT FIRE,
THE HOLY ONE OF ISRAEL
LED HIS PEOPLE
THROUGH THE DESERT SOJOURN
TOWARD THE PROMISED LAND.

SO TOO,
IN THE FAITH CLOUD OF OUR DAY
AND THE NIGHT FIRE OF OUR HOPE,
THE HOLY ONE,
THE RISEN ONE,
OF THE UNIVERSAL ISRAEL,
LEADS HIS PEOPLE THROUGH THE DESERT SOJOURN
TOWARD THE PROMISED LAND,
FILLED WITH THE MILK OF BEATITUDE
AND THE HONEY OF TRINITARIAN LOVE. +

+OUR DAILY BREAD
IS LIFE
IN THE BREAD FROM HEAVEN,
CHRIST JESUS.

ARE WE NOT TO FEED OUR CHILDREN
THE BEST OF BREAD TO COME?

FOR LOVE
IS GIVING THE BELOVED
WHAT IS TRULY FOR THEIR BEST.

AND THE IMMORTAL BREAD FROM HEAVEN,
THE BREAD OF ANGELS,
CHRIST JESUS OUR LORD,
IS TRULY THE BEST OUR BELOVED CAN HOPE FOR.

AND WHEREVER THIS MANNA MAY FALL
-THIS IS GOD'S WILL FOR US-
-THE PLACE OF SANCTIFICATION AND WITNESS-
WE MUST WITNESS
TO THE BREAD WHICH GIVES EVERLASTING LIFE
IN THE PERPETUAL WITNESS OF SACRIFICIAL LOVE.   +

+WE PRAY FOR OUR DAILY BREAD.
AND THEN WE WAIL AND MOAN AND CRY
FOR THE LUXURIES OF THE WORLD.

NOT ONE OF US CAN CARRY THE BURDEN
OF THE MORAL GUIDANCE
AND THE SALVIFIC STRUGGLE
OF THE SON'S AND DAUGHTERS OF GOD.

NOT A MAN-EVEN A STRONG MAN-
CAN CARRY THE CROSS ALONE!

THAT IS WHY WE NEED THE CHRIST, THE SAVIOR OF MAN.
HE ALONE CARRIES HIS CROSS!

AND IN DOING SO
-CARRYING THE CROSS OF UNIVERSAL SALVATION-
WE ARE EMPOWERED TO CARRY OUR CROSS...
AND JUST MAYBE, HELP ANOTHER ALONG *THE WAY.* +

+GOD DOES NOT HATE THEM, AND LOVE US!
    HE HATES SIN AND LOVES VIRTUE!
SO IN RESCUING THE POOR FROM PERSECUTION,
HE ENRICHES THE SAVED TO SAVE THE RICH,
TO SHOW THEM JUST HOW POOR THEY REALLY ARE.

FOR COMMUNION IN GOD, THROUGH CHRIST JESUS
        IS COMMUNION IN THE SHEPHERD-
SEEKING ALL THE LOST SHEEP OF GOD'S BELOVED ISRAEL. +

+I AM A SINNER BY NATURE, A SINNER BY CHOICE, A SINNER BY
WEAKNESS, AND A SINNER BY IGNORANT BLISS.
YOU KNOW MY PLIGHT AND UNDERSTAND MY STRUGGLE
BETTER THAN I, KNOWING MY HEART AND SOUL AND MIND,
WOVEN IN YOUR WILL EVEN BEFORE MY BIRTH.
SAVE ME, IN THE INFINITE GRACE OF YOUR SORROWFUL SUFFERING.
CLEANSE ME OF THE SIN WHICH WEIGHTS ME DOWN,
AND SULLIES MY LOVE.
REDEEM ME IN YOUR LOVE, AND I WILL LIVE TO POINT *THE WAY*
-TO TRUTH AND FREEDOM IN MERCY. +

+THE LIFE OF THE MESSIAH
IS FOUND WITHIN THE BODY OF THE LIVING CHRIST,
WITHIN THE COMMUNION OF GOD AND MAN,
THE COMMUNION OF BROTHER AND SISTER
TO BROTHER AND SISTER,
ENLIVENED IN THE VERY LIFE OF CHRIST
IN THE HOLY SPIRIT
WHICH TURNS BREAD AND WINE
INTO THE VERY BODY AND BLOOD OF MERCY HIMSELF.

YET COMMUNION IS MORE THAN AN IDENTITY.
IT IS A COVENANT WITH THE HEALER AND REDEEMER OF MAN.
IT IS A CALLING-A DEMAND WHICH COMES FROM A GIFT-
A DEMAND TO HEAL ONES BROTHER,
A CALLING TO REDEEM ONES SISTER,
IN THE GIFT OF THE LIFE OF THE EUCHARISTIC LORD. +

+WITHIN THE BOAT OF TURMOIL AND SUFFERING,
ONLY THE SINCERE PRAYER OF THE HUMBLE BELIEVER
DRAWS THE SAVIOR TO COME NEAR
ON THE WATERS OF FAITH AND HOPE.

APPROACHING, BECKONING US TO ENTER THE PASCHAL FLOOD,
WE WILL EVENTUALLY SINK, AS PETER SANK,
IN THE FINITE LIMITS OF OUR EVER CEASING PRAYER.

BUT THE GOODNESS,
AND THE BEAUTY,
AND THE TRUTH
OF THIS NEAR DEATH EXPERIENCE
IS THE SWIFTNESS OF THE LORD OF COMPASSION-
WHO SAVES SO DEARLY
AS TO ENKINDLE NEWBORN TRUST AND LOVE. +

+WHO ARE YOU LORD? FROM THE CROSS YOU ANSWER.
WHAT IS MY PURPOSE? FROM GETHSEMANE YOU SPEAK.
WHERE DOES ALL THIS LEAD? COMING ON A CLOUD YOU SMILE.
WHEN WILL I SEE JUSTICE? FROM MY REPENTANCE YOU SAY 'NOW.'
HOW MAY I SEE YOUR FACE? IN POVERTY AND MERCY YOU ANSWER.
WHY? 'FOR *I AM* LOVE.' +

+DON'T KID YOURSELF.
GOD LOVES A GOOD FIGHT!
FROM THE WRESTLE WITH JACOB,
TO THE TUSSLE WITH THE HEART AND MIND OF MOSES,
AND IN FULFILLING ALL THE HOPES AND DESIRES
FOUND IN OUR SPIRITAL STRUGGLES,
CHRIST JESUS
FOUGHT THE GOOD AND GLORIOUS FIGHT
FROM UPON HIS CROSS
SO THAT WE
-NOT UNLIKE HE IN HIS GETHSEMANE BATTLE-
WOULD BECOME PRAYER WARRIORS IN THE SPIRIT
-WHO INTERCEDES IN MERCY FROM THE CROSS-
FOR THE SALVATION WON WITHIN THE WAR,
WHERE FEAR AND TREMBLING ON ONES KNEES
BRINGS STRENGTH FOR VICTORY
IN DEFEATING THE EVIL ONE. +

+SEEK THE LORD FOR HEALING!
SHOUT FOR THE PITY OF THE DIVINE PHYSICIAN!
BEAT DOWN THE VERY DOORS OF HIS CHURCH!

SEEK WHAT YOU DO NOT DESERVE,
IN THE GRACE WHICH IS GIVEN WITHOUT MERIT,
IN THE BELOVED DISPOSITION OF REPENTANCE.

THOUGH A SINNER,
SEEK THE BREAD OF ANGELS
BY CALLING UPON THE MERCY OF THE COMPASSIONATE CHRIST.

"LORD, I AM NOT WORTHY TO RECEIVE YOU!
BUT ONLY SAY THE WORD, AND I SHALL BE HEALED." +

+AS A NATIVE, THE FORIEGNER MAY BE SEEN AS A THREAT.
    THIS MAY LEAD TO PREJUDICE AND EXCLUSIVENESS.
YET BECOME THE FORIEGNER FOR JUSTONE DAY;
PERCEIVING YOUR THREAT FELT IN THE HEART OF THE NATIVE.
THIS MAY LEAD TO CONVERSION AND TO COMPASSION-
THE ALL INCLUSIVENESS OF THE LOVE OF THE SUFFERING CHRIST. +

+FROM THE DESERT TREK NEAR SINAI,
TO THE SINS OF OUR FATHERS,
WE, I, HAVE CONTINUED TO REJECT
THE SIMPLE AND PURE MERCY OF GOD.

WE SO EASILY FORGET THE SIGNS AND WONDERS
OF SINS FORGIVEN
AND THE RECONCILIATION
WHICH LEADS TO SIMPLE AND PURE COMMUNION WITH GOD.

WE SO EASILY FORGET
THE SUFFERING MEDIATION OF THE MOSES OF GOD,
THE CHRIST OF MAN,
HE WHO TOOK UPON HIMSELF
-IN SIMPLE AND PURE INNOCENCE-
OUR SINS AND THE VILENESS OF THE DEVIL'S ATTACK,
DEFLECTING GOD'S JUST WRATH,
BRINGING FORTH GOD'S ABUNDANT MERCY,
IN SIMPLE AND PURE OBEDIENCE AND LOVE. +

+GOD REVEALED,
REVEALS THE VERY REVELATION OF THE MYSTERY
OF THE SON OF REDEMPTION,
WHICH ALWAYS LURKS BEHIND THE VERY CLOUDS
OF OUR SIN, OUR DESPAIR, AND OUR DOUBT.

ALMIGHTY,
THE VERY SON OF GLORY
DESIRES OUR REPENTANCE .
THEN,
HE SHALL BURST FORTH,
MELTING THE CLOUD IN THE FORGIVENESS OF SIN,
SET AFIRE IN THE TORCH OF HIS CROSS.

FOR WE ARE TRULY LOST
IN THE SNARES OF MORTAL SIN.
NO god, NO MAN,
NO INVENTION OF THE MIND
CAN SAVE US.
FOR SALVATION ALONE IS CHRIST JESUS! +

+TO TRULY MEDITATE ON THE ACTS OF THE LORD
IS TO SEE HOLINESS
AND OMNIPOTENCE
AND CREATIVITY
AND POWER,
-*AWESOME POWER*-
DERIVING FROM WITHIN THE SOUND OF DIVINE MIGHTY THUNDER,
RESOUNDING IN THE BEATING OF THE SACRED HEART OF MERCY.

FOR THE WATERS PART AT THE SIGHT OF THE CHRIST.
AND THE MOUNTAINS QUAKE UPON HEARING HIS MIGHTY WHISPER.
FOR JESUS IS THE MIGHTY SHEPHERD OF HIS BELOVED FLOCK.
WOLVES BEWARE! +

+LORD JESUS,
TEACH ME HOW TO LOVE, AS YOU LOVE, UNTO DEATH AND BEYOND.
LORD JESUS,
TEACH ME HOW TO SUFFER, AS YOU SUFFERED ON YOUR CROSS,
WHICH PERPETUATES MERCY FOREVER.
LORD JESUS,
TEACH ME HOW TO LIVE, AS YOU LIVE, IN SELFLESS SELF-GIVING,
SO THAT I MAY LEARN THE TRUE JOY OF LIFE,
THE TOTAL GIVING OF MYSELF.
LORD JESUS,
TEACH ME YOUR *WAY.* +

+MY NATURAL SCENT
REVEALS FEAR AND MISTRUST AND DESPAIR.
I SO WISH FOR THE AROMA OF FAITH AND HOPE AND CHARITY.

YET ON MY OWN,
THE MUSKY SCENT OF THE NATURAL MAN
REVEALS BUT A WHIFF OF FINITE LIMITS.

BUT WITH THE RISEN ROSE OF THE FLOWERING GOSPEL WITHIN,
MY FINITE NATURE MAY FREELY CHOOSE
TO TAKE UPON ITSELF THE GENTLE YOKE
AND THE FRAGRANT AROMA
OF THE INFINITE FLOWER OF SALVATION,
JESUS CHRIST THE LORD. +

+AS GREAT AND GOOD AS MOSES WAS,
A PROPHET UNPARALELLED,
HE BOWED TO THE MYSTERY AND THE GOODNESS AND THE WILL
OF THE PROVIDENTIAL GOD OF THE PEOPLE OF ISRAEL.

AS GREAT AND GOOD AS JOHN THE BAPTIST WAS,
-*NO MAN GREATER THAN HE*-
HE BOWED TO THE LAMB AND THE SERVANT AND THE SON
OF THE BENEFICENT GOD OF THE NEW COVENANT IN BLOOD.

AND AS GREAT AND GOOD AS JESUS THE CHRIST IS,
-FULLY GOD AND FULLY MAN-
HE BOWED TO THE FATHER
IN SUFFERING
AND IN IGNOMINOUS DEATH
TO RISE A NEW PEOPLE OF THE HEAVENLY JERUSALEM. +

+**CONFLICT** MUST LEAD TO COMPASSION.
FOR EVERY MAN, WOMAN AND CHILD
FAILS ANOTHER AT ONE TIME IN THEIR LIFE.
COMPASSION MUST LEAD TO DIALOGUE-
AIMED AT RECONCILIATION, NOT REVENGE.

FOR THE STRONGER MAN,
MODELED ON **CHRIST** JESUS,
DOES NOT DELIVER A RETALIATORY BLOW,
BUT EXTENDS AN ARM OF AID,
WHICH COMES FROM A HEART AND A MIND
CONVERTED IN THE MERCY OF THE CRUCIFIED CHRIST...
HE WHO EXTENDED HIS ARMS ON THE **CROSS**
IN DIVINE AND TRIUNE LOVE. +

+LOVE IS THE GREATEST GOOD!
BUT LOVE MUST BE AN EVER GROWING REALITY.
FOR LOVE IS NOT AN ABSTRACT, BUT AN ORGANIC REALITY.
LOVE IS LIFE! AND LIFE IS LIVED IN LOVE!
TO CEASE TO LOVE FOR EVEN ONE MOMENT IS TO DIE IN SIN.
GOD IS LOVE! AND WE MAY ONLY LOVE IN GOD!
THEREFORE, LIFE IN CHRIST IS LOVE IN GOD,
AND LOVE IN GOD IS LIFE ETERNAL. +

+THE PRAYER OF THE CHRIST,
WAS THE WILL OF THE FATHER.
AS HE BORE THE CROSS OF GOD'S WRATH,
AND THE CROWN OF CELESTIAL IGNOMINY,
WHILE HANGING INNOCENTLY AS GUILT,
HE CRIED FOR LIFE, *OUR LIFE,* AND HE RECEIVED THE TOMB,
AND THE DESCENT INTO HELL,
FOR THE SPLENDID AND MAJESTIC ELEVATION
OF THE LORD OF ALL
IN THE SPIRIT OF MERCY
FOR THE LIFE OF MAN
IN THE LOVE OF THE FATHER,
WHICH NEVER FAILS TO AMAZE! +

+GOD'S VICTORY
-WON THROUGH THE BLOOD OF CHRIST ON HIS CROSS-
IS FOR LIFE AND LOVE.

AS JEPHTHAH VOWED A LIVING SACRIFICE FOR *HIS* VICTORY,
AND NOT THE LORD'S,
GOD'S VICTORY IN LIFE AND LOVE ELUDED HIS GRASP.

AS HIS DAUGHTER WAS GIVEN AS A SACRIFICE
FOR A VOW IN PERSONAL VICTORY,
HIS LOSS WAS TRULY THE LOSS OF GOD'S VICTORY,
IN AND THROUGH THE CRUCIFIXION AND RESURRECTION
OF HIS BELOVED SON IN LIFE AND LOVE.

THE LESSON THAT ALL CAN LEARN
IS IN *OUR* VICTORY,
AT THE COST OF GOD'S VICTORY IN CHRIST,
WE LOSE LIFE AND LOVE,
AND REAP ONLY SORROW AND DEATH. +

+LIFE, FOR A VERY GOOD MAN, CAN END IN A FLASH IN THE HANDS
OF A MUCH LESSER MAN. *SEE JOHN AND HEROD!*
LIFE, FOR THE GREATEST OF MEN, CAN END IN BLOOD AND SORROW
IN THE HANDS OF LESSER MEN. *SEE CHRIST AND FALLEN HUMANITY!*
LIFE, FOR THE WORST OF SINNERS, CAN BE SAVED IN A FLASH IN THE
PIERCED HANDS OF THE GREAT GOD MAN. *SEE JESUS THE MESSIAH!* +

+I HAVE JESUS OR I HAVE FEAR…
AND LUST AND ENVY AND ANGER AND HURT
AND THE QUEST FOR VAIN GLORY,
AND THE DESIRE TO PROVE A POINT,
AND THE ILLUSION OF GAINING REVENGE,
AND A BATTLE AGAINST A WORLD,
A PERCEPTION AND A DECEPTION WHICH NEVER WANES,
DAY UPON DAY, STRUGGLE UPON STRUGGLE,
IN THE SAME BATTLE WITH DIFFERENT COMBATANTS,
NEVER WON-
ALL THE WHILE GRAYING AND TIRING AND LOSING FAITH AND HOPE
-IN MYSELF-
UNTIL DEATH ENDS THE WAR!
I HAVE JESUS OR I HAVE NOTHING! +

+THE ALMIGHTY,
WHO MELTS MOUNTAINS AS WAX,
CAME AS A BABE,
DEPENDANT ON HUMAN CARE.

AS THE ALPHA,
AND THE OMEGA,
THE OMNIPOTENT AND ETERNAL WORD,
HE DIED ON A CROSS, THE LOT OF A CRIMINAL,
INNOCENT, THOUGH BEARING ALL OUR CRIME.

AS DIVINITY, ETERNAL,
WITHOUT BEGINNING OR END,
HE WAS BURIED AS A POOR MAN IN ANOTHER MAN'S TOMB.

AND *HE ROSE*,
AS FORTY DAY WITNESS,
AND ASCENDING MEDIATOR,
TO THE LOVE OF THE FATHER
IN THE SPIRIT OF OBEDIENT MERCY.
OBEDIENCE THAT ROCKS THE WORLD!
FOREVER WITNESSING FOR OUR PETITIONS
-BEARING THE WOUNDS OF FAITHFULNESS-
IN THE LIVING PRESENCE
OF THE FATHER AND THE SPIRIT OF LOVE. +

+THE COVENANT IN BLOOD,
AND THE LAW OF THE SPIRIT,
IS TO LEAD THE DISCIPLE IN *THE WAY* OF REPENTANCE,
ON THE ROAD OF HOLINESS,
IN FAITH THROUGH CHALLENGE,
IN HOPE THROUGH SUFFERING,
AND IN LOVE THROUGH ALL THAT THE WORLD,
THE FLESH,
AND THE DEVIL
WILL THROW OUR WAY AS OBSTACLE,
AND SNARE,
IN DOUBT AND DESPAIR,
WHICH WILL ONLY BE OVERCOME IN LOVING TRUST
THROUGH GRACE AND SPIRIT
ON THE CROSS OF OUR WEAKNESS
AND IN THE RESURRECTION OF OUR LIFE
IN THE VERY LIFE OF CHRIST,
HUMBLE AND DEPENDANT ON THE FATHER,
HE WHO IS THE SOURCE OF OUR STRENGTH! +

+FORGIVEN IN THE NAME OF JESUS,
FATHERS AND MOTHERS
IN THE FATHERHOOD OF GOD,
SONS AND DAUGHTERS
IN THE FAITHFULNESS
OF GOD'S BELOVED FIRST BORN,
WE HAVE COME TO KNOW OUR HEAVENLY FATHER
IN AND THROUGH HIS SON,
-THROUGH WHOM ALL GOODNESS COMES-
IN THE SPIRIT
-WHO EMPOWERS THE FAITHFUL TO OVERCOME ALL EVIL-
IN HOLDING TO ALL TRUTH,
WHILE DENYING THE BODY
AND THE EYE
AND THE HEART
OF ALL THAT IS PASSING,
THAT THE BODY, THE EYE, AND THE HEART
MAY ONLY SERVE
THE LORD OF ETERNAL LOVE. +

+OH BLESSED ANNA, SO OLD AND GRAY.
OH SORROWFUL ANNA, WIDOW OF EIGHTY-FOUR.
OH FAITHFUL ANNA, FIXTURE IN GOD'S HOLY TEMPLE.
OH HOPEFUL ANNA, SERVING HIM NIGHT AND DAY.

OH ANNA, SO FAITHFUL, SO PURE, SO DEVOUT, WHAT DID YOU SEE?

WHAT MOVED YOUR HEART TO A BURST OF PRAISE
AND THE PRONOUNCMENT OF PROPHETIC DELIVERANCE?

WHAT DID YOU SEE IN THAT POOR COUPLES ARMS,
IN THE EYES OF THAT BABY BOY? +

+AS I STRUGGLE TO MEET THE NEEDS OF THE DAY,
THE DEMONS OF WEAKNESS AND PRIDE AND FEAR
ATTACK MY ENERGY,
MY CREATIVITY,
MY PATIENCE,
AND MY DEVOTION.

THESE DEMONS LIVE WITHIN ME,
IN THOUGHTS AND DESIRES AND ACTS.

BUT, IN ME, THEY ARE NOT OF ME-
FOR I AM A REDEEMED CHILD OF GOD.

FOR I LIVE IN CHRIST
AND STRUGGLE IN GRACE,
DYING TO THE DEMONS,
ONLY TO RISE IN THE SON. +

+AS I WALK-A WOUNDED SOUL-
IN THE STREETS OF TURMOIL, HURT, AND PRIDE,
I HAVE A CHOICE TO CHOOSE INSIDE.   RHYME
VENGEANCE FROM HURT AND POWER FROM PRIDE,
ARE CHOICES I CHOOSE-IN FEAR AND DESPAIR-
IN WOUNDS THAT I SEEK TO HIDE.
BUT *COMPASSION* FROM PRAYER, AND PEACE IN GRACE
ARE CHOICES I CHOOSE-IN FAITH AND HOPE-
IN HIS WOUNDS IN BLOOD WHERE MERCY IS FOREVER SUPPLIED. +

+ LOVE IS GOD'S WORD.
LIFE IS CHRIST'S BEING.
OUR LIFE IS HIS LIGHT
-UNCONQUERABLE LUMINESCENT LOVE-
AS WITNESSED BY THE WILD DESERT PROPHET
WHO PREPARED *THE WAY* IN REPENTANCE AND GRACE.

AS THE MORNING STAR BROKE NEW DAY ON GOD'S CHOSEN PEOPLE,
THEY CONCEIVED AN ECLIPSE OF HEART, MIND AND SOUL.
REJECTED, THEY REMAINED IN DARKNESS.
ACCEPTED, THEY WERE ADOPTED IN THE TURBULENT SEA OF LOVE.

GOD BECAME MAN
-IN THE EYES OF FAITH-
AS GRACE REVEALED TRUTH IN WORD BECOME SAVIOR.

DIVINE, OF GREATNESS TRANSCENDENT,
HE DESCENDED BEYOND MODESTY TO SAVE THOSE HE LOVED.

AND GRACE BEYOND PERCEPTION
FLOODS THE HEARTS AND MINDS OF THOSE WHO BELIEVE,
THOSE WHO SEE THE FATHER IN THE FACE OF THE SON-
IN THE SPIRIT WHO ILLUMINATES ALL TRUTH IN THEIR LOVE. +

+IN THE MYSTERY OF GOD'S TIME,
IN THE SUBMISSIVE WITNESS OF THE BETHLEHEM STAR,
THE WORD WAS BORN OF WOMAN,
SUBJECT TO THE LAW,
TO REDEEM THE SLAVES OF THE ELEMENTS,
CONVERTING THEM TO CHILDREN OF THE ETERNAL.

AND REALIZATION OF REDEMPTION IN ADOPTION
IS THE GRACED AND FILIAL CRY FOR FATHERLY LOVE.

FOR BONDAGE IS BROKEN
AND CHILDHOOD IS SECURED
IN THE WEAPONRY OF FAITH AND HOPE.
AND PROOF OF INHERITANCE-IN THE KEY OF CHRIST-
IS FOUND IN THE KINGS OWN TREASURE-
WITHIN THE CHEST OF HIS UNFATHOMABLE SACRED HEART. +

+*A JOLLY OLD CHRISTMAS RHYME*

CHRISTMAS IS FAMILY, HOLY, POOR, AND DEVOUT.
CHRISTMAS IS SHEPHERDS AND ANGELS SCURRYING ABOUT.
CHRISTMAS IS MARY PONDERING SO DEEP.
CHRISTMAS IS TRANSFORMED SHEPHERDS LEADING GOD'S SHEEP.
CHRISTMAS IS THE FEW INSPIRED SO BOLD-
BELIEVING AND HOPING IN WHAT THEY'VE BEEN TOLD.
CHRISTMAS IS DAILY IN BURDEN AND CHORE.
CHRISTMAS IS LOVE'S BABE KNOCKING AT OUR HEART'S DOOR. +

+ANTI-CHRIST IS ANTI-TRUTH,
AND ANTI-CHRIST IS ANTI-FATHER,
IN THE SPIRIT OF ANTI-LOVE.

BUT FAITH IS BIRTH IN BAPTISM AND CROSS,
ALIVE IN THE SPIRIT WHO ROSE THE SON.

AND THE FAITH KEPT LIVING
IN THE HOPE OF GOD'S LOVE
WILL SEE UPON THE HORIZON
THE DAWNING OF PROMISED BEAUTY
IN HEAVEN'S BEATITUDE TO COME.

SO KEEP THE FAITH!
AND DWELL IN HOPE!
FOR THE LOVE OF GOD IN THE COMING CHRIST
LIVES RIGHT *NOW* IN YOU! +

+IN THE DARK OF DISMAY, IN THE CLOUD OF CONFUSION,
BEHOLD THE COMING LIGHT!
ATTRACTIVE, RESPLENDENT PERFECTION DRAWS-GRACEFULLY-
ALL MEN TO THE DIVINE HEART, SACRED IN LOVE!
NOTICE THE CONVERSION OF HEARTS!
NOTICE THE SUBTLE, YET SWIFT, CROSS-BORN VICTORY!
PERCEIVE! AND LIVE! GRACE UPON GRACE AWAITS.
THE WORLD OF THE REPENTANT, AND THE CONVERTED,
AND THE BELEIVING
IN THE CROSS AND THE EMPTY TOMB, THIS WORLD WILL BE YOURS! +

+THE SON IS THE JUSTICE OF WHICH I SEEK!
THE BELOVED IS THE RIGHTEOUSNESS OF WHICH I DESIRE!
THE VIRTUE OF CHRIST IS PEACE FOR THE WORLD.
I PRAY FOR VIRTUE AND WORK FOR PEACE.

FOR SERVICE TO THE FATHER IS KINGSHIP IN THE SON
IN THE SPIRIT OF JUSTICE, RIGHTEOUSNESS AND PEACE.

FOR JUSTICE AND RIGHTEOUSNESS AND PEACE
ARE FOUND IN FREEDOM FROM SIN
GAINED SOLELY IN THE VICTORY
OF THE CRUCIFIED AND RISEN SON. +

+REVELATION HAS BEEN GIVEN TO THE SELECT, THE BLESSED,
THE FEW, THE PROPHETS AND APOSTLES
SUMMONED TO CARRY THE GOSPEL MESSAGE
OF UNCONDITIONAL AND UNFATHOMABLE MERCY
FOR ALL MEN, WOMEN AND PEOPLES
IN ALL LANDS FOR ALL TIME
IN LIVING FAITH IN THE PURPOSEFUL PASSION
OF THE CHRIST,
AND LIVING HOPE IN THE PROMISED RESURRECTION
IN GOD'S SON,
IN THE LOVE OF THE SPIRIT
MANIFEST IN GRACED VICTORY
VIA THE BLOOD SHED ON CALVARY. +

+GOD LIVES.
ADAM AND EVE RECEIVED LIFE.
DISOBEDIENCE BROUGHT FORTH DEATH.
ALMIGHTY LIFE DESCENDED HUMBLY INCARNATE.

DEATH SHUDDERED
AS MIRACLE AND MERCY WALKED THE DIRT PATH.
LIFE DIED-OBEDIENTLY, PAINFULLY-
SO THAT DEATH WOULD BE CONQUERED DEFINITIVELY.

WE LIVE TO DIE TO SELF IN THE LIFE OF THE RISEN ONE.
HE WHO DIED OUT OF LOVE TO CONQUER DEATH-
SO THAT DEATH IS BUT GATEWAY TO LIFE ETERNAL. +

+THE PRACTICE OF RELIGION
-AND THE STATUS THIS GAINS-
WILL NOT PREPARE ONE FOR THE COMING CHRIST
IF ONES EYES ARE NOT SET ABOVE
AND ONES HEART NOT TORN ASUNDER
IN SHEEPISH NEED OF THE SHEPHERD OF GOD'S PEOPLE.

FOR EMPTY PRACTICE OF THE CHRISTIAN RELIGION
WILL NOT RESERVE A SEAT
AT THE BANQUET OF THE LORD
UNLESS ONE SEEKS
FOR THE ILLUMINATING LIFE GIVING LIGHT
OF THE MORNING STAR
AND TRAVELS A LONG AND NARROW PATH
ARRIVING WITH GIFTS
OF REPENTANCE AND CONTRITION AND NEWFOUND DEVOTION,
FALLING TO ONES KNEES,
WORSHIPPING THE NEWBORN CHRIST,
WITNESSING TO THE BABE IN THEIR HEART,
SWADDLED IN THE CLOTH OF A NEWLY CONVERTED HEART. +

+OUR PRAYERS
ARE ANSWERED,
BECAUSE WE FOLLOW THE COMMANDMENT OF LOVE,
IN THE LIFE OF THE SON OF LOVE,
IN THE SPIRIT OF REPENTANCE AND HUMBLE OBEDIENCE.

OUR HOPE
IN THE SPIRIT OF TRUTH,
IS SURE-IN THE FAITH-
AND GRACED FROM ABOVE
IN CHRIST JESUS,
WHO DIED FOR OUR SIN AND WAS BURIED BELOW.

OUR MISSION
IS A MISSION OF MERCY,
RISEN IN THE CHRIST FROM ABOVE,
GRACED IN THE LANGUAGE OF RESURRECTION,
SPREAD IN THE SPIRITED DOVE
IN FAITH, HOPE AND LOVE. +

+JESUS IS THE SON OF GOD,
THE KING OF NATIONS,
THE LORD OF ALL DOMAINS.

THE CROSS IS THE MEANS OF DELIVERANCE,
THE *WAY* OF THE SAVED,
THE WATERS OF ADOPTION AND KINGSHIP.

I AM NOW A SON AND DAUGHTER OF GOD!
A SERVANT KING TO THE NATIONS.
A LORD OF ALL DOMAINS.

SO, SON AND DAUGHTER, LORD AND STEWARD,
BE WISE! FEAR GOD!
TAKE SHELTER AT THE FOOT OF HIS CROSS! +

+AFTER THE GRACE OF THE BAPTIZER
HAS STRICKEN YOUR HEART
WITH SORROWFUL GUILT
IN LIGHT OF THE DARKNESS IN YOUR SIN,
THE LORD WILL APPEAR IN THE DARKEST OUTER REGION-
IN THE ZEBULUN AND NAPHTALI OF YOUR EMPTINESS-
TO PROCLAIM HIS PASCHAL PREROGATIVE,
HEALING DISEASE,
DRIVING OUT DEMONS,
PROCLAIMING THE GOODNESS OF GOD
IN MERCY AND PEACE AND RECONCILIATION
WITH THE FATHER
IN THE SPIRIT
OF THE RISEN SON
WHO CONQUERS SIN AND DEATH VIA OBEDIENCE AND SUFFERING
IN THE MERCY WHICH ABOLISHES ALL EVIL. +

+**THE** CHRISTIAN LIFE IS THE LIFE OF THE SHEEP
ENLIVENED IN TH LIFE OF THE SHEPHERD.
FOR, WITHOUT THE SHEPHERD, THE SHEEP ARE IN CONSTANT PERIL.
WEAK, AND WITHOUT DIRECTION, THEY ARE BUT PREY FOR WOLVES.
BUT IN THE TRUE PRESENCE OF THE SHEPHERD,
THEY LIVE BY HIS VOICE ALONE,
FLOURISHING IN HIS GOODNESS, HIS GRACE, AND HIS LOVE. +

+PRIOR TO CHRIST, AND AFTER HIS ASCENSION,
THE FAITHFUL CHILDREN OF GOD
HAVE OFFERED THEIR PRAYER
FOR THE JUSTICE AND THE RIGHTEOUSNESS OF THE ROYAL SON.

IN OUR HOMELAND,
OVER SEAS,
AND ABROAD,
THE SPIRIT OF THE RISEN SAVIOR
CRIES INCESSANTLY FOR THE POOR,
AND THE ORPHAN AND THE WIDOW-
THE CRY FOR PEACE AND JUSTICE!

AND THIS CRY HAS BEEN ANSWERED
-IN THE GROOM AND HEAD
OF THE BRIDE AND BODY,
OF THE UNIVERSAL KING-
IN HE WHO GRACES VIRTUE,
VIRTUE WHICH CONQUERS ALL EVIL
AND HEALS THE TRULY REPENTANT SOUL. +

+JESUS,
MY LORD AND MY SAVIOR,
TAKE PITY ON ME!

FOR I AM BUT A SHEEPISH MAN,
WEAK, LOST, STUMBLING ON DANGEROUS GROUND,
IN NEED OF A STRONG AND COMPASSIONATE SHEPHERD.

I AM BUT A FAMISHED WANDERER,
EMPTY, WOUNDED
-CIRCLING MY OWN GRAVE IN SELF-DESTRUCTIVE VICE-
IN NEED OF THE FORGIVENESS AND THE FOOD
WHICH RECONCILE AND TRANSFORM
IN REPENTANCE AND VIRTUE
IN THE BODY OF MERCY
AND THE BLOOD OF LOVE
IN THE CHRISTOF MAN
AND THE SON OF THE LIVING GOD,
JESUS THE LORD. +

+WHY ARE THE FISHERMEN
MISSING THE FISHER OF MEN?

WHY DO THE SHEEP RUN ASTRAY,
MISSING THE SHEPHERD OF SALVATION?

WHY, WHEN WITNESSING IN THE WORD
WALKING ON WATER,
DOES FEAR OVERCOME FAITH?

WHY, WHEN FIVE LOAVES AND TWO FISH
FEED FIVE THOUSAND,
DO WE STILL DOUBT?

WHAT WOULD OUR SAVIOR SAY?
"COURAGE! IT IS I! DO NOT BE AFRAID." +

+JESUS IS OUR JUSTICE,
JESUS IS OUR RIGHTEOUSNESS,
JESUS IS OUR CHARITY.

IN HIM ALONE ARE WE PLEASING TO THE HEAVENLY FATHER ABOVE.

JESUS IS OUR REDEMPTION,
JESUS IS OUR VIRTUE,
JESUS IS OUR DIGNITY,
JESUS IS OUR HOPE.

IN HIM ALONE ARE WE SAVED. IN HIM ALONE WE LIVE.

MAY WE PRAISE HIM, ALWAYS!
MAY WE SHARE HIS LIGHT.
MAY THE WORLD SUBMIT TO HIS MERCY.
MAY ALLELUIA BECOME OUR SINGLE WORD! +

+IF YOU SPEAK THE TRUTH OF JESUS CHRIST
AND NO ONE LISTENS,
REST ASSURED,
GOD HAS SPOKEN THROUGH YOU! +

+SCARRED DEEPLY FROM SIN,
UGLY AND EMPTY IN LUST AND ENVY AND MALICE,
JESUS THE LORD PEERED INTO MY EYES...
AS IF I WERE OF BEAUTY.

THE SINGLE SECOND LOOK OF LOVE
DROVE ME DEEP IN CONTRITION TRUE!

REPENTANCE BECAME MY ONLY BREATHE!
I CRIED: HEAL ME! IF BUT WITH ONLY A TOUCH!

EAGER IN TRANSCENDENT DIGNITY,
THE LORD OF THE UNIVERSE WILLINGLY TOUCHED THIS WORM!

AND BUTTERFLY FAITH
SPRUNG WINGS OF HOPE
AS MERCY CAME NEAR IN LOVE! +

+REPENT.
RENEWED, SING ANEW!
ALLELUIA!

MAKE YOUR *LIFE*
MUSIC
TO THE VERY EAR OF GOD,
SING PRAISE,
PLAY TUNES OF THANKSGIVING
TO OUR LORD AND SAVIOR.

PLAY THE SYMPHONY OF HUMAN WEAKNESS
ELEVATED TO THE HEAVENS
IN THE GLORY OF GOD THE FATHER
IN JESUS CHRIST OUR LORD!

FOR THE SONG IS WITHIN OUR HEARTS-
IN THE SPIRIT OF OUR REDEMPTION.
THUS, WE SING JOYFULLY
IN FAITH AND HOPE-GOSPEL BOUND-
IN THE LIFE AND THE PASSION
OF THE RISEN SON OF GOD. +

+JESUS,
THE WORD OF THE FATHER,
THE FULLNESS OF THE SPIRIT,
PEACE AND JUSTICE AND INTEGRITY FOR MAN.

GENTLE AND COMPASSIONATE,
HE IS UNWAVERING JUSTICE.

FAITHFUL AND MERCIFUL,
HE IS UNCONQUERABLE SALVATION.

COVENANT IN BODY AND BLOOD,
LIGHT IN MERCY AND TRUTH,
JESUS IS THE FACE AND THE HEART OF OUR LOVING GOD.

HE IS FREEDOM FOR PRISONERS,
SIGHT FOR THE BLIND,
AND LIGHT FOR THOSE
IN THE DARKNESS OF HOPELESSNESS AND DESPAIR.

HE IS LIFE ETERNAL, AND SALVATION TRUE.
HE IS JESUS THE LORD, OUR CHRIST AND OUR GOD. +

+JESUS IS THE TORCH OF THE ISRAELITE!
THE FIERY FLAME OF THE CHRISTIAN!
THE LIGHT FOR THE WORLD!

THE JEW IS THE FIRST TO BE CHOSEN.
THE CHRIST, BORN OF JEWISH STOCK.

THE CHRISTIAN IS THE CHILD OF THE SPIRIT-
WITHIN THE COMMUNION OF MERCY AND GRACE.

BUT THE JEW
AND THE CHRISTIAN
ARE THE BODY OF GOD,
THE LIGHT OF SALVATION,
THE MISSIONARIES OF MERCY,
THE VERY ARMS OF THE LOVING GOD. +

+JESUS SEEKS THE LOST AND LONELY SHEEP
OF THE TRIBE OF VIRTUE!
HE TEACHES, UNLIKE MEN, WITH AUTHORITY
IN *HIS WAY* OF SALVATION!
DEMONS AND DISCIPLES OF DEMONS
KNOW HIM WELL!
FOR HE IS THEIR EXIT, THEIR REPRESSION,
AND THEIR DEMISE!
LIKEWISE, THE DISCIPLES OF GOD'S MERCY AND LOVE
ALSO KNOW HIM WELL!
FOR HE IS THEIR ENTRANCE, THEIR DELIVERANCE,
AND THEIR LIFE!
FOR HE IS MERCY FOR THE REPENTANT,
THE JUST JUDGE FOR ALL EVIL.
HE IS THE REWARD AND THE REWARDER OF ALL HEARTS,
HEAVEN TO LOVERS,
HELLFIRE TO THE MALISCIOUS. +

+THE MOTHER OF YOUR SERVANT IS ILL-
"STRAIGHTWAY" YOU GO TO HEAL HER.

THE BROTHERS AND SISTERS OF YOUR SERVANT
ARE SICK AND WEAK AND WOUNDED
IN SPIRIT AND MIND AND BODY-
"STRAIGHTWAY" YOU GO TO THEM AND HEAL THEM.

AND THE WORLD OF YOUR SERVANT
IS SAD AND HURT AND SICK IN SPIRIT-
"STRAIGHTWAY" YOU GO IN SPIRIT AND BODY
TO THOSE OF FAITH AND HOPE,
AND IN LOVE YOU HEAL THEM. +

+WHEN WE TRUST GOD TO DELIVER US A KING,
WE RECEIVE A SHEPHERD WHO PROTECTS US!
WHEN WE TRUST GOD TO DELIVER US A KING,
WE RECEIVE A LAMB WHO SAVES US!
WHEN WE TRUST GOD TO DELIVER US A KING,
WE RECEIVE A BABY WHO TRANSFORMS US!
WHEN WE TRUST GOD TO DELIVER US A KING,
WE RECEIVE HIS SON WHO LOVES US! +

+THROUGH CHRIST,
MAN RECEIVES FREELY WHAT NEVER WAS OBTAINABLE IN TOIL,
WHAT PRAYERS AND TEARS DESIRED.

THROUGH JESUS,
GRACE AND GLORY IN PEACE AND JOY
CROWN OUR HEADS IN FAITH AND HOPE AND CHARITY.

THROUGH HIS PASSION AND RESURRECTION,
WE LIVE *NOW* AND HOPE FOR DAYS ETERNAL-
AFTER DEATH'S CONQUERED GRAVE.

THROUGH HIS BODY AND BLOOD,
SALVATION IS IMMANENT
IN THE ACCESSIBLE MYSTERY
OF CHRIST'S EUCHARISTIC PRESENCE.

THROUGH HIS SPIRIT,
WE TRUST IN GOD IN EVERYTHING,
LIVING WITHIN THE KINGDOM OF THE LORD-
IN OUR HEARTS, IN OUR FAITH,
AND IN HOPE'S GRACED FERVENT CHARITY. +

JESUS CHRIST INCARNATE, IMMANENT, ALIVE!
+THOUGH MANY PEOPLE WITH MANY TALENTS AND MANY DESIRES,
WE ARE ONE IN ONE SPIRIT, IN ONE LOVE, ON ONE MISSION,
IN ONE LORD, FOR ONE GOOD, IN ONE TRUTH,
IN AND FOR THE LOVE OF OUR ONE FATHER,
THE ALMIGHTY FATHER OF OUR ONE SAVIOR,
WHO SANCTIFIES US IN THE ONE HOLY SPIRIT
WHICH BUILDS US UP IN THE ONE FAITH
AND THE ONE HOPE IN THE ONE BODY OF LOVE,
THE BODY OF CHRIST, THE BRIDE OF THE LORD,
THE FLOCK OF THE SHEPHERD, THE PEOPLE OF GOD,
THE CHURCH OF CHRIST, THE CHURCH WHO IS ALIVE IN CHRIST,
THE CHURCH IN, THROUGH, AND FOR CHRIST,
THE CHURCH CHRIST,
THE UNIVERSAL HOPE OF MAN, THE LIGHT TO THE GENTILES,
THE CATHOLIC CHURCH. +

+CRYING FOR A SIGN OF JESUS IN OUR LIFE,
WE RUN TO HIS MOTHER MARY TO INTERCEDE FOR US
-IN MERCIFUL GRACE AND REDEMPTIVE BREAD AND SALVIFIC WINE-
IN THE HOPE OF MARRIAGE-IN FAITH AND SACRAMENT AND PRAYER-
WITH THE GOOD SHEPHERD WHO PROTECTS,
AND THE GENTLE LAMB WHO FORGIVES,
IN LIFE AND FREEDOM AND LOVE.

AND OFFERING OUR LIFE IN REPENTANCE,
AS WATER IN JARS OF CLAY,
WE HOPE IN FAITH,
IN THE COMMUNION OF LOVE,
FOR THE MIRACLE OF TRANSFORMATION,
AS OUR LIVES TAKE ON UNSURPASSABLE FLAVOR
IN THE WINE OF THE COMPASSIONATE CHRIST. +

+THE SACRIFICE OF ONES WILL
IS THE GREATEST SACRIFICE
ASIDE FROM THE GIFT OF ONES LIFE.

AND A DISCIPLE OF CHRIST,
OFFERING ONES WILL
IN HUMBLE OBEDIENCE
FOR THE SAKE OF BLESSED RELATIONSHIP WITH JESUS
IS IMITATING IN A MOST INTIMATE WAY
THE OFFERING OF CHRIST'S WILL IN GETHSEMANE
TO THE WILL OF THE FATHER
IN THE UNITY OF THEIR LOVE
IN THE SPIRIT OF SACRIFICIAL AGAPE,
THE LOVE WHICH REVEALED HIMSELF ON THE CROSS.

FOR IN OFFERING OUR WILL
TO THE WILL OF GOD,
WE TASTE GLORY IN SUFFERING,
UNITED TO CHRIST CRUCIFIED
AND AWAIT-IN THE SPIRIT OF LIFE EVERLASTING-
THE SUBLIME JOY OF CHRIST RISEN WITHIN US! +

+THE CROSS THE CROSS THE CROSS,
FAITH'S WAY, HOPE'S ENDURANCE, LOVE'S WITNESS. +

GOD THE SPIRIT

"ALTHOUGH LOVE IS AN ESSENTIAL NAME OF GOD, AS WE HAVE SEEN, THE TERM IS ALSO USED SPECIFICALLY AS A PERSONAL NAME IN GOD; AS SUCH IT IS PROPER TO THE THIRD PERSON OF THE TRINITY. THE HOLY GHOST (SPIRIT) IS LOVE."
ST THOMAS AQUINAS
SUMMA THEOLOGICA QQ 37

"ALL THE SOVEREIGNTY AND FREEDOM OF THE WORLD COMPARED TO THE FREEDOM AND SOVEREIGNTY OF THE SPIRIT OF GOD IS UTTER SLAVERY, ANGUISH, AND CAPTIVITY. "
ST JOHN OF THE CROSS
THE ASCENT OF MOUNT CARMEL

+THE END TIME JUDGE
PLACES MANY A PAGAN ALONG OUR PATH.

IT IS OUR CHOICE TO VIEW THESE PEOPLE
AS GRACE OR AS OBSTACLE.

FOR THE JUDGE WHO TESTS US DAILY
IS ALSO THE MERCIFUL FATHER
WHO GRACES US IN THE BODY AND BLOOD OF HIS CRUCIFIED SON,
SO THAT THROUGH *THE SPIRIT OF THE RESURRECTION*
WE MAY COOPERATE IN OUR SALVATION,
BRINGING NEWLY FOUND BROTHERS AND SISTERS OF CHRIST
ALONG *THE WAY.* +

+I CANNOT SAY THAT I UNDERSTAND EVERYTHING
FROM THE LIPS OF THE LORD.
THIS I CAN SAY: I TRUST IN HIS LOVE,
FOR HIS LOVE IS WITNESSED IN HIS DYING FOR ME,
HIS DYING FOR ME
WHEN ALL I EVER GAVE HIM WAS SIN AND SILENCE.
I TRUST IN HIS CHURCH.
THERE, A GREATER UNDERSTANDING CAN BE FOUND
FOR A SPIRITUAL CHILD LIKE ME.

FINALLY, I TRUST IN THE *HOLY SPIRIT,*
FROM THE HEART,
IN A FAITH LANGUAGE SOMETIMES BEYOND WORDS. +

+SEEK GOD WITHIN…
SEEK GOD IN THE SILENCE OF HEARTFELT DEVOTION.
FEAR THE LORD IN THE HUMILITY OF TRUE SELF-REFLECTION.
REPENT AS A CHILD, FOR GOD IS A COMPASSIONATE FATHER.
PRAY TO ANGELS, PRAY TO SAINTS,
FOR THEY ARE THE MESSANGERS OF OUR PETITIONS,
AND THE COURIERS OF GOD'S GRACE.
AND THEY TRAVEL IN THE POWER OF THE MIGHTY WIND
OF *GOD'S HOLY SPIRIT*
UP AND DOWN THE LADDER BETWEEN HEAVEN AND EARTH,
BUILT UPON THE CROSS OF THE CRUCIFIED AND RISEN CHRIST. +

+I HAVE NEVER SEEN GOD,
BUT I HAVE FELT HIS TOUCH
IN THE MERCY AND LOVE AND COMPASSION
OF HIS SACRAMENTS, IN HIS WRITTEN WORD,
IN THE CHARITY OF HIS BELOVED DISCIPLES,
AND IN THE STRANGEST AND MOST POWERFUL TESTIMONY
TO HIS TRUTH...
THE LOVE WHICH WELLS UP INSIDE OF ME,
BURSTING FORTH IN SPONTANEOUS AND UNPROVOKED CHARITY.

CONTRASTING MY OWN NATURAL DEPRAVITY,
THIS TESTIFIES TO SUPERNATURAL LOVE AS *GOD'S SPIRIT* IN ME! +

+**THE** WORLD IS NOT FRIEND,
AND CERTAINLY NOT END!
AS CHRIST, WE MUST MEND,   *RHYME*
AND IN TEMPTATION NEVER BEND.
FOR THIS IS THE PLACE OF SHARING GOD'S GRACE,
IN MERCY AND LOVE AS GIFTS FROM ABOVE,
WHILE CARRYING ONES CROSS, AND AVOIDING SATAN'S DROSS,
IN FAITH AND IN HOPE, IN GOD'S CHURCH, IN GOD'S POPE.
FOR WE ARE LIGHTAND WE ARE BEACON
AND WE ARE SALTAND WE ARE GOD'S DEACON.
IN LOVE WE WILL WIN,
AS CHRIST CONQUERED SIN,
IN TREMBLING AND FEAR, SALVATION DRAWS NEAR,
BRINGING FRIEND, CHANGING FOE, *IN THE SPIRIT WE MUST GO!* +

+**WHEN** OTHERS FLOURISH IN ACTS OF MERCY,
AND CHARITY ABOUNDS FROM THEIR MOUTH AND THEIR HANDS,
WHILE YOU LANGUISH IN THE DESERT
OF DRY MINISTRY AND SEEMINGLY FRUITLESS EFFORT,
ALWAYS KEEP IN MIND, CLOSE TO YOUR HEART,
AS FUEL FOR YOUR SOUL,
THAT AN OASIS AWAITS AND THE DESERT WILL END
IN THE CESSATION OF PRIDE
AND THE DISCOVERY OF GREENER PASTURE
IN THE JOY OF GOD'S GOOD WORK IN ANOTHER BROTHER.
FOR IN THAT JOY WILL FLOW THE *TRUE SPIRIT* OF THAT CHARITY
WHICH WILL SURELY MOVE ANOTHER. +

IN MEMORY OF FATHER CHARLES MALLEN, CSSR-
FATHER, SHEPHERD, BROTHER, FRIEND

+THE FIRE OF GOD'S LOVE
IS MUCH TOO HOT FOR THE ICY COLD HEART
OF THE MAN AND WOMAN OF MALICE.

BUT FOR THE BELOVED DISCIPLE,
ALREADY ON FIRE *IN THE SPIRIT* OF THE CRUCIFIED FIRESTORM,
THE BLAZE OF GOD IS BUT DELIGHT AND JOY!

YET FIRE DESIRES TO SPREAD!
FOR THE FIRE OF GOD'S LOVE YEARNS
TO PURGATE
THE LUKEWARM DISCIPLE,
AND CONSUME THE LOST AND THE COLD
IN THE UNFATHOMABLE HEAT
OF THE FURNACE OF AL MERCY
IN THE SACRED HEART OF THE MESSIAH,
HE WHO CONVERTS THE HEART IN ONE AMEN
FROM ICY DEATH TO FIERY LIFE
FOR LOVE ALONE.

THUS, THIS SPARK OF CHRIST'S FLAME,
THIS FAITHFUL DISCIPLE,
THIS MERCIFUL FATHER,
THIS VIGILANT SHEPHERD,
THIS COMPASSIONATE BROTHER,
AND THIS PERSEVERING FRIEND,
SPREAD THE FIRE OF CHARITY-
IN HIS LIFE, HIS LEGACY, AND THE SPIRIT OF LOVE ETERNAL. +

+I MUST DEPART THE LAND OF MY CAPTIVITY,
HASTILY,
WITHOUT PROVISIONS,
WITH ONLY THE UNLEAVENED DOUGH
OF FAITH
AND HOPE
AND CHARITY
IN THE HOLY SPIRIT OF MY SAVIOR-
HE WHO WILL PROVIDE FOR WHAT I TRULY NEED. +

+ARMED WITH THE WEAPONRY OF TRUST AND LOVE,
THE INVISIBLE SPIRIT OF THE GOD I CANNOT SEE
SENDS ME FORTH TO BATTLE THE PRINCIPALITIES OF THE WORLD,
THROUGH FAITH AND HOPE AND CHARITY.

THE WORLD, ARMED WITH VISCIOUS TOOLS OF TORTURE,
IN MALICE AND REJECTION AND PERSECUTION AND SEDUCTION,
THRUST FORWARD BY THE gods OF THEIR OWN EYES,
DOES BATTLE THROUGH DESPAIR AND FEAR AND HATRED.

THE BATTLE, IF FAITHFULLY FOUGHT ON MY PART,
ENDS WITH ME, BLOODIED AND BEATEN ON A CROSS!

YET, THIS IS VICTORY!
FOR FAITHFULLY, GOD WILL RAISE ME TO LIVE AGAIN!

AND IN MY RESCUE,
MY ENEMY WILL SEE THE VISIBLE SPIRIT OF GOD ALL THE CLEARER!
AND THE CROSS OF THE CRUCIFIED CHRIST WILL TRIUMPH AGAIN! +

+BEFORE I DIE,
MY GREATEST HOPE
IS THAT MY CONSCIENCE WILL BEAR WITNESS
TO MY HEART
THAT I GAVE MY BEST,
THE GIFT OF MY LIFE,
AND ALL MY GOODNESS,
FOR THE BELOVED FEW,
BESTOWED UPON MY LIFE,
BY THE SPIRIT OF GOD,
HE WHO MYSTERIOUSLY ELUDES MY GRASP.

AS OF NOW,
MY CONSCIENCE CONVICTS ME
OF MALPRACTICE, AND IRRESPONSIBILITY, AND SELFISHNESS,
AND THIS MYSTERIOUS SPIRIT
-HE WHO ELUDES MY GRASP-
CHALLENGES ME TO CHANGE FOR THE BETTER,
REALIZING MY GREATEST HOPE
IN GOD REVEALING *AGAPE* LOVE. +

+GOD SCATTERS PROUD ARMIES AND GATHERS NEEDY CHILDREN.
TO THE WARRIOR OF PRIDE, GOD GIFTS PURGATION.
TO THE CRUSHED AND THE PERSECUTED,
THE TRULY POOR IN SPIRIT,
GOD PROVIDES A HOME.

BOW YOUR HEAD,
BEND YOUR KNEE,
PRAY,
AND RECEIVE GRACE!

DENY! DENOUNCE! DEFEND YOUR HONOR!
REMAIN INDIGNANT TO DIVINE WILL,
AND DIE A THOUSAND DEATHS…
ALL WITHOUT THE RESURRECTION OF GRACE,
IN THE HOLY SPIRIT OF GOD'S ETERNAL LOVE.

LOVE, WHICH IS GIVEN IN SPIRIT…
AND RETURNED IN SANCTITY. +

+AS THE LORD IS BOTH *LAMB* AND *LION*,
WE MUST BE BOTH LAMB AND LION
FOR OUR BROTHERS AND SISTERS IN CHRIST.

FOR THE WORLD IS FULL OF RAVENOUS WOLVES,
SEEKING TO DEVOUR THE PURE AND GENTLE SHEEP.

AND AMONG THE FLOCK,
LIE IN HIDING
WOLVES UNDER THE GUISE OF SHEEP,
READY TO WOUND WITH THE DAGGER OF THEIR LYING TONGUES.

FOR THE FLOCK MUST ADHERE TO CHRIST'S VICAR SHEPHERD,
FOLLOWING FAITHFULLY IN COMMUNION
WITH HIS BELOVED BRIDE,
HIS CHURCH,
ALLOWING *THE HOLY SPIRIT OF GOD*
TO GUIDE HIS PILGRIM PEOPLE HOME…
WHERE THE LOVING FATHER AWAITS WITH OPEN ARMS. +

+JESUS WAS CONSECRATED TO THE FATHER'S TRUTH
THROUGH THE WOOD AND THE NAILS OF HIS BLESSED CROSS.

HIS DESIRE WAS AND IS ALWAYS,
FOR OUR CONSECRATION TO HIS TRUTH,
ONE IN BEING WITH THE FATHER,
FOR THE RECONCILIATORY COMMUNION OF GOD AND MAN
IN CHRIST
FOUND THROUGH THE WOOD AND THE NAILS
OF OUR STRUGGLES, BURDENS, AND SUFFERINGS,
FOR OUR SALVATION,
THE SANCTITY WHICH IS FOUND
IN THE HOLY SPIRIT OF CHRIST
IN THE COMMUNION OF THE SAINTS
WITHIN THE CHURCH OF CHRIST'S BROTHERS AND SISTERS,
HIS BRIDE IN THE UNIFYING SPIRIT OF LOVE,
THE LOVE WHICH VIVIFIES OUR HEARTS
AND GLORIFIES THE FATHER OF ALL,
ALL THAT IS PURE AND GOOD IN CREATION. +

+*PENTECOST IS FIRE AND WIND!*
THE BIRTH OF THE CHURCH OF JESUS CHRIST
UNLEASHED COURAGE IN COMPASSION,
VIRTUE IN REPENTANCE,
AND FAITH AND HOPE IN THE HUMBLE REALIZATION
OF BEING LOVED UNCONDITIONALLY.

WITHIN THE PERSEVERING WIND OF THE SPIRIT,
THE VERY FIRE OF GOD'S LOVE,
IN CHRIST INCARNATE,
RISEN IN BODY AND SACRAMENT,
WE PROCLAIM WHAT WE LIVE!
CHRIST JESUS *ALIVE* FOR THE SALVATION OF MANKIND. +

+THE LANGUAGES AT BABEL LED TO BABBLE!
THE TONGUES AT PENTECOST LED TO SALVATION!
MAN'S SCHISM FROM GOD'S WILL ONLY LEADS TO CONFUSION.
MAN'S DOCILITY TO GOD'S SPIRIT ONLY LEADS TO SALVATION.
MANY LANGUAGES, ONE FAITH! MANY PEOPLES, ONE HOPE!
MANY SOULS, ONE HOLY SPIRIT IN ONE EVERLASTING LOVE! +

+UNITY IS A DIVERSITY OF EXPRESSION
IN COMMUNION WITH THE ONE SOURCE
OF ONE FAITH IN ONE HOPE AND ONE LOVE
EQUALING ONE TRUTH,
PERVADED, GRACED, AND PROVIDED
IN FREE DIVINE CREATIVITY
IN ONE HOLY SPIRIT
FOUND IN DIVERSE CHARISMS, DIVERSE VOCATIONS,
DIVERSE CULTURES, AND DIVERSE LANGUAGES,
IN THE MINISTRY OF ONE MERCY
FOR THE LOVE OF ONE SHEPHERD FOR THE MANY LOST SHEEP,
FOR THE GLORY AND HONOR OF THE ONE FATHER,
THE FATHER OF JESUS CHRIST OUR LORD. +

+*FEAR* IS THE NATURAL CONSEQUENCE
OF SEPARATION FROM THE LORD.
COURAGE COMES IN THE REAL PRESENCE OF CHRIST.
FROM HIS PRESENCE COMES COMMUNION IN THE SPIRIT!

IN THE COMMUNION OF THE SPIRIT,
WE WALK TO THE ENDS OF THE EARTH,
SHARING THE GOSPEL,
DISPENSING GOD'S MERCY,
AND WITNESSING TO HOPE IN GRACE AND VIRTUE,
THROUGH THE LOVE OF GOD,
FOUND IN THE LIVING BODY OF CHRIST, HIS CHURCH. +

+THROUGH SEASONS OF DISSAPOINTMENT
AND DESERT TREKS IN ADDICTIVE DRYNESS,
I STILL CRY TO THE LORD OF MERCY.

AND EVEN THOUGH MY POCKETS ARE EMPTY
AND MY PANTS HAVE HOLES,
THE SPIRIT OF THE LIVING GOD OF MERCY
FILLS ME WITH PERSISTENCE AND HOPE.

FOR ONE DAY,
I WILL REALIZE MY PURPOSE,
GOD'S HIDDEN PLAN FOR ME.
THEN TRUTH WILL REVEAL...THE TRUTH OF ME. +

+IN SEEKING POVERTY AND HUMILITY,
SHAME WILL NEVER REMAIN YOUR LEGACY.

FOR GOD FORGIVES AND TRANSFORMS
AND RAISES THE DEAD FROM SIN,
SHAMEFULLY LOST IN THEIR PRIDE,
ENGULFING THEM IN THE OPEN ARMS OF HIS FATHERLY MERCY,
TRANSFORMING THEM IN THE CLEANSING BLOOD
OF HIS BELOVED SON,
RAISING THEM UP AS NEWBORN SAINTS IN THE WATERS OF BAPTISM,
AND GIVING THEM LIFE AND NOBILITY
IN THE *UNCONQUERABLE SPIRIT* OF HIS *EVERLASTING LOVE.* +

+I AM FORGIVEN AND GRACED AND ENCOURAGED,
TO SEE MYSELF IN THE LIGHT OF THE IMAGE I REFLECT,
WITHIN THE LIFE OF CHRIST,
BESTOWED UPON ME IN SANCTIFYING GRACE
THROUGH THE HOLY SPIRIT IN THE SACRAMENTS OF GOD'S CHURCH.

FROM THIS GRACED REFLECTION
I AM TO FORGIVE AND GRACE AND ENCOURAGE
IN HUMBLE OBEDIENCE TO THE MANDATE OF THE LORD,
TO LOVE CHRIST IN THE POOR, AS CHRIST LOVES THE POOR IN ME. +

+LITTLE THOUGH I AM, MY STRENGTH ABOUNDS IN THE LORD!
TAKE WITNESS AND HOPE LITTLE ONES!
LITTLE THOUGH WE ARE, OUR STRENGTH ABOUNDS UNITED IN HIM.
TAKE WITNESS AND HOPE SCATTERED FAMILY!
SINNERS THOUGH WE ARE!
OUR PERFECTION ABOUNDS AS WE ABIDE IN HIM.
SEEK HIS LIFE, AND SHINE AS HIS LIGHT!
FIND STRENGTH
AND COMFORT
AND PURPOSE
WITHIN THE LIVING SACRIFICE OF THE EUCHARISTIC LORD!
FOR HIS LIFE IS FOUND WITHIN *THE SPIRIT*
WHO INCARNATES,
REDEEMS,
ASCENDS,
AND ALWAYS RETURNS AS LOVE. +

+CHRIST IS THE GREAT AMEN!
FOR SALVATION IS THE GIFT
WHICH ALLOWS FALLEN AND DISOBEDIENT HUMANITY,
THROUGH THE GLORIOUS EFFECT
OF THE MERCIFUL CONDESCENSION OF THE SAVIOR,
TO UTTER IN PERFECTED DEVOTION:
THE AMEN
OF THE GETHSEMANE LORD,
THE AMEN
OF THE FLAGELLATION,
THE AMEN
OF THE CRUCIFIXION,
THE AMEN
OF THE TOMB AND THE DESCENT...
SO THAT IN THE HOLY SPIRIT OF THE RESURRECTED LORD,
WE MAY ASCEND TO GOD
IN FAITH AND HOPE
WHILE LIVING HERE AND NOW
IN THE LOVE WHICH SANCTIFIES AND READIES
ALL MEN FOR CHRIST'S TRIUMPHANT RETURN. +

+THE LETTER IS MEANT TO POINT TO THE SPIRIT!

THE LETTER IS BOTH SIGN AND SYMBOL,
EFFECTING ENLIGHTENMENT IN THE BLIND OF SPIRIT,
FOR THE VISION OF THE SANCTIFYING SPIRIT,
IN THE POWER OF THE ALMIGHTY SPIRIT.

THE LETTER
SERVES AS THE VOICE
AND THE CALL OF THE SPIRIT;
A CONDUIT OF GOD'S GRACE
-IN GOD'S LOVE-
THROUGH HUMAN LANGUAGE
-IN DIVINE TRUTH-
FOR THE SALVATION OF MANKIND
IN BAPTISMAL HOLINESS BEGOTTEN OF CHRIST'S CROSS
FOR THE JOY OF THE ANGELS AND SAINTS
IN THE COMPANY OF JESUS AND MARY,
ALL FOR THE GLORY OF GOD THE FATHER. +

+THE SPIRIT CRIES WITHIN ME
FOR THE REMEMBRANCE OF MERCY,
AND GRATITUDE FOR GRACE UPON GRACE IN SINS FORGIVEN...
AND GOD COME NEAR,
IN SACRAMENTS OF LOVE AND LIFE RESTORED.

FOR THE FATHER
SENT THE SON
TO REDEEM MANKIND,
IMPARTING THE SPIRIT OF HIS UNFAILING LOVE
WITHIN OUR HEARTS
SO THAT STRENGTHENED IN THE BODY AND BLOOD
OF HIS SON, OUR SAVIOR,
WE WOULD REVEAL TO ALL MEN AND WOMEN
THE ABBA OF CHRIST
WHOSE SPIRIT HEALS ALL WOUNDS
AND RECONCILES THE SPLIT BETWEEN MAN AND PERFECT LOVE. +

+WE ARE BUT VESSELS OF CLAY;
UNABLE TO PROMISE IN CERTAINTY,
NEVER TO CREATE PERFECTLY,
EVER TO STRUGGLE IN FIDELITY.

FOR THIS, WE MUST SEEK FOR HUMILITY.

FOR GOD'S PROMISES ALONE ARE CERTAIN,
GOD'S CREATION ALONE IS PERFECTION,
AND GOD'S FIDELITY ALONE IS FOREVER UNBROKEN
IN THE EASE OF HIS ALMIGHTY ESSENCE.

THIS ASSURES GRACE IN FAITH AND HOPE
WHICH SPRINGS FROM THE HEART OF CLAY,
TO PERFECTION IN THE HEART OF CHRIST,
FROM THE CHARITY OF THE SANCTIFYING SPIRIT
WHOSE GRACE TRANSFORMS NATURE
IN THE PERFECT LOVE OF THE HEAVENLY FATHER. +

+EVANGELIZATION AND ECUMENISM
ARE THE VERY BREATHE OF THE LUNGS OF THE LORD,
IN THE WIND OF THE SPIRIT OF PENTECOST. +

+HOPE IS MEMORY EXERCISED IN FAITH,
REVEALING THE MERCIFUL LOVE OF GOD
IN ALL SINFULNESS VANQUISHED
WITHIN THE HOLY SPIRIT OF RECONCILIATION,
ISSUING FORTH FROM THE VOICE OF GOD,
IN THE ONE WORD WHICH BRINGS NEW LIFE,
THE ETERNAL WORD OF MERCY, CHRIST JESUS THE LORD. +

+THE BLOOD OF THE MOSAIC COVENANT
WAS THE BLOOD OF A BEAST.
THOUGH THE PEOPLE PROMISED FIDELITY,
ONLY GOD KEEPS HIS PROMISES.

THE BLOOD OF THE NEW COVENANT
IS THE BLOOD OF THE CHRIST.
THOUGH THE PEOPLE PERENIALLY STRUGGLE WITH FIDELITY,
GOD FULFILLS HIS PROMISE DAILY
IN THE PERFECT SACRIFICE OF CHRIST
ON THE ALTAR OF PERFECT LOVE,
FROM THE TABLE OF THE LAST SUPPER,
TO THE CROSS ON CALVARY,
THROUGH THE RESURRECTION IN THE VERY SAME SPIRIT,
THE SPIRIT WHICH PERPETUATES THIS PERFECT ACT OF LOVE
IN THE MOST HOLY EUCHARIST. +

+"WHAT RETURN CAN I MAKE TO YAHWEH,
FOR ALL HIS GOODNESS TO ME?"

JUST A LITTLE MORE TRUST, JUST A LITTLE MORE FIDELITY.

FOR CHRIST HAS DIED, FOR ME.
AND HIS SACRIFICE, THOUGH JOYFUL IN REDEMPTION,
COST THE FATHER MUCH SUFFERING.

JUSTICE AND MERCY HAVE SPOKEN THROUGH CHRIST.
THE WORD OF GOD HAS FULFILLED THE FATHER'S PLAN.
NOW WE, IN TURN, ARE CALLED TO OFFER OURSELVES
IN CHRIST'S PERFECT THANK OFFERING,
WALKING FAITHFULLY IN *THE HOLY SPIRIT,*
WHICH RAISES LIFE IN CHRIST "IN THE LAND OF THE LIVING." +

+ IT IS EASY TO LOVE THOSE
WHO LOVE US FIRST.

BUT THE LOVE OF THE SAINT
IS THE LOVE OF CHRIST,
WHO LOVES BEYOND RESPONSE.

FOR NAILED TO THE CROSS,
CHRIST LOVED TO THE LAST DROP
OF HIS MOST PRECIOUS BLOOD,
LOVING UNTO DEATH,
REDEEMING THROUGH PERSECUTION,
AND DESCENDING TO THE DEAD.

LOVING BEYOND THE RESPONSE,
HE ROSE TO NEW LIFE;
RISEN, HE SHARES *HIS LIFE-GIVING SPIRIT*,
WHICH TRANSFORMS THE HEART OF MAN,
SO THAT MAN MAY LOVE BEYOND THE RESPONSE. +

+SALVATION HAS ALREADY BEEN WON
BY THE MIGHTY RIGHT HAND OF GOD
THROUGH THE CROSS AND RESURRECTION OF THE CHRIST.

*NOW IS THE TIME OF THE SPIRIT
AND THE CHURCH*,
JOINED AS BODY TO HER HEAD
AND AS BRIDE TO HER GROOM,
THE SAVIOR OF MAN,
JESUS CHRIST.

NOW IS THE TIME TO BECOME OUR SALVATION!
NOW IS THE TIME TO SHARE GOD'S MERCY!
THIS IS THE PLACE,
WHEREVER WE ARE,
TO LIVE OUR FAITH,
BECOME OUR HOPE,
SO THAT GOD'S LOVE IN US
MAY CALL THE LOST TO JOIN CHRIST'S BODY
IN SALVATION ALREADY WON! +

+WHEN JESUS ADMONISHES US TO LOVE OUR ENEMY,
HE IS CUTTING US TO THE DEEPEST RECESSES
OF OUR SOUL, WHERE spirit AND SPIRIT MEET
IN THE GIFTED TREASURE CHEST OF THE CONSCIENCE,
WHERE FAITH AND HOPE ARE BOTH TESTED
AND UNLEASHED
AS MERCY FOR THE PURPOSES OF GOD'S LOVE.

WITH THE TWO EDGED SWORD OF THE GOSPEL,
JEUS WEILDS LOVE'S WEAPON
IN THE HEALING WOUND OF DOUBLE RECOGNITION:
TO LOVE EVERYONE,
EVEN OUR ENEMY,
IS TO BE HOLY AS GOD ALONE IS HOLY.
AND TO LOVE ONES ENEMY
IS TO PATIENTLY EXPECT GOD'S GRACE
TO CONQUER THEIR SINFULNESS
IN THE DUE TIME OF DIVINE LOVE. +

+CHRIST IS THE JOYFUL OBEDIENCE OF HUMANITY!

HIS BROTHERS AND SISTERS ENJOY HIS POWER AND HIS BLESSINGS
IN TRANSFORMED HEARTS, WHICH TRANSFORM OTHERS.

CHRIST IS LIGHT IN THE ECLIPSE OF SIN;
TRUE TO HIS EVER-FAITHFUL PRESENCE.

ALWAYS GIVING, HIS GRACE HUNTS INEXHAUSTABLY...
FOR REPENTANCE, AND CONVERSION, AND SANCTITY,
AND HONOR IN SAINTHOOD,
-IN THE SPIRITOF HOLINESS-
FOR THE GLORY OF OUR FATHER IN HEAVEN. +

+WINE AND WOMEN, AND WAR AND WAGES ARE BUT HARBINGERS
OF WORRY, WEARINESS AND WORN OUT SAGES.
GOLD AND GLORY AND ALL THE NEW RAGES
BURN THE GOOD BOOK OF LIFE TO THE VERY LAST PAGES.
BUT LIFE IN GOD'S SPIRIT BRINGS JOY SO DEEP,
FOR LOVE DESTROYS ALL REASONS TO WEEP. +

+**TO GIVE** OUR OF SHEER LOVE
IS TO GIVE FROM WITHIN THE SILENT CLOUD
OF THE HOLY SPIRIT OF ANONYMOUS AND TRUE HUMILITY,
AS FOUND IN THE FIRST THIRTY YEARS OF THE NAZARENE.
TO PRAY OUT OF PURE FAITH AND HOPE
IS TO PRAY IN THE DARKNESS OF GETHSEMANE,
WITH ALL COMPANIONS ASLEEP,
AND ONLY THE FATHER TO LISTEN…
AND RESPOND.
TO FAST OUT OF SHEER AGAPE,
IS TO FAST FROM WITHIN THE HONEST DECEPTION
OF EXTERNAL CALM,
RESERVING INTERNAL SUFFERING
AS A GIFT OF LOVE
OFFERED TO THE FATHER
IN *THE HOLY SPIRIT*
AND THE SACRAMENT OF THANKSGIVING,
WRAPPED IN THE SUBLIME SACRIFICE OF THE SUFFERING SERVANT. +

+FORGIVENESS IS THE SEED OF FORGIVENESS,
WHICH GENERATES AN ATMOSPHERE
CONDUCIVE TO A GARDEN
RESPLENDENT
IN THE FLOWERING OF AUTHENTIC PEACE AND JUSTICE
IN THE *SPIRIT* OF GENUINE RESPECT FOR HUMAN DIGNITY,
WHICH CAN ONLY COME FROM THE HOLY SPIRIT
OF THE ONE TRUE DIGNIFIED HUMAN,
THE GOD-MAN
WHO DIVINIZED THE FALLEN CHILDREN OF ADAM AND EVE,
RAISING THEM AS ADOPTED SONS AND DAUGHTERS,
IN THE SANCTITY WHICH COMES IN LIVING PASCHAL FAITH,
-FOLLOWING THE WAY OF THE CROSS-
WHICH ALWAYS POINTS TOWARD THE OPEN ARMS
OF THE LOVING PRODIGAL FATHER. +

+WE ARE NAMED BY OUR PARENTS IN THE FLESH.
WE ARE RE-NAMED IN BAPTISM IN THE HOLY SPIRIT!
NO LONGER ABRAM BUT ABRAHAM, NO LONGER SIMON BUT CEPHAS.
GOD HAS A PLAN FOR WHO WE REALLY ARE.
ALL WE MUST DO IS OBEY. +

+FAITH IS NOT A BARRIER TO DANGER!
FAITH IS NOT A GUARANTEE OF SUCCESS!
FAITH CANNOT WARD OFF THE ATTACK OF THE MALISCIOUS!

FAITH, HOWEVER, WARDS OFF DESPAIR
AND COWARDICE
AND RESIGNATION
IN THE DIVINE GRACE OF HOPE
AND COURAGE
AND PERSEVERANCE
IN THE DYNAMIC PRAYER
OF THE WARRIOR OF COMPASSION
AND THE KNIGHT OF MERCY
WILLING TO DIE AS THE MARTYR OF LOVE-
BELEIVING IN ALL CIRCUMSTANCES
IN THE MOST HOLY SPIRIT OF THE CHRIST WHO SAVES! +

+MY DAILY *ROUTINE,*
OF RITES AND RITUALS AND HABITS,
MIGHT JUST BE THE MAJOR OBSTACLE
TO A SPONTANEOUS NEIGHBORLY INTERCHANGE
OF FORGIVENESS AND RECONCILIATION,
WHICH COMES FROM A HEART IN TUNE
WITH THE INTIMATIONS
OF THE UNPREDICTABLE,
EVER CREATIVE
AND ALWAYS CHARITABLE HOLY SPIRIT. +

+ZECHARIAH'S TONGUE LAY HEAVY IN HIS MOUTH
TIL HIS HEART AQUIESED TO THE WILL OF GOD.
THEN PRAISE IN POWER POURED FORTH!
JOHN'S PRESENCE LAY HID IN THE WILDERNESS
TIL *THE SPIRIT OF GOD* SUMMONED HIM FORTH
IN THE FIRE OF BAPTISMAL TRUTH.
THEN PRAISE IN POWER POURED FORTH!
CHRIST'S SALVATION GREW HUMBLY IN THE WOMB OF MARY,
AND THE PROVIDENTIAL OBSCURITY OF NAZARETH,
TIL THE WILL OF GOD *IN THE SPIRIT OF ALL LOVE*
ANNOUNCED *IMMANUEL NOW!*
THEN PRAISE IN *POWER* POURED FORTH! +

+GOD IMPREGNATES THE SOUL
WITH THE SEED OF LOVE IN HIS SON.

GOODNESS AND TRUTH AND BEAUTY
ARE BORN OF THE HOLY SPIRIT.

THE VIRUS IMPLANTED IN THE SOUL
SANS THE SPIRIT OF GOD,
THIS IS A VIOLENT *RAPE-*
PERPETUATED BY THE FATHER OF LIES.

MALICE AND DECEIT AND DECAY
ARE CONSEQUENCES OF EVIL.

LIKE ABRAM AND SARAI,
WE MUST CHOOSE BETWEEN PATIENCE AND VIGILANCE
IN THE PROMISE OF GOD,
OR DESPAIR AND IMPULSIVITY
IN THE IMMEDIATELY GRATIFYING SPIRIT OF EVIL. +

+THOUGH OUR SINS
FILL THE SHORES OF OUR SOUL
WITH SAND,
GOD'S MERCY
FILLS EVERY CROOK AND CAVERN OF OUR HEART
WITH THE OCEAN OF HIS MERCY.

FOR THE SANDS OF SIN MAY DRY OUR FAITH,
AND CHOKE OUR HOPE,
BUT *THE SPIRIT OF THE ABBA OF LOVE*
QUENCHES OUR THIRST
IN THE MERCY OF HIS LIVING WATER
-HIS SON AND HIS WORD,
OUR LORD AND OUR SAVIOR-
FROM THE ROCK OF OUR SALVATION,
AS THE CORNERSTONE OF THE HOUSE BUILT ON ROCK
-BUILT WITH THE STONES OF REPENTANT MAN-
THE CHURCH WHICH WITHSTANDS ALL STORMS,
IN THE RENEWAL OF OUR FAITH AND HOPE
IN THE BLOOD SHED IN GOD'S LOVE FOR MAN. +

+I HAVE IT ON CHRIST'S AUTHORITY…
FROM SACRED SCRIPTURE:
TO WALK THE TALK IS TO WALK CHRIST'S *WAY*,
BUT TO TALK THE TALK WITHOUT THE WALK
IS TO ABANDON THE NARROW AND THE FEW,
TO WALK ON THE WIDE WITH THE MANY.

FOR A HOUSE BUILT UPON ASCETIC AND PIOUS SELF-CENTEREDNESS
IS A HOME SET FOR DESTRUCTION IN THE STORM.

BUT A HOUSE BUILT UPON *THE SPIRIT OF LIVING FAITH,*
THIS IS A HOME SET UP ON THE ROCK OF PERSEVERANCE
IN THE HOPE AND THE CHARITY WHICH OVERCOMES ALL STORMS
IN THE SANCTITY WHICH GLORIFIES THE LORD. +

+GOD FULFILLS EVERY PROMISE,
ANSWERS EVERY PRAYER, IN A LIFETIME!

A CENTURY WRINKLED,
AND ABRAM BECAME ABRAHAM.
A CENTURY WORN,
AND ABRAHAM REALIZED GOD'S PROMISE IN ISAAC.

AFTER NINETY YEARS OF STRUGGLING FIDELITY,
SARAI BECAME SARAH,
AND FINALLY BORE MIRACULOUS FRUIT
IN DELIVERING ABRAHAM THE FIRST OF MANY!

TIME TAKES NO HOLIDAY!
THE CALENDER MARCHES ON!
SILENCE AND FRUSTRATIONS BETRAY TRUTH.

FOR THE SPIRIT OF GOD'S LOVE
FULFILLS OUR FAITHFUL HOPE
THROUGH ALL DAYS! +

+GO TO CONFESSION!
LOVE IN MERCY IS WAITING!
FACING SINFULNESS IS AN EXERCISE IN HOLINESS,
AND THE SUREST SIGN OF THE HOLY SPIRIT IN ACTION! +

+REVERANCE AND DEVOTION LEAD *THE WAY*
TO FAMILIAL SUCCESS IN THE VIRTUES OF FIDELITY AND CHARITY
WHICH BLESS IN THE PROSPERITY OF THE LITTLE CHURCH,
THE LITTLE COMMUNITY, THE VITAL CELL OF THE BODY,
A FAMILY ALIVE IN CHRIST!

FOR FEAR OF THE LORD AND LOVE OF HIS SON
BRING FORTH *THE TREASURE OF THE HOLY SPIRIT*
IN THE STRENGTHENING OF THE FAMILY
IN THE SACRAMENTAL UNION OF MARRIAGE,
THE VOCATION OF PARENTHOOD,
AND THE BLESSING OF CHILDREN,
THROUGH BLOOD AND ADOPTION,
AND THE PARENTHOOD OF EXTENDED FAMILY,
TO INCLUDE THE SPIRITUAL PARENT,
IN THE RAISING OF GOD'S CHILDREN
AS PROPHETS, PRIESTS AND SERVANT KINGS
TO LIVE IN THE SPIRIT
WITHIN THE BODY
OF INCARNATE COMPASSION, MERCY AND SALVATION. +

+LIFE AND EVIL ARE IMCOMPATIBLE!
LIFE IS PURE GOODNESS.
THE DESIRE FOR LIFE IS PURE FAITH AND HOPE.
THE PROTECTION OF LIFE IS JUSTICE BORN FROM ABOVE!

EVIL IS THE NEGATION OF LIFE,
THE DESIRE FOR DEATH,
AND THE DESTRUCTION OF THE LIVING,
INFECTED FROM BELOW!

GOD, THEREFORE, IS FOUND IN LIFE!
FOR WHEREVER –THE DESIRE FOR, AND THE PROTECTION OF–
THIS MOST BLESSED GIFT IS FOUND,
THERE THE CREATIVE HOLY SPIRIT WILL BE! +

+FROM THE ARK OF THE VIRGIN,
CHRIST OFFERS THE PERFECT HOLOCAUST,
WHICH ABATES THE JUST WRATH–DRYING THE FLOOD OF SIN–
REPLACING IT WITH *THE SPIRIT* OF LIVING WATER. +

+THE SPIRIT OF THE LORD,
IN OUR CONSCIENCE,
WITH OUR MIND,
IN OUR HEART,
WITH OUR SPIRIT,
IMMERSING OUR VERY SOUL
IN ABSOLUTE DARKNESS
-IN THE SPICE OF THE DEVIL, OUR CHOSEN VICE-
AWAKENS US TO RUN!

THE ONLY CHOICE IN TEMPTATION
IS TO HEARKEN TO THE VOICE OF THE HOLY SPIRIT WITHIN,
RUNNING TO SAFETY IN GOD'S OPEN ARMS...
NEVER TURNING BACK!

FOR THE FIRE AND BRIMSTONE OF VICE EMBRACED
IS EQUALLY MORTAL
IN THE GLANCE BACKWARD OF THE SALTY SINNER,
LOST IN THE NOSTOLGIA OF LUST. +

+IF CHRIST IS TRULY IN OUR BOAT,
WITH FAITH AND HOPE ASSERTING HIS NEARNESS,
AND THE APOSTOLIC CAPTAIN AND HIS EPISCOPAL FIRST MATES
ASSURING US OF HIS REAL PRESENCE,
WHY DO WE FEAR THE STORMY SEAS?
BECAUSE STORMS MEASURE FAITH!
TRUE FAITH
IS NEVER REVEALED IN CALM AND PLACID DAYS,
BUT IN TH TUMULT OF THE RAVAGING STORMS OF THE NIGHT!
FOR THE CROSS DARKENED THE SKY,
REFLECTING THE DOUBT OF HIS DISCIPLES SANS MARY AND A FEW.
ONLY THE LIGHT OF THE RESURRECTION
IN THE RISING OF GOD'S SON,
DID ILLUMINATION AND CLARITY AND FAITH
COME TO THE DISCIPLES.
AND THE SPIRIT OF THE LORD
-RAISING CHRIST DAILY IN OUR HEARTS-
IN THE ONE SACRIFICE OF CHRIST'S CROSS
-IN THE EUCHARIST OF GOD'S CHURCH-
REVEALS THE LORD, RESTING NEAR, WITHIN OUR STORMS. +

GOD OUR BEATITUDE

"LOVE IS THE ORIGIN AND SOURCE OF ALL GOOD THINGS. WHOEVER WALKS IN LOVE CAN NEITHER STRAY NOR BE AFRAID. LOVE GUIDES, LOVE PROTECTS, LOVE LEADS TO THE END.
FROM THE OFFICE OF READINGS, FEAST OF ST STEPHEN

"YOUR ARMS, MY JESUS, ARE THE ELEVATOR WHICH WILL TAKE ME UP TO HEAVEN. THERE IS NO NEED FOR ME TO GROW UP; ON THE CONTRARY, I MUST STAY LITTLE, AND BECOME MORE AND MORE SO.
ST THERESE OF LISIEUX
THE LITTLE WAY OF SAINT THERESE OF LISIEUX
INTO THE ARMS OF LOVE

"OUR HEARTS WERE MADE FOR THEE. THEY ARE RESTLESS UNTIL THEY REST IN THEE, O GOD."
ST AUGUSTINE OF HIPPO
DE CIVITATE DEI, BOOK XIV, CHAPTER 3

+THE HOLY SPIRIT AND GRACE...
THESE ARE THE GIFTS OF LOVE
FROM THE FATHER, THROUGH THE SON,
FOR OUR SALVATION, AND THE SALVATION OF ALL.

THEREFORE,
DECEPTIVE LIVING AND HYPOCRICY
MUST BE VANQUISHED IN THE MERCY OF GOD,
DOING DEATH TO SELF, IN REPENTANCE AND HONEST LIVING,
IN FAITH AND HOPE AND TRUST IN CHRIST JESUS OUR LOVE.

PRAYER IN THE SPIRIT
-WHO BESTOWS GOD'S LOVE-
MUST BE OFFERED IN THE TRUE RELIGION OF CHARITY
-EXTENDED MORNING, NOON, AND NIGHT-
IN THANKSGIVING AND PRAISE,
FOR LIFE AND MERCY AND LOVE RECEIVED UNDESERVEDLY. +

+AS I ENTER THE CHAPEL,
I VIEW THE STAIN GLASS DEPICTION OF YOU
AS THE LOVING SHEPHERD,
HOLDING A DEARLY BELOVED LITTLE LAMB LIKE ME.

YOUR CARICATURE IS SO BEAUTIFUL,
SO REASSURING, SO UNCONDITIONAL IN LOVE-
FOR A RATHER SMALL, AND QUITE HONESTLY,
HOMELY CREATURE LIKE ME.

I IDENTIFY SO STRONGLY WITH THIS ARTFUL DEPICTION OF YOU
AS SHEPHERD
AND ME AS SMALL AND HOMELY.

THOUGH WOUNDED AND WEAK,
THROUGH MY FAITHLESSNESS AND BITTER ANGER TOWARD YOU,
YOU HOLD ME *NOW*, AND PROMISE TO HOLD ME FOREVER-
IN MERCY, WHICH OVERCOMES MY PAIN
AND RAISES MY LOVE
IN RESURRECTION AND LIFE
- THE UNIMAGINABLE HEIGHT
OF AGAPE TRINITARIAN LOVE. +

+AS I LAY IN MY BED,
BARELY AWAKE IN GRACED VIGILANCE,
I AM STARTLED BY THE BURST OF A SPIRIT-BLOWN TRUMPHET.

AND A VOICE,
AN ANGELIC VOICE
SINGS OF THE COMING OF THE LORD.

I AM BLINDED BY A LIGHT!
SO BRIGHT!
THAT DAY TURNS INTO NIGHT!

AND I SENSE LONG LOST FRIENDS
AND DEPARTED FAMILY
REGAINING SENSE AND CONSCIOUSNESS
AS I AM SWEPT UP IN RARIFIED AIR
TO MEET THE LORD IN PEACE AND JOY ETERNAL,
FOUND SOLELY IN THE TRUEST OF LOVE. +

+FAITH IN CHRIST
IS FAITH IN TRUE CHARITY FOR VARIOUS IMPOVERISHMENTS,
GENUINE LIBERTY EXTENDED TO UNATTRACTIVE CAPTIVITY,
SIGHT SHARED IN COMMON BLINDNESS,
AND COMMUNION IN FREEDOM
SHARED IN ACKNOWLEDGED COMMON DEPRAVITY…
IN AN ENDLESS YEAR OF THE KINGDOM OF GOD.

YET THIS FREEDOM IN CHARITY EXTENDED
PRESUPPOSES OUR BLINDNESS TOWARD CHRIST
WHO IS
NEXT TO US IN THE PEW,
NEXT TO US IN OUR HOME,
NEXT TO US ON THE ROAD,
AND NEXT TO US IN THE MIRROR.

WILL WE THROW HIM OFF THE BROW OF THE CLIFF,
OR WILL WE ACKNOWLEDGE HIM IN MERCY AND LOVE? +

+*S*ALVATION *IS NOW, NEVER EV*ADE *R*EPENTANCE! +

+WHEN YOU ARE ALONE, UNAPPRECIATED, CUT OFF,
-AS IF INVISIBLE-
JESUS PROCLAIMS:
YOU MATTER TO ME!
YOU ARE MY BELOVED!
I WOULD HAVE DIED FOR YOU AND YOU ALONE!

I LOVE YOU IN A *WAY* YOU WILL NEVER FULLY COMPREHEND
UNTIL WE MEET
IN THE LOVING EMBRACE
OF THE PRODIGAL FATHER,
AND THE SPIRIT OF MY LOVE FOR YOU,
THE SPIRIT OF UNCONDITIONAL
SACRIFICIAL
MERCIFUL
AND ETERNAL LOVE. +

+A THIEF IN THE NIGHT WILL COME! WILL WE BE READY?

FOR THE NIGHT IS BUT ABSENCE OF LIGHT,
AND THEIVERY IS BUT ABSENCE OF GOODNESS.

AND THROUGH FAITH, IN THE GRACE OF HOPE,
AND THE SPIRIT OF LOVE,
WE ARE NOT VOID OF LIGHT AND GOODNESS.

FOR GOD IS FAITHFUL!
AND IF WE STAY IN THE LIGHT,
HIS GOODNESS WILL CONQUER THE DARK THIEVERY OF DEATH! +

+**MY FEAR** IS BUT A LACK OF FAITH
IN THE SALVIFIC LIGHT OF CHRIST.
MY DESIRE IS BUT PARTICIPATION AND ACCEPTANCE
IN THE BREATHE OF CHRIST'S SPIRIT
AND THE LIFE OF HIS BODY.
MY FAITH AND MY HOPE SEEK THE TOUCH OF GOD,
FOR THE KISS OF PEACE, AND THE EMBRACE OF MERCY...
IN THIS DAY!
MY LOVE, SOLELY IN GRACE, SEEKS FOR HOPE AND PERSEVERANCE
IN PASCHAL EXPRESSION, SIMPLY TO GLORIFY ABBA. +

+WHEN YOU PRAY FOR ME,
YOU PLANT ME FIRMLY BY THE RIVER OF LIFE!
WHEN YOU COMMEND MY FAITH,
YOU REAFFIRM ME IN THE GRACE OF HOPE!
WHEN YOU REPRIMAND ME
FROM THE COMPASSIONATE PERSPECTIVE OF A FELLOW SINNER,
YOU PLANT THE SEED OF VIRTUE
IN HUMILITY AND REPENTANCE AND TRUE CONTRITION.

LOVE BEGETS LOVE!
FOR THE SAINT IS SEED FOR SANCTITY,
AND A BEACON OF LIGHT
ON THE DARK AND NARROW ROAD TOWARD ETERNITY. +

+WE ARE BUT TREES,
PLANTED IN THE SOIL OF OUR LIFE SITUATION,
NOT OF OUR OWN VOLITION.

YET, WHEREVER OUR LOCATION,
WHATEVER OUR SITUATION,
THE LORD BESTOWS THE SON AND THE WATER
FOR LIFE AND FOR GROWTH.

OUR ROOTS ARE CONSTANTLY BATHED
IN THE SPIRIT OF LIVING WATER.

OUR BRANCHES ARE LOVINGLY PRUNED
BY THE HAND OF THE PRODIGAL GARDENER.

AND THE SON,
THE BRIGHT LIGHT OF LIFE,
HE BURNS IN PERPETUAL PASSION
FOR THE VERY LIFE OF THIS TREE,
AND FOR ALL THE TREES
IN GOD'S CREATED GARDEN. +

+CHRIST IS NOT JESUS' LAST NAME!
CHRIST IS THE ESSENCE OF WHO HE IS!
HE IS MERCY!
CHRIST JESUS MERCY! +

+THE PATH OF THE HONEST
WINDS THROUGH AN INEVITABLE STRETCH OF TRECHERY.

THE PATH OF THE HUMBLE
IS SULLIED WITH DEBRIS FROM PRIDEFUL WARS.

THE ROAD IN HOLINESS
IS FULL OF BANDITS IN THE BUSH,
DEMONS AND DESTROYERS SCARRED WITH EVIL INTENTION!

YET, GOD IS THE WIND AT OUR BACK!
CHRIST IS THE FORERUNNER OF ALL OUR PATHS!
AND THE SPIRIT OF LOVE IS THE DRAGONSLAYER,
SENT TO PROTECT OUR SOUL. +

+THIRTY SILVER PIECES?
WHAT WAS JUDAS THINKING?
OR, MORE LIKELY,
IS THAT HOW PATHETIC MAN BECOMES
UNDER THE BOOT OF SATAN?

YET I,
WHO HAVE EATEN AT THE TABLE OF THE LORD,
AM I NOT JUDAS IN SIN?
IS IT NOT ALSO THE REWARD OF MY DIABOLICAL CHOICES
THIRTY PIECES OF DEATH?

AND WHICH TREE WILL I CHOOSE TO RUN TO?
THE HANGING TREE OF DESPAIR,
OR THE CRUCIFORM TREE OF MERCY? +

+I STARE AT THE CROSS FROM THE VANTAGE POINT OF DEPRAVITY.
IN PRIDEFUL HYPERTROPHY, LUST RUN AMOK,
ENVY VOLCANIC, GREED PERSONIFIED,
AND ANGER EXPLOSIVE, SELFISHNESS HAS BECOME MY ESSENCE.
AND I SEE A MAN ON THE CROSS; THOUGH I DON'T RECOGNIZE HIM.
FOR HE IS NOT ANGRY OR PROUD OR SPEWING WITH VICE,
BUT BOLD AND RADIANT, SHINING FORTH IN SUFFERING,
FULL OF THE POWER OF WHICH I AM MOST IN NEED OF,
 THE POWER OF LOVE! +

+I AM BANISHED...YOU OPEN THE DOOR.
I AM LEFT FOR DEAD...YOU RETURN MY LIFE.
I AM BELITTLED AND ROBBED...YOU BUILD ME UP IN COURAGE,
REFRESHING ME FROM YOUR BOUNTY OF GRACE.

I AM WOUNDED AND WEAK, DRAINED OF COMPASSION...
YOU PICK ME UP, HEAL MY WOUNDS,
REFRESHING MY HEART WITH MERCY.

REBORN FROM YOUR CROSS,
I DIE TO SELF IN RESURRECTION...
LIVING FOREVER UPON YOUR RETURN. +

+SAVE ME IN GRACED COMPASSION SHARED!
    SAVE ME IN GRACED FAITH EXPRESSED!
SAVE ME IN GRACED PERSEVERANCE PRACTICED!
SAVE ME IN GRACED HUMILITY WILLINGLY SUFFERED!
SAVE ME IN GRACED REVERENCE,
GRACED DEVOTION,
AND GRACED REPENTANCE,
WITH EYES THAT SEE *MY* SIN AND *YOUR* SALVATION,
WITH EARS THAT HEAR THE CRY OF THE POOR,
WITH HANDS THAT AID THE NEED OF A BROTHER,
WITH A HEART REDEEMED FROM SIN,
TRANSFORMED FROM STONE TO FLESH,
WITH ONE TOUCH FROM *THE ONE* WHO WAS LIFTED UP
IN SUPREME SUFFERING, DYING FOR LIFE, RISING IN LOVE,
AND REIGNING FOREVER AS LORD,
FOR THOSE OF FAITH IN JUSTICE,
FOR THOSE OF HOPE IN PEACE,
AND FOR THOSE BORN OF THE LOVE WHICH NEVER DIES. +

+THE CHRIST I WORSHIP
KNOWS MY TEMPTATION,
KNOWS MY FRAILTY,
AND UNDERSTANDS THE DANGER THAT I FACE.

FOR HE TOO WAS TEMPTED, PERFECTED IN PERIL UNTO DEATH.
FROM THIS HE ROSE, FROM THIS I PRAY.
HE HEARS AND PROTECTS AND GRACES. IN THIS I LIVE! +

+IN THE DARK NIGHT OF THE GARDEN STRUGGLE,
WITHIN THE BETRAYAL OF JUDAS
AND THE SWINGING OF SIMON'S SWORD,
AMIDST HIGH PRIESTLY ACCUSATIONS
AND PETER'S DENIAL,
BEFORE PILATE'S PROBES AND QUESTIONS POSITED,
THROUGH ANGRY MOBS,
THROUGH SCOURGING TERROR, MOCKING, TORMENTS OF ALL KIND,
CARRYING THE BURLY BEAM,
BEATEN AND BLOODY,
NAILED TO A CROSS,
TORMENTED BY A THEIF,
VIEWING THE ANGUISH OF YOUR BLESSED MOTHER,
DYING SLOWLY, PAINFULLY, DESERTED,
ALONE BEARING THE ATTACK OF ALL EVIL…
YOU THOUGHT OF ME,
AND PERSEVERED TO THE END, FOR MY SALVATION! +

+THE ENEMY CHARGES AFTER US FULL TILT.
OF OUR OWN ABILITY, WE ARE DOOMED TO BEING OVERCOME.

BUT IN FAITH,
THE DARK CLOUD OF GOD'S MYSTERY
BRINGS FORTH COMFORT AND STRENGTH,
AND IN HOPE,
THE ANGEL OF GOD IS THERE TO GUIDE OUR EVERY STEP-
THROUGH THE PARTED WATERS IN GOD'S ETERNAL LOVE.

FOR FIDELITY TO GOD *ALWAYS* DROWNS THE ENEMY! +

+**THANKS AND PRAISE** ARE BUT A REASONABLE RESPONSE
TO THE GOD WHO SAVED US
IN THE MIDST OF OUR REJECTION OF HIM.
FAITH AND HOPE, MANIFESTED IN TRUST,
REASONABLY RESPONDS TO *THE ONLY ONE*
WHO LOVES US UNCONDITIONALLY.
AWE AND REVERENCE ARE THE ONLY REASONABLE RESPONSE
TO GOD'S OMNIPOTENT WISDOM
IN THE LIFE, DEATH AND RESURRECTION
OF OUR LORD AND SAVIOR JESUS CHRIST. +

+GOD HAS BLESSED US WITH APOSTOLIC WITNESS!
NOT MERELY A BIBLE WHICH FELL FROM HEAVEN,
BUT THE FLESH AND BLOOD,
BODY AND SOUL WITNESS OF STRUGGLING SAINTS JUST LIKE US!

AND THESE WITNESSES,
IN PERSECUTION AND STRIFE,
HAVE HANDED ON THE WORD OF GOD,
WHO IS CHRIST JESUS OUR LORD.

THE INCARNATE WORD OF GOD,
IN SPIRIT, SACRAMENT, WORD AND CHURCH,
DWELLS AMONG US!

MERCY AND SALVATION REACH DOWN FROM HEAVEN!
PEACE AND JUSTICE WALK THE EARTH!
FAITH AND HOPE COOPERATE IN LOVE EMMANUEL! +

+*I AM IN EASTER EVE'S TOMB.*
BOTH BETRAYED AND BETRAYER,
ON LIFE'S HOLY THURSDAY,
I HAVE DIED A SORT OF DEATH IN WOUNDEDNESS,
IN SIN AND DESPAIR ON LIFE'S GOOD FRIDAY.

EVERYDAY SEEMS LIKE HOLY SATURDAY,
IN SILENCE AND EMPTINESS AND LONELINESS.

AND ONLY A FAINT GLIMMER OF HOPE
KEEPS THIS CORPSE LIKE SOUL IN EXPECTATION
OF THE NEVER TOO SOON ARRIVAL
OF EASTER SON-DAY. +

+MY ONLY HOPE IS THAT YOUR LOVE IS TRULY EVERLASTING.
MY ONLY HOPE IS THAT YOUR SALVATION IS TRULY MINE TO SEEK.
MY ONLY HOPE IS FOR YOUR POWER
AND MY WEAKNESS
TO MEET IN MERCIES EMBRACE.
MY ONLY HOPE IS THAT CHRIST REJECTED, CHRIST CRUCIFIED,
AND CHRIST RISEN
WILL SAVE A SINNER LIKE ME. +

+IN FAITH AND HOPE,
PROVEN IN LOVE,
IS HIDDEN WITHIN US
THE SPIRIT
WHO BRINGS ABOUT OUR TRANSFORMATION IN CHRIST.

THOUGH WE LIVE, WE HAVE DIED.

OUR FIRST DEATH IS A GIFT OF LOVE
FROM THE PASSION TREE
FOUND IN US THROUGH BAPTISM.

THEREFORE,
WHILE WE WALK THE EARTH
AND STEWARD GOD'S CREATION,
MINISTERING TO THE MESSIAH'S MISSION,
OUR HEART, OUR MIND, AND OUR SOUL
MUST LEAD OUR BODY IN HEAVENLY PRIORITY
FOR THE SALVATION OF ALL ON GOD'S GREEN EARTH! +

+EASTER MORN
IS THE GRACED SEIZURE OF HOPE
WHICH FLASHES IN ONES HEART AND MIND,
ENERGIZING ONES SOUL TO ROLL AWAY THE STONE OF DESPAIR
AND *RISE UP* ONCE MORE IN REJUVENATED FAITH
EMBRACING-IN PARADOX- THE CROSS,
WHICH NEVER ENTOMBS IN DESPAIR,
BUT ENLIVENS AND GIVES LIFE GIVING SPIRIT
TO A BLESSED SUFFERING
WHICH LEADS TO ETERNAL LIFE IN THE LOVE OF THE RISEN LORD. +

+AS CHRIST IS THE CORNERSTONE OF OUR FAITH,
RESURRECTION IS THE CORNERSTONE OF OUR HOPE.
FOR WITHOUT CHRIST OUR FAITH IS VOID,
AND WITHOUT RESURRECTION OUR HOPE IS DEAD.
FOR CHRISTIANITY WITHOUT CHRIST IS IMPOSSIBLE,
AND CHRIST WITHOUT RESURRECTION IS UNACCEPTABLE!
FOR LOVE WITHOUT *AGAPE* IS MERE SENTIMENT,
AND SENTIMENT WITHOUT THE RISEN ONE
IS BUT THE DESPERATE AFFECTIONS OF THE DYING IN THEIR SIN. +

+DAVID,
THOUGH DEAD AND BURIED,
FORESHADOWED THE KING OF GLORY
IN THE PROPHETIC PSALM OF RESURRECTION.

LIKEWISE, PETER,
THOUGH WEAK AND IMPETUOUS,
FORESHADOWED THE SPIRIT OF PERFECT WITNESS
IN PREACHING THE BAPTISM OF NEW LIFE IN CHRIST.

FROM THE RESURRECTED KING OF GLORY
AND THE SPIRIT OF PERFECT WITNESS,
WE ARE TO SPREAD THE GOOD NEWS
-IN LIVES HOLY, FOR THE GLORY OF THE FATHER-
OF GOD'S GOODNESS AND TRUTH AND BEAUTY,
AND HIS GIFT OF ETERNAL LIFE. +

+I BEG FOR RICHES,
  I BEG FOR FAME,
I BEG FOR POWER,
I BEG FOR GLORY!

AND THE LORD TAKES NO INSULT!
AND MY PRAYERS ARE ANSWERED!

YET NO RICHES, NOR EARTHLY FAME, NOR POWER,
NOR PERSONAL GLORY ARRIVE!

THEN I ENTER THE CONFESSIONAL…
AND PROCEED TO THE COMMUNION OF GOD AND MAN IN CHRIST.

AND I AM BLESSED *RICH* BEYOND COMPARE!
I AM *FAMOUS* AMONG ANGELS AND SAINTS!
I RECEIVE GOD'S *POWER* IN REPENTANCE AND HUMILITY!
AND I *GLORY* IN THE IMAGE OF THE PERFECT MAN,
JESUS CHRIST MY LORD! +

+*TRUST* IN THE SANDSTORM,
-BLIND, AND LED BY THE SPIRIT-
HOPE *FAITHFULLY* FOR LOVE'S INEVITABLE OASIS. +

+JESUS,
LIVING WATER AND REFINERS FIRE,
GENTLE LAMB AND ROARING LION,
SUFFERING SERVANT AND STEELY SHEPHERD,
MERCIFUL SAVIOR AND END TIME JUDGE,
LOVE INCARNATE AND ETERNAL WORD,
THE WAY, THE TRUTH AND THE LIFE. +

+YOUR WAY, YOUR PATH, YOUR TRUTH, MY SALVATION.
YOUR GOODNESS-MY DIRECTION!
MY FEAR...YOUR WISDOM,
MY HUMILITY...YOUR GUIDANCE,
MY POVERTY...YOUR PRESENCE,
-GRACE, GRACE, GRACE-
MY FAITH, MY HOPE, MY LOVE...YOUR ETERNAL LIFE. +

+IF ONLY WE WEREN'T SO MAGNIFICENT,
FOR THEN WE MIGHT THEN SENSE THE MAGNIFICENCE OF GOD!

FOR,
WE CALLED FOR A WARRIOR AND RECEIVED A BABY!
WE CALLED FOR A WAR AND RECEIVED THE GOSPEL OF PEACE.
WE SOUGHT FOR A NATION AND RECEIVED THE CHURCH.
WE SOUGHT FOR A TEMPLE ANE RECEIVED THE EUCHARIST.
WE SOUGHT FOR AN EVELASTING KINGDOM,
AND FROM THE CROSS
-AND THE EMPTY TOMB-
ROSE FULFILLMENT! +

+THE RECIPE FOR CONVERSION AND EVERLASTING SANCTITY
EXPRESSED IN VIRTUE IS:
SINGING AND BLESSING AND SHARING THE GLORIOUS MERCY
OF GOD
BORN ANEW
EACH AND EVERY DAY,
MANIFEST IN WILLING AND LOVING ACTS
OF JOYOUS COMPASSION,
INSPIRED BY GIFTS RECEIVED IN LIFE AND LOVE AND LIBERTY,
FOUND IN THE SPIRIT OF THE GIVER OF ALL GOODNESS IN GRACE,
THE FATHER OF OUR LORD AND SAVIOR JESUS CHRIST. +

+GRACE DISCIPLINES DESIRE,
PROTECTING FOR CHRIST WHAT IS HIS ALONE.

FOR GRACE,
WHICH SAVES,
FLOWS CO-TERMINOUS
WITH THE BLOOD SHED ON CALVARY.

FOR THE SAVIOR HAS SAVED US
NOT FOR OURSELVES,
BUT FOR HIMSELF.

GRACE EMPOWERS US TO CHOOSE
"THE WAY, THE TRUTH, AND THE LIFE"
OF CHRIST, OUR GLORY. +

+THE WORLD WILL BE BUSY WITH WORLDLY THINGS.

BUT THE DISCIPLE MUST REMAIN FAITHFUL
TO THE WORK OF HIS AND HER MASTER.

FOR THE SPIRIT OF GOD IS AT WORK IN ALL THINGS!

AND MAN IS LOST IN THE FIELD AND SEEMINGLY FORGOTTEN.
BUT ANGELS EVER HOVER WITH SIGNS AND SONGS OF JOY!

AND THE DISCIPLE MUST BE READY TO WITNESS
TO GOD'S CREATIVITY
IN THE BIRTH OF CHRIST IN THEIR HEARTS
FOR ALL THE WORLD TO SEE! +

+SIMEON THE PROPHET LIVED-EXPECTANTLY-
FOR THE CONSOLATION OF GOD.

THOUGH RAIN IN STORM, AND HEAT IN DESERT
CERTAINLY FELL ON HIS PATH,
SIMEON ALWAYS SOUGHT TO THE HORIZON
FOR THE SCANTEST HINT
OF THE OUTBREAK OF THE MORNING STAR,
AND THE BIRTH OF GOD'S WONDERFUL MERCY. +

+JESUS IS THE LAMB WHO DIVIDES,
THE LION WHO UNITES,
THE SAVIOR WHO JUDGES,
AND THE JUDGE WHO IS MERCY HIMSELF!

WHO, AMONG MEN, IS STRONG ENOUGH, LARGE ENOUGH,
OR WISE ENOUGH,
TO WRAP THEIR ARMS -COMPLETELY-
AROUND THE WONDER AND THE MAJESTY
OF GOD REVEALED
IN JESUS CHRIST OUR LORD. +

+UNSURE? LOVE!
IN THE DARK? TURN!
SEEK THE LIGHT WHICH SEEKS YOU FIRST!

JUDGE THE TREE, NOT BY ITS FIRST FRUITS,
BUT BY WHERE ITS ROOTS ARE PLANTED.

FOR ALL TREES ARE BUT IMPERFECT,
AND THE IMPERFECT WILL BEGET IMPERFECTION.

BUT IMPERFECTION,
PLANTED HUMBLY AND OBEDIENTLY IN LOVING PERFECTION,
WILL SOON DELIVER THE FRESH FRUIT OF ETERNAL LOVE. +

+CHRIST GROWS SILENTLY AND EFFECTIVELY
IN THE BOSOM OF THE FAITHFUL AND PATIENT
PROPHET AND PROPHETESS
WHO TRULY SEEK "THE CONSOLATION OF GOD AND THE
DELIVERANCE OF JERUSALEM."

THE HIDDEN LIFE OF THE HUMBLE SERVANT,
PRAYING, REPENTING, SERVING, PERSEVERING,
RAISES TO MATURITY THE CHRISTMAS GIFT
OF CHRIST INCARNATE WITHIN,
AND IN GOD'S TIME
THE SPIRIT WILL BAPTIZE YOU
AND BLESS YOU WITH THE DESERTS
OF THE CROSS, THE TOMB, AND THE RISEN LIFE OF CHRIST. +

+"SING YAHWEH A NEW SONG!"
LET GOD'S CREATION
PARTICIPATE IN THE PRAISE AND GLORY
DESERVED OF THE FATHER OF ALL GOOD GIFTS
IN JESUS CHRIST,
THE HOLY SPIRIT,
THE MOST HOLY EUCHARIST,
WORD AND TRADITION,
THE SAINTS...
IN EVERY MAN, WOMAN, AND CHILD,
AND ALL OF GOD'S CREATION,
ALL CREATURES BIG AND SMALL,
LAND, AIR, AND SEA...
THEREFORE,
LET LIFE FLOURISH,
LET TRUTH FLOW FREE,
AND LET GOD REIGN AMONG US
IN OUR HEARTS, OUR MINDS, OUR BODIES, AND OUR SOULS,
SINGING A NEW SONG OF LOVE
IN THE NEW CREATION OF HOLINESS,
IN THANKSGIVING FOR MERCY RECEIVED. +

+WORD OF GOD,
INCARNATE CHRIST, EUCHARISTIC LORD,
LAMB, LION, SAVIOR, SHEPHERD...
SAVE ME FROM MY OWN DREADFUL DOUBT,
MY OWN CALLOUS AND UNFORGIVING JUDGMENTS,
MY OWN THANKLESSNESS AND SELFISHNESS,
MY OWN COWARDICE, ENVY AND LUST.

REMIND ME,
SPIRIT OF TRUTH,
OF MY SORDID PAST, GOD'S WELCOMING ARMS,
MY JOY IN RESURRECTION FROM MORTAL SIN,
AND THE SUBLIME LIFE OF THE EUCHARISTIC CHRIST,
IN COMMUNION WITH GOD AND MAN,
IN PERSONAL WHOLENESS OF LIFE
IN FAITH AND HOPE AND LOVE WHICH SPRING ETERNAL
AS GRACE FROM THE HEART OF THE CRUCIFIED AND RISEN CHRIST,
MY LORD, MY LIFE, MY LOVE. +

FAITH OVER DOUBT

"AND JESUS SAID TO HIM, 'IF YOU CAN! ALL THINGS ARE POSSIBLE TO HIM WHO BELIEVES.' IMMEDIATELY THE FATHER OF THE CHILD CRIED OUT AND SAID, 'I BELIEVE; HELP MY UNBELIEF.'"
MARK 9: 23-24
THE HOLY BIBLE
REVISED STANDARD VERSION/SECOND EDITION
IGNATIUS PRESS

"MAN'S GREATNESS LIES IN BEING FAITHFUL TO THE PRESENT MOMENT. WE MUST BE FAITHFUL TO THE PRESENT MOMENT OR WE WILL FRUSTRATE THE PLAN OF GOD FOR OUR LIVES."
FATHER SOLANUS CASEY O.F.M. CAP

+A LOVING CHRISTIAN
APPEARS AS A FAITHFUL JEW.

FOR AN UNFAITHFUL JEW
CAN NEVER BE A LOVING CHRISTIAN.
FOR CHRIST ALONE IS THE FAITHFUL JEW.

AND ONLY IN OBEDIENCE AND LOVING IMITATION OF CHRIST
MAY THE CHRISTIAN PLEASE THE GOD OF ISRAEL.

FOR THE LAW OF GOD,
WRITTEN ON TABLETS OF STONE,
IS THE SAME LAW ALIVE IN CHRIST,
AND LIVEABLE IN LOVE IN HIS HOLY SPIRIT.

SO LOVING CHRISTIAN,
LOVE THE LAW OF GOD!
LOVE THE LORD WHO IS LAW!
LOVE THE SPIRIT WHO MAKES US LAWFUL-
MAKING A LIVING CHRISTIAN AND A FAITHFUL JEW. +

+WE ARE BUT BEACH,
IN STORM AND INVASION.

CLOUDS AND WIND AND RAIN AND COLD
BEAT US DOWN
AS WARRIORS WITH WEAPONS INVADE OUR HOMELAND.

TOO MANY TO CONQUER,
SO MUCH TO WITHSTAND,
WE RUN TO GOD'S MOUNTAIN,
WE SEEK SHELTER WITHIN HIS ROCK.

IMPENETRABLE IS HIS LOVE,
UNCONQUERABLE IS HIS MERCY.

IF ONLY IN PERSEVERANCE
WE SHALL BE SAVED IN FAITH,
FOR HE SHALL BE VICTORIOUS-FOR US AND OUR SALVATION-
IN HIS ALMIGHTY LOVE. +

+IN SOLIDARITY WITH THE BAPTIZER,
WE WANDER THESE STREETS
AMONG QUESTIONS OF WHO WE ARE.

KNOWING, IN FAITH, OF WHO WE ARE,
WE KNOW OF WHOM WE ARE SENT,
AND WE KNOW OF WHAT WE MUST DO.

FOR WE CRY OF REPENTANCE,
AND PAVE THE PATH
OF THE STRAIGHT AND NARROW *WAY*.

AND WE WASH WITH WATER AND OIL,
AND FEED ON BREAD AND WINE,
IN THE OBEDIENCE OF HOPE-FILLED FAITH...
KNOWING, IN SPIRIT AND GRACE,
THAT SOMEONE GREATER THAN US WILL COME,
IN HOLY MERCY AND DIVINE LOVE. +

+IN OUR DARK PERCEPTION
OF PERFECTION,
A LIGHT SHINES BRIGHTLY!

THIS LIGHT,
THE SPIRIT OF LOVE
BETWEEN THE FATHER AND THE SON,
ILLUMINATES THE OBJECT OF OUR LOVE
FOR THE FATHER
AND THE SON
IN THE SPIRIT
WHO OFFERS OUR NEIGHBOR
AS LIVING SACRIFICE
TO THE LOVE OF CHRIST WITHIN US.

FOR *FAITH IN CHRIST*
IS CHILDHOOD IN THE FATHER,
AND LOVE FOR OUR SIBLING
-IN THE SPIRIT OF SACRAMENTAL COMMUNION-
IS LOVE FOR GOD
THROUGH THE BODY OF HIS SON. +

+AS JESUS READ THE SCROLL OF THE PROPHET ISAIAH,
HE FULFILLED THE PREDICTION OF THE TEXT IN SPIRIT AND TRUTH
AS EVANGELIST
AND REDEEMER
AND HEALER
AND SHEPHERD,
UNTO PERFECTION.

AS I READ THE GOSPEL OF LUKE,
AND THE WORDS OF THE PROPHET ISAIAH,
I AM CHALLENGED BY THE WORDS OF THE TEXT
TO BELIEVE IN SPIRIT AND TRUTH,
TO REPENT OF MY SINS,
AND TURN TO THE LORD
FOR MERCY AND GRACE,
SO THAT I MAY EVANGELIZE
AND REDEEM
AND HEAL
AND SHEPHERD,
IN THE PERFECTION OF OUR LOVING GOD. +

+*LIGHTNING FAST,*
OUR FAITH IS STRENGTHENED,
OUR LOVED ONES PRAYED FOR,
OUR WALK GRACED FOR PEACE,
WITHIN THE *FLASH* OF A EUCHARISTIC SECOND.

FOR MERCY SEEKS THE CHILDREN *OF FAITH,*
THOSE LIKE JACOB WHO WRESTLED WITH LORD,
EVER STRUGGLING FORWARD
FOR THE LOVE OF THE LIVING GOD.

AND IN STRUGGLING IN FAITH,
MOVED FORWARD IN HOPE,
 WE BECOME THE ISRAEL OF GOD,
GIFTED IN THE LAW AND THE SPIRITM
KNOWING THE NECESSITY OF THE CROSS,
WILLING TO UNDERGO ALL SUFFERING,
IN THE EFFICACY OF GOD'S GRACE,
BORN IN THE WOUNDS OF THE RISEN CHRIST. +

+FEAR BREEDS INSECURITY
AND INSECURITY BREEDS MISTRUST
AND MISTRUST BREEDS ANGER
AND ANGER TENDS TO LASH OUT INAPPROPRIATELY,
WHICH LEADS TO GUILT AND ISOLATION
- THE BEGINNING OF FEAR
AND MISTRUST AND ANGER AND LASHING OUT AND GUILT-
FURTHERING ISOLATION FROM GOD AND MAN.

WHEN FEAR PEAKS OUT
FROM THE DEPTHS OF ONES SOUL,
SECURITY IS FOUND SOLELY IN *A LEAP OF FAITH*
IN THE FORGIVENESS OF THE MERCIFUL GOD
IN MERCY WHICH VANQUISHES ANGER
IN APPROPRIATE ACTS OF CHARITY
WHICH LEADS TO JOY IN COMMUNION WITH GOD AND MAN
IN THE SACRAMENTS OF RECONCILIATION
AND IN THE MOST HOLY EUCHARIST
WHERE CHRIST TRANSFORMS THE HEART
FROM FEAR TO FAITH
AND FROM MISTRUST TO DEVOTION
IN THE COMMUNION OF LOVE
WHERE ANGER GIVES WAY TO CHARITY. +

+POWER EMENATES
FROM THE SOUL, WISE AND HUMBLE IN GRACE,
WHICH PERCEIVES SERVITUDE TO GOD
IN PREPARING *THE WAY* IN CHRIST
AS HIS OR HER GREATEST GLORY.

AS THEY WILLINGLY SHRINK FROM THEIR PRIDE,
THEY BLOSSOM AS HUMBLE REFLECTIONS
OF THE ONE WHO PERFECTS THEM
IN THEIR *OBEDIENCE OF FAITH*
-WHICH HOPES SOLELY IN THE CHARITY OF GOD-
AS *THE CRUCIFIED CHRIST,* FAITHFULLY OBEYED UNTO DEATH,
HOPING ONLY IN ONENESS WITH THE FATHER'S WILL,
RISEN IN THE SPIRIT OF CHARITY,
WHICH IS THE LOVE OF THE FATHER AND SON
IN THEIR PERFECT COMMUNION AS ONE GOD. +

+THE ROAD WELL TRAVELED,
BUT SO OFTEN ABANDONED,
IS THE ROAD OF THE LOVE FOR GOD.

FOR THIS ROAD IS *THE WAY,*
PAVED IN THE BLOOD AND THE PASSION
OF THE BELOVED SON
AND SUFFERING SERVANT OF GOD.

BUT THIS WAY,
 ON THIS ROCKY AND NARROW ROAD,
IS A STEEP CLIMB IN FAITH,
AS OUR LOVE IN THE SPIRIT
GROWS IN STRUGGLE AND DARKNESS
FROM GRACE -AS THE MEANS AND THE CONSOLATION OF GOD-
TO HIS VERY ESSENCE
AS GOODNESS, TRUTH AND BEAUTY.

THANKFULLY, GOD IS MERCIFUL!
AND HIS CHURCH, IN SPIRIT AND GRACE,
IN SACRAMENT AND IN FELLOWSHIP,
ALLOWS FOR GROWTH IN LOVE
THROUGH LOVE,
FROM LOVE HIMSELF.   +

+AS WE LIE IN THE DARKNESS IN THE DIMNESS OF VISION IN FAITH,
WE ARE SUMMONED IN WAYS IMPERCEPTIBLE
TO MIND, HEART AND SOUL.

WE MUST CALL UPON APOSTOLIC WISDOM AND DISCERNMENT-
IN PATIENCE AND IN HOPE.

ONLY THEN IN THE THIRD CALL OF THE LORD
WILL WE DISCERN THE SUMMONS TO DISCIPLESHIP
WITH AN ANSWER FULL OF INTEGRITY,
READY AND WILLING TO FOLLOW THE LAMB OF GOD
IN THE SPIRIT OF TRUTH
IN *THE WAY* OF THE WILL OF THE FATHER ALMIGHTY.

THEN, WHEN CALLED, THE WORD WILL BE FULFILLED WITHIN US. +

+<u>FAITH HEALS ALL WOUNDS</u>

MANGLED IN THE WOUNDS OF POOR CHOICE,
I CRAWL IN PAIN AND SHAME TO MY ONLY HOPE OF SALVATION.
REVEALING MY WOUNDS
AND MY WEAKNESSES AND MY SINS,
I AM HEALED INSTANTLY IN LOVE.

AS I LEAVE,
MY HEALER COMMANDS ME TO SIN NO MORE!
I KNOW, AND HE KNOWS,
THAT THIS IS IMPOSSIBLE FOR ME.
YET ALL THINGS ARE POSSIBLE IN HIM WHO HEALS THE CONTRITE! +

+<u>FAITH AND SANITY CARRY THE SAME COMPASS</u>

WHEN WE CLAMOR FOR A KING
AND IGNORE THE KINGSHIP OF GOD,
WE BECOME PAWNS AND SLAVES
TO THE WHIMS OF ANOTHER MAN.

WHEN WE SEEK A RULER
AND IGNORE THE RULE OF OUR LORD,
WE HAND OVER OUR DIGNITY AND CHARITY
TO THE DEPRAVITY OF ANOTHER MAN'S SOUL.

WHEN WE SEEK TO BE LIKE THE WORLD
AND FORGET THE LOVE OF ITS CREATOR
WE LOSE SIGHT OF HIS IMAGE WITHIN,
AND PERCEIVE ONLY THE ANIMAL IN MAN.

WHEN WE SEEK FOR A KINGDOM WON IN WAR
WE FORGET THE KINGDOM TO COME IN PEACE,
AND WE TURN FROM THE PRINCE OF LIGHT
ONLY TO FALL IN THE SNARE OF THE PRINCIPALITIES OF DARKNESS.

WHEN WE IGNORE THE PROPHETS
ONLY TO TURN OUR EAR TO THE PAGANS,
WE FALL BLIND AND DEAF TO THE WORD OF GOD
AND SUFFER THE SLOW DEATH OF THE BABEL OF MAN. +

+THE KENOSIS OF CHRIST
IS THE PARALLEL, YET, SUPERIOR ANALOGY
TO *THE LEAP OF FAITH.*

FOR MAN LEAPS IN FAITH
FROM ABSOLUTE DESPAIR AND UNCERTAINTY
TO HOPE IN A PROMISE GREATER THAN ONESELF.

BUT CHRIST LEAPT FROM HEAVEN,
FROM THE FATHER,
FROM PERFECT LOVE,
INTO THE ABYSS
OF SIN, DOUBT, DARKNESS AND DEATH.

THIS SALVIFIC LEAP DESERVES OUR DEVOTION. +

+JESUS, MARY AND THE CROSS
ARE INTIMATELY INTERWOVEN
WITH THE DISCIPLE THAT HE LOVES.

THE GIFT OF MARY,
GIVEN AS EXEMPLAR AND MOTHER
OF CROSS CONTEMPLATIVE CHRISTIANITY
IS A SUMMONS TO LAY OUR HEAD
ON JESUS' BREAST
-ATOP HIS SACRED HEART-
WHILE LIVING A LIFE OF FAITH, HOPE AND CHARITY
IMAGING HER IMMACULATE HEART
IN GLORIFYING GOD THE FATHER
AS HANDMAID AND SAINT
IN THE LIGHT OF HER SON
IN THE SPIRIT OF OBEDIENT FAITH. +

+TWO SIDES OF A LEAF…FALLING FROM A TREE…
ONE SIDE *FAITH* IN GOD'S LOVE,
THE OTHER, DESPAIR AND FEAR IN ISOLATION.
FLUTTERING IN THE WIND, MAN'S SOUL
WAFFLES BETWEEN HOPE AND RESIGNATION.
THE ONLY STABILITY PROVIDED
IS THE CRASH OF THE LEAF ON THE SOLID GROUND OF GOD. +

+FOR THE UNAFFIRMED, THE UNLOVED...
KEEP THE PROMISES OF SACRED SCRIPTURE
CLOSE TO YOUR HEART.

FOR THOSE WOUNDED IN ABUSE AND PERSECUTION,
THOSE WHO FIND TRUST A NEAR IMPOSSIBLE CHALLENGE...
TRUST IN THE CROSS AND THE EMPTY TOMB!

FOR THOSE WHO FEAR
THAT THEY CANNOT EXPRESS SUFFICIENT GRATITUDE
TO GOD FOR ALL HIS MERCY...
UNITE YOURSELF TO THE EUCHARIST IN FAITH,
FOR THIS IS THANKFULNESS HIMSELF,
PAR EXCELLENCE. +

+*OUR FAITH IS RESURRECTIONAL*
IN THE HOPE OF MARY OF MAGDELA,
WHICH INSPIRES US TO RUN TO MOTHER CHURCH
FOR THE GUIDANCE OF THE HOLY SPIRIT,
ENTRUSTED BY CHRIST TO THE SUCCESSOR OF PETER-
AND IN THE LOVE OF THE LORD
-GIVEN AT THE FOOT OF THE CROSS-
TO MARY,
FOR THE CARE OF HER NEW SON, JOHN,
AND TO ALL GOD'S ADOPTED CHILDREN
IN THE BAPTISM WHICH ENSUES FROM THE CROSS,
WHERE OUR CRUCIFIED SAVIOR DIED FOR OUR SINS
TO RISE AS BELOVED ELDER BROTHER
TO A MULTITUDE OF HEAVENLY BROTHERS AND SISTERS
IN THE LOVE OF THE FATHER
AND THE FELLOWSHIP OF THE HOLY SPIRIT
AS THE COMMUNION OF SAINTS IN CHRIST. +

+PRAISE GOD, DRAWING INWARD IN FAITH,
POINTING OUTWARD IN HOPE.
GOD CREATES, I BELIEVE! GOD REDEEMS, I BELIEVE!
GOD CONQUERS, I BELIEVE! GOD REIGNS, I BELIEVE!
GOD HEARS OUR PRAYER! GOD KNOWS OUR PAIN!
GOD IS WORKING FOR OUR GOOD IN ALL THINGS!
IN FAITH, HOPE AND CHARITY, GOD'S SALVATION IS NOW! +

+EXHAUSTED IN MANY FUTILE EFFORTS
TO CATCH BUT A FEW FISH,
I PLACE MY DIRECTION IN THE HANDS OF JESUS.

FOR SEARCHING FOR THE FISH OF MERE SURVIVAL
HAS LEFT ME HUNGRY, POOR AND DISILLUSIONED.

IT IS HIGH TIME I HANDED MY NETS OVER TO THE LORD.

FOR HIS CATCH IS MY ETERNAL SALVATION.
AND MY EFFORTS,
NOW GRACED COOPERATION,
IN FAITHFUL TRUST,
HOPEFUL OBEDIENCE,
AND LOVING PERSEVERANCE,
IS THE BEGINNING OF AN ADVENTURE
AND RELATIONSHIP
WITH THE FISHER OF MEN-
AND THE GUARANTEED CATCH OF PURPOSE, PEACE AND JOY. +

+IMMANUEL
IS THE CHILD OF A STEPFATHER,
HE WHO EXEMPLIFIED HUMBLE AND OBEDIENT *FAITH*.

IMMANUEL
IS THE CHILD OF A MOTHER,
IMMACULATELY CONCEIVED,
AS THE TABERNACLE OF SALVATION
AND THE MOTHER OF OUR ETERNAL HOPE.

IMMANUEL
IS THE CHILD OF THE SPIRIT-
THE SPIRIT WHO OVERSHADOWS *FAITHFULNESS*,
HOPE IN GOD,
AND THE LOVE OF HIS PROVIDENCE.

IMMANUEL
IS THE CHILD OF THE FATHER,
HE WHO IS LOVE,
HE WHO SPARES NOTHING FOR HIS CHILDREN. +

A SIMPLE FAITH PROPOSAL

+MAYBE
OR FEET TOUCH THE GROUND
AND OUR HEAD IS IN THE AIR
FOR MORE THAN LOCOMOTION.

MAYBE
OUR FEET WALK THE EARTH
AND OUR MIND, IN THE SPIRIT OF CHRIST,
REACHES TO THE HEAVENS
IN AN INCARNATE MARRIAGE OF FLESH AND BLOOD
AND BODY AND SOUL.

MAYBE
AFTER THE CHRIST,
HEAVEN IN THE SPIRIT
ENTERS THE BODY AND SOUL OF MAN
THROUGH A MIND AND A SPIRIT
ENLIGHTENED WITH THE WISDOM OF THE LOVE OF GOD
THROUGH THE RECEPTION OF THE MOST HOLY EUCHARIST
IN THE HOLY SPIRIT,
WHICH REVEALS THE INTERSECTION OF HEAVEN AND EARTH. +

+LOOK TO THE HEAVENS OR LOOK TO THE DUST,
THIS IS THE ULTIMATE CHOICE OF LIFE.
LIVING OR DYING-THIS IS OUR CHOICE!

FOR THE FLESH FORMED FROM THE DUST OF THE EARTH
IS OUR OLD AND NATURAL SELF,
WHICH ONLY LEADS TO IDOLATRY AND NATURAL DEATH.

BUT THE SPIRIT IN THE HEAVENS, BREATHED INTO US AS GIFT,
THIS IS OUR NEW AND SUPERNATURAL SELF,
WHICH LEADS TO TRUE WORSHIP AND RESURRECTION UNTO LIFE.

FOR IN FAITH, HOPE AND LOVE, THE SPIRIT IN THE HEAVENS
RENEWS THE DUST OF THE FLESH,
OFFERING EVERY MOMENT OF LIFE TO THE CREATOR HIMSELF,
AS THANKSGIVING FOR THE GIFT OF LIFE EVERLASTING. +

HOPE OVER DESPAIR

"SPE SALVI FACTU SUMUS"-IN HOPE WE WERE SAVED, SAYS ST PAUL TO THE ROMANS, AND LIKEWISE TO US. ACCORDING TO THE CHRISTIAN FAITH, "REDEMPTION-SALVATION-IS NOT SIMPLY A GIVEN. REDEMPTION IS OFFERED TO US IN THE SENSE THAT WE HAVE BEEN GIVEN HOPE, TRUSTWORTHY HOPE, BY VIRTUE OF WHICH WE CAN FACE OUR PRESENT: THE PRESENT, EVEN IF IT IS ARDUOUS, CAN BE LIVED AND ACCEPTED IF IT LEADS TOWARDS A GOAL, IF WE CAN BE SURE OF THIS GOAL, AND IF THIS GOAL IS GREAT ENOUGH TO JUSTIFY THE EFFORT OF THE JOURNEY."
POPE BENEDICT XVI
SPE SALVI-ON CHRISTIAN HOPE

"THE POSSIBILITY OF DESPAIR, WE ARE TOLD, IS 'MAN'S ADVANTAGE OVER THE BEAST' AND 'THE CHRISTIANS ADVANTAGE OVER NATURAL MAN...' TO BE CURED IS 'THE CHRISTIAN'S BLESSEDNESS.'"
SOREN KIERKEGAARD
THE SICKNESS UNTO DEATH

"LET US HOLD FAST THE CONFESSION OF OUR HOPE WITHOUT WAVERING, FOR HE WHO PROMISED IS FAITHFUL..."
HEBREWS 10:23 RSV-SECOND EDITION-IGNATIUS

OUR CHRISTIAN HOPE

+CHRIST ETERNAL,
THE FACE OF THE UNCHANGING GOD,
EVER FAITHFUL,
HOLDING ALL LIFE COMPASSIONATELY,
CREATOR AND SUSTAINER, REDEEMER;
-OUR MEANS AND OUR END,
OUR STRENGTH AND OUR PURPOSE,
OUR GRACE AND OUR BEATITUDE-
IN REVERENT FEAR OF YOUR WISDOM, TREMBLING IN BLESSED AWE,
WE ARE GRACED IN THE PASSING OF A SWIFT, YET DIM, REFLECTION
OF YOUR PERFECT LOVE.

IN MERCY PRESERVE US,
IN WISDOM REFINE US, IN LOVE REDEEM US,
BRING US NEAR TO PRAISE YOU,
WITHIN THE UNFATHOMABLE BLISS
-WHICH WE TERM HEAVEN-
IN THE LIVING COMMUNION OF PERFECT LOVE,
FATHER, SON AND SPIRIT. +

+THE KINGDOM OF GOD,
THE UNCONQUERABLE, UNFATHOMABLE,
INSCRUTIBLE, SOVERIEGN REIGN
OF THE MOST HOLY TRINITY
WITHIN THE HEARTS AND MINDS
OF THE BRETHREN OF THE NEW ADAM,
NEWLY CREATED IN THE LOVE OF THE CRUCIFIED,
WHERE ONE SOLITARY DROP OF HIS PRESCIOUS BLOOD
RENEWED ALL CREATION PAST, PRESENT AND FUTURE-
THIS KINGDOM IS AMONG US NOW!

YET ONLY IN FAITH MAY ONE PERCEIVE THIS REALITY.
AND ONLY IN HOPE MAY ONE RECEIVE ITS FULFILLMENT.
AND ONLY IN LOVE
DID ONE ACHIEVE THIS DESIRE;
THE WILL OF THE FATHER,
MAN PERFECTED IN BEATITUDE FOREVER. +

+FROM BRIGHTNESS TO BRIGHTNESS
   AND DARKNESS TO DARKNESS
-IN STEALTH SPIRITUS SILENCE-
THE WORD, THE TRUTH, THE SPIRIT OF THE LORD,
ANNOUNCES THE COMING OF THE LOVER-
THE KING AND SAVIOR OF MAN.

IN FAITH AND IN *HOPE,*
LOVE IS FOUND IN MERCY,
WHERE LIFE BEGINS AND DEATH BECOMES BUT GATEWAY.

FOR FAITH AND HOPE
UNITES ONES HEART
IN THE ONE TRUE ETERNAL FORCE-
THE LOVE THAT IS GOD. +

THE DESPAIR OF THE WORLDLY

+WILL I MISS THE LORD ENMESHED IN MY WORK?
WILL I PROVE NON-VIGILANT ENTHRALLED IN MY PLEASURES?
WILL I MISS HIS SECOND COMING DROWNING IN MY WORRIES?
WILL I PASS ON THE PAROUSIA IN DOUBT AND DESPAIR?
WILL I MISS HEAVEN'S BOAT WEIGHED DOWN IN RICHES?

WILL I RENDER A JUST ACCOUNT ON JUDGMENT DAY,
WHEN LOVE NEVER EXTENDS PAST THE TIP OF MY NOSE?

WILL HELL BE FINE FOR ME,
ABSORBED AS I AM
IN THE LIFEWORKS OF A LONESOME LORD? +

OUR HOPE IN SUFFERING

+PATIENCE IN SUFFERING, CLUNG TO IN FAITH KEPT LIVING,
-FOUND IN THE FORGED *HOPE* OF PAST PASCHAL PURGATION-
GIVES BIRTH-THROUGH ANGELIC TOUCH- TO A MAN OF STRENGTH
-DIVINE STRENGTH-FORTIFIED IN MERCIFUL LOVE.
FOR PERSEVERANCE BUILDS CHARACTER,
AS THE PASSION BUILT THE RESURRECTION,
AND ADAM'S FALL PROVIDED FOR THE REDEMPTION IN CHRIST. +

OUR HOPE IN CHRIST

+SING AN ENTRANCE SONG!
ENTER THE PRESENCE
OF LOVE AND LIFE AND JOY
IN THANKGIVING!

IN ISAAC
AND EGYPT AND HEROD AND CHRIST,
THE FIRST BORN IS THE SEED OF OUR SALVATION!

FOR AS ABRAHAM'S OBEDIENCE
AND PHARAOH'S FIRST BORN
LED TO LAMENTATIONS IN HEROD'S MASSACRE,
CHRIST THE LORD,
THE FIRST BORN OF ALL CREATION
FELL SEED FROM THE TREE OF OUR SALVATION
-TO THE SHOUTS OF EARTHLY DERISION,
AND HEAVENLY JOY-
SPRUNG FORTH
IN THE NEWFOUND TREE OF LIFE
FOUND IN HIS GLORIOUS RESURRECTION! +

+HOPELESS?
  HELPLESS?
EXHAUSTED? FRUSTRATED? BEWILDERED? ANGRY? DEEPLY HURT?
PERSECUTED? MISUNDERSTOOD? FORGOTTEN? REVILED? LOST?
LONELY? POOR? HUNGRY? DESTITUTE?

WONDERFUL!

SO MUCH THE BETTER TO THROW OFF THE WORLD!
SO MUCH THE BETTER TO FIND YOURSELF IN GOD!

SO MUCH THE BETTER TO HUMBLE YOURSELF...
IN NOTHINGNESS,
FINDING EVERYTHING IN GOD'S ALMIGHTY WILL.
SO MUCH THE BETTER TO LIVE ANEW
IN THE MERCY OF GOD,
ONE DAY AT A TIME. +

A PRAYER FOR HOPE FULFILLED

+STAND, OH STAND ST MICHAEL!

AND AFTER THE CATACLYSM,
AFTER THE SECOND FALL,
SPARE THE HOLY REMNANT,
THE PEOPLE OF ALL ISRAEL,
THE SHEEP AFTER THE LAMB,
THE FLOCK OF THE SHEPHERD,
THE CHILDREN OF GOD, THE SIBLINGS OF THE CHRIST.

OH ST MICHAEL,
AWAKEN THOSE ASLEEP.
SOUND THE TRUMPHET! HARKEN THE ANGELS!
ANNOUNCE THE COMING OF THE LORD!

FOR JUSTICE, SWEET JUSTICE HAS ARRIVED!
AND MERCY, WONDERFUL MERCY IS HERE!

HEAVEN AND HELL AWAIT OUR DESIRE!
FOR EVERY MAN'S DESIRE
WILL SHINE EVER SO BRIGHTLY IN VIRTUE,
AND EVER SO DARK IN DISGRACE.
FOR WE ILL GET WHAT WE DESIRE!
THE JUSTICE AND MERCY OF GOD. +

THE SACRAMENT OF HOPE FULFILLED

+ONE IS THE SACRIFICE.
PERFECT IS ITS ESSENCE.
PERPETUAL IS ITS NATURE.
EFFICACIOUS IS ITS EFFECTIVENESS.
LOVE IS ITS DRIVING FORCE.
HOLINESS IS ITS EFFECT.
THE FATHER ITS ORIGINATOR.
THE SON ITS PROGENITOR.
THE SPRIRIT ITS SEED.
THE RESURRECTION ITS FRUIT.
HEAVEN FULFILLED ITS GOAL. +

THE HOPE OF ALL TAX COLLECTORS AND SINNERS

+SUFFERING FROM SELF INFLICTED WOUNDS,
IN GREED AND DECEIT, HE HUNGERED-IN CURIOUS ANXIETY-
FOR THE LIVING ANSWER TO HIS *DYING HOPE.*

WHILE ALL AROUND HIM,
AS RIGHTEOUS INDIGNATION AND PROPER ACCUSATION
SPED AT HIM LIKE HOSTILE ARROWS,
HE STOOD FIRM IN HUMBLE REPENTANCE,
WHILE THE LORD OF ALL MERCY
SOUGHT TO DINE WITH HIM IN THEIR NEW FOUND RECONCILIATION.

FOR,
THE TAX COLLECTOR AND THE SINNER,
SEEKS
AND REPENTS
AND RECEIVES NEW LIFE:
"TODAY SALVATION HAS COME TO THIS HOUSE,
BECAUSE THIS MAN TOO IS A SON OF ABRAHAM." +

+UNAWAKE AND UNAWARE,
WHAT MIGHT HAVE BEEN MY FATE
IF PROVIDENTIAL ATTENTION
WAS NOT GRACED UPON MY POOR AND SLEEPING SOUL?

UNAWAKE AND UNAWARE,
WHAT MIGHT HAVE BEEN MY FATE
IF MERCIFUL ATTTENTION
WAS NOT GRACED UPON MY WEAK AND SINNING SPIRIT?

UNAWAKE AND UNAWARE,
WHAG MIGHT HAVE BEEN MY FATE
IF PASCHAL SUFFERING
WAS NOT GRACED UPON MY SINFULLY INHERITED BEING?

UNAWAKE AND UNAWARE,
WHAT MIGHT *STILL* BE MY FATE
IF MY MEMORY IN FAITH AND *HOPE*
FAIL TO RECALL DIVINE LOVE? +

+FOR THOSE OF BUT A SPARK OF HOPE,
HOPE BUILDS
UPON FAITH.

FOR THOSE WHO FREELY CHOOSE TO DOUBT,
DOUBT DESTROYS IN DESPAIR.

AND HOPE IS A GIFT,
THERE FOR THE TAKING-
ASK, SEEK, KNOCK...

BUT DESPAIR IS THE REJECTION OF A GIFT,
THE REJECTION OF LIFE-
AND DEATH TO ONES SOUL.

FOR YES IS FOR LIFE,
AND NO IS FOR DEATH,
AND GRACE PROVIDES FOR,
AND DESIRES OF,
ALL TO SAY YES...
YET RESPECTS ALL WHO SAY NO. +

HOPE IN COURAGE FROM FAITH GRACED

+TO HELL WITH THE POPULAR!
WHAT IS WRONG IS WRONG AND WHAT IS RIGHT IS RIGHT.
TO HELL WITH THE RULERS AND PRINCIPALITIES OF OUR DAY!
WHAT IS GOOD IS GOOD
AND WHAT IS EVIL IS EVIL.
POLITICS BE DAMNED!

FOR GOD IS GOD
AND MAN IS MAN
AND THE LAW,
WRITTEN ON OUR HEARTS,
PASSED ON THROUGH OUR ANCESTORS,
REVEALED IN THE HOLY BOOK
-AND THE SACRED TRADITION-
STILL STAND...
IF ONLY WE DO TOO! +

+YOUR *PRESENCE* IS MY COMFORT AND MY HOPE!
AS YOU CALL ME NEAR, ENTERING MY ABODE,
YOU DRAW ME INTO YOUR HEART SO SACRED.

CONSUMED, ASSUMED,
DRAWN HEAVENLY,
THE DEMONS WITHIN RETREAT.

THOUGH SALVATION BE FROM THE CROSS,
IT IS PERPETUATED SACRAMENTALLY AS GIFT
IN THE INTIMACY OF LOVE.

DYING, YOU VANQUISHED EVILS STRONGHOLD.
RISING, YOU EMPOWERED GOODNESS IN THE FLESH.
HENCEFORTH,
GOD IS FOREVER REVEALED AS THE JUST AND MERCIFUL SAVIOR.

OH COME AGAIN DEAR LORD!
SAVE THE JUST! FORGIVE THE REPENTANT!
DESTROY OUR LAST ENEMY!
REIGN VISIBLE IN OUR BLINDNESS.
REIGN SUPREME IN OUR WEAKNESS.
IN LOVE, GIVE US LIFE,
IN HOLINESS GIVE US PERFECTION,
IN YOUR GLORY GIVE US PURPOSE IN PRAISE! +

+SO RICH AND POWERFUL ON MONDAY.
EMPOWERED IN THE POWER OF THE PREVIOUS DAY'S SON.
DEFEATED IN BATTLE
-EMBITTERED AND ENRAGED-TUESDAY COMES.
WEDNESDAY WE STUMBLE, AND WE ASK WHY?
AS THE METTLE OF OUR HOPE IS TESTED IN FIRE.
THURSDAY SO DARK, LIFE SO CRUEL.
DESPAIR SERENADES US AS UNAVOIDABLE MELODY.
FRIDAY QUIET...AND DRY! WHAT WENT WRONG?
SATURDAY WE PERCEIVE WHAT ALWAYS WAS,
AND WE REPENT AND WE ARE FORGIVEN,
AND IN GRACE AND PEACE WE ARE RECONCILED.
SUNDAY WE ARE FED IN RICHES AND POWER.
ALIVE IN THE POWER OF ONE! +

+THE FATHER IS THE MOUNTAIN PEAK OF GLORY!
THE SON THE ROSE OF THE GARDEN DIVINE.
THE SPIRIT THE BROOK FOR SALVATIONS THIRST.
GOD, AND OCEAN OF FORGIVENESS.
THE SAINTS AND ANGELS, FISH FOR LIFE.
THE TRINITY, THREE KNOWN IN ONE UNFATHOMABLE MYSTERY.
GRACE AND SPIRIT, A LOVING GIFT UNDESERVED.
JESUS CHRIST, THE REASON FOR OUR HOPE. +

+SIGNS OF LIFE
ARE SIGNS OF GOD AMONG US.

FOR IMMANUEL IS
BIRTH AND BAPTISM AND FORGIVENESS AND REDEMPTION...
AND STRENGTH IN SUFFERING,
AND HOPE IN FACING DEATH...
AND THE *WAY* BEYOND.

AS THE SIGNS OF THE TIMES
ARE THE SIGNS OF LIFE'S CURRENT CONDITION,
THE SIGNS OF LOVE IN MERCY,
WHICH STAND IN STARK CONTRAST TO THE WORLD,
-AS RIPE FRUIT IN A BARREN FIELD,
AND AS A DIVINE OASIS IN A MAN MADE DESERT-
STAND AS THE SOURCE OF HOPE AND STRENGTH
WHEN FACED WITH THE FUNDAMENTAL CHOICE
BETWEEN LIFE IN CHRIST AND DEATH IN SIN. +

+ON A DYING TREE, A SHOOT OF HOPE SPRUNG UP,
FROM AN IMPROBABLE CAUSE, FOR THE FOLLY OF GREAT JOY.

FOR THE TREE OF MAN, DYING IN DISOBEDIENCE,
WAS SAVED BY THE PLANTER AND THE PRUNER
AND THE PROVIDER OF ALL GOOD FRUIT;
THOUGH THIS TREE WAS NOT NECESSARY,
AND THE GOOD FRUIT SPARSE.

FOR ON GOD'S TREE WAS THIS TREE SAVED.
AND THE FRUIT FROM GOD'S BLESSED TREE,
THE FRUIT OF THE SPIRIT, WAS SALVATION AND GREAT JOY. +

+THE DESERT OF HUMAN IGNORANCE
SHARES SANDS IN ALL, INCLUDING ME.

THE OASIS OF WISDOM,
OF COMPASSION,
OF HONESTY,
OF INTEGRITY,
IN THE LIVING WATERS OF THE HOLY SPIRIT,
SEEKS TO FLOW IN ALL, INCLUDING ME.

THE FREEDOM TO CHOOSE
BETWEEN
MALICE, ENVY, PRIDE AND REVENGE
OR
FAITH, HOPE, JUSTICE AND MERCY
IS FOUND IN ALL, INCLUDING ME.

THUS IS MY HOPE
IN THE VYING SPIRIT-
VICTORY IN THE FLESH,
IN THE CHRIST OF GOD,
VICTORY IN ALL, INCLUDING ME. +

+SEEK GOD
WITH THE EARNESTNESS
OF A HUMBLE SINNER
SEEKING GOD'S SALVATION!

SEEK FOR GOD'S DESIRE
IN JUSTICE FOR THE POOR,
AND MERCY FOR THE UNFORGIVEN.

WORSHIP IN GENUINE THANKSGIVING AND PRAISE!

FOR GOD IS OUR ABBA,
OUR LIFE,
OUR LOVE,
OUR HOPE,
AND OUR SALVATION! +

+TAKE SOLACE MY POOR FRIEND,
IN THE MYSTERY OF THE POOR CHRIST AMONG US.

FOR NOW WE ARE AS DIRT,
INVISIBLE TO THE EYE OF THE RICH.

WE ARE AS TOOLS IN A BOX,
FOR MERE DIRTY WORK,
HIDDEN WHEN FEAST AND CELEBRATION ARRIVES.

BUT AMONGST US IS THE LORD!
RICH IN POWER, HE IS POOR FOR US.
OUR SUFFERING IS JOINED WITH HIS.
THIS IS THE POOR MAN'S HOPE! +

+THE DEACON OF GOD MUST BE FIRM IN CONVICTION,
SOLID IN CHARACTER, FAITHFUL TO ONE SPOUSE,
COMPOSED, COMPASSIONATE, COURAGEOUS,
A DEDICATED TEACHER, AND EARNEST PREACHER,
TEMPERATE IN JOY, PERSEVERING IN SORROW,
TRUSTWORTHY, A CONCERNED FATHER, AN INTERESTED HUSBAND,
AND A MAN SEARCHING-ALWAYS-HUMBLY, REPENTANTLY,
FOR HIS ONLY HOPE,
HIS ONLY SALVATION,
IN JESUS HIS CHRIST. +

+WE ARE THE FAMILY OF CHRIST'S DISCIPLES,
THE BODY OF THE MESSIAH OF THE WORLD.
WE ARE THE CHURCH!
THE CHILDREN "OF THE LIVING GOD."
WE ARE THE EVANGELISTS OF GOSPEL SALVATION;
PROTECTORS AND PROPOSERS
OF UNDYING
AND UNCHANGING
DIVINE TRUTH.
WE ARE THE TEMPLE OF THE SPIRIT OF GOD WHO IS LOVE!
WE MAKE VISIBLE HE WHO MADE VISIBLE
THE GOD TRANSCENDENTLY INVISIBLE,
YET MERCIFULLY IMMANENT,
HE WHO IS OUR *UNENDING HOPE FOR GLORY.* +

LOVE PERFECTED IN SUFFERING

"THE CROSS OF LIFE, ACCEPTED AND EMBRACED AND UNITED WITH THE CROSS OF CHRIST, PURIFIES THE SOUL OF THE UNDIVINE IN IT AND ASSIMILATES IT EVER MORE TO GOD. THE SOUL THUS LOSES ITS OWN EVIL LIFE TO FIND ITS TRUE LIFE. THE CROSS, BEING THE INSTRUMENT OF LIFE, IS THE KEY TO HAPPINESS."
EDWARD LEEN   WHY THE CROSS?

"HUMAN SUFFERING HAS REACHED ITS CULMINATION IN THE PASSION OF THE CHRIST. AND AT THE SAME TIME IT HAS ENTERED INTO A COMPLETELY NEW DIMENSION AND A NEW ORDER: IT HAS BEEN LINKED WITH LOVE...TO THAT LOVE WHICH CREATES GOOD, DRAWING IT OUT BY MEANS OF SUFFERING, JUST AS THE SUPREME GOOD OF THE REDEMPTION OF THE WORLD WAS DRAWN FROM THE CROSS OF CHRIST..."
POPE JOHN PAUL II   SALVIFICI DOLORIS

+MY LIFE IS RENEWED,
AS YOUR IMAGE IS GIVEN BACK TO ME,
AND I PRAISE YOUR GLORY IN THE RESPLENDENT SON OF MERCY!

FOR MY PRIDE IS WOUNDED
AS MY WOUNDS ARE HEALED.
MY RICHES DIMINISH
AS MY POVERTY IS REWARDED.
MY FULLNESS IS EMPTIED
AS MY NOTHINGNESS RECEIVES YOUR GLORY!

FOR VAIN GLORY IS DEATH,
AND FAITHFUL DEATH IS GLORY!

AS LIFE IN SELF BRINGS HELL-
HELL FOUGHT FAITHFULLY BRINGS LIFE!

AS FOR INJUSTICE,
THE UNJUST KINGS OF THE WORLDLY HELL
SUBJECT THE FAITHFUL AS THE FUEL FOR THEIR FIRE!

BUT IN THE JUSTICE OF THE CRUCIFIED ONE,
THE FUEL OF EARTHLY PERSECUTION
BECOME THE FATHER'S KINGS IN THE NEW WORLD TO COME. +

+I BEG FOR HEALING
AND THINGS GET WORSE.
I BEG FOR MERCY
AND A COLD WORLD GETS COLDER.
I BEG FOR INSIGHT
AND RECEIVE GREATER CONFUSION.
I PRAY FOR PURPOSE AND FEEL THE BITTER STING OF REJECTION.

MY PRAYER IS WEAK!
MY HEART EVER SO FAINT.
MY MIND BEFUDDLED.
AND I THROW UP A HAIL MARY,
HOPING AGAINST HOPE FOR A MIRACLE,
IN THE IMMACULATE CONCEPTION
OF A PRAYER ANSWERED. +

+DEFEAT IS OFTEN IN YOUR GRACE.
EXILE IS OFTEN IN YOUR LOVE.
HUMILIATION IS OFTEN IN YOUR MERCY.
SHAME IS OFTEN YOUR GREATEST GIFT.

FOR IN SIN WE ARE BUT PROSTITUTES AND SINNERS,
REVILED IN THE STENCH OF OUR OWN SELFISH PRIDE.

BUT IN REPENTANCE WE ARE WASHED CLEAN,
REVEALING DIGNITY AND BEAUTY,
NOT OF OUR OWN MAKING.

FOR WE ARE THE IMAGE OF ONE INFINITELY GREATER! +

+JESUS IS BUT ONE SMILE AWAY,
ONE HUG AWAY,
ONE GREETING AWAY.

JESUS IS AS NEAR AS BUT ONE PERSECUTION BORNE PATIENTLY,
ONE SACRIFICE OF TIME AND ATTENTION GIVEN-
WHEN PERSONAL CONVENIENCE SAYS OTHERWISE.

JESUS BRINGS SALVATION
WHEN WE LEND AN EAR EVEN WHEN WE ARE FATIGUED,
WHEN WE SHARE EVEN WHEN SELFISHNESS SUMMONS,
WHEN WE FORGIVE EVEN WHEN WE STILL HURT,
WHEN WE APOLOGIVE AND RECONCILE
IN HUMILITY AND SINCERITY
FOR PEACE AND FELLOWSHIP,
WHICH TRULY PLEASES GOD.

FOR WE ARE QUITE OFTEN,
THE ONLY BRIDGE TO FAITH,
THE ONLY LINK TO HOPE,
THE CLOSEST BODY OF LOVE,
IN THE HOLY SPIRIT WHO INSPIRES ALL VIRTUE
FROM THE BELOVED CHRIST
WHO EMPOWERS ALL LOVE
FOR THE SALVATION
OF ALL OF THE ALMIGHTY FATHER'S LOST CHILDREN. +

+THE SACRIFICE OF ONES WILL
IS THE GREATEST SACRIFICE
ASIDE FROM THE GIFT OF ONES LIFE.

AND THE DISCIPLE OF CHRIST,
OFFERING THEIR WILL IN HUMBLE OBEDIENCE
FOR THE SAKE OF BLESSED RELATIONSHIP WITH JESUS,
IS IMITATING IN A MOST INTIMATE WAY
THE OFFERING OF CHRIST'S HUMAN WILL
IN GETHSEMANE
TO THE WILL OF THE FATHER
IN THE UNITY OF THEIR LOVE
IN THE SPIRIT OF SACRIFICIAL AGAPE,
THE LOVE WHICH REVEALED HIMSELF ON THE CROSS.

FOR IN OFFERING OUR WILL
TO THE WILL OF GOD
WE TASTE GLORY IN SUFFERING,
UNITED TO CHRIST CRUCIFIED,
AND AWAIT-IN THE SPIRIT OF LIFE-
THE SUBLIME JOY OF CHRIST RISEN WITHIN US. +

+"NEW WINE, FRESH SKINS!
FROM CONFESSION TO COMMUNION
WE ARE RENEWED IN THE NEW WINE OF CHRIST
SHED FOR LOVE OF HIS FATHER
IN THE SPIRIT WHO EMPOWERS PERFECTION
FOR THE SALVATION OF MAN
IN THE INCARNATE GIFT
OF LIVE DIVINIZED IN CHRIST
AS THE DISCIPLE WALKING THE PASCHAL WAY
IN FAITH HUMBLE, AND HOPE OBEDIENT,
IN THE LOVE OF GOD
POURED OUT IN THE SPIRIT
IN THE COMMUNION OF EUCHARISTIC THANKSGIVING
WHERE GOD AND MAN ARE RECONCILED
IN THE LIFE OF CHRIST
AND THIS LIFE AS ONE BODY
REACHES TO THE VERY ENDS OF THE WORLD
TO FULFILL GOD'S MESSIANIC MISSION OF MERCY. +

+GOLIATH COMES IN MANY FORMS.

HUGE FEROCITY, WITH DEADLY INTENT,
IS FOUND IN THE WIND AND THE WAVES OF THE WORLD!

THE REALITY OF EVIL,
BOTH NATURAL AND DIABOLICALLY SPIRITED,
INVADES US FROM WITHOUT…
AND FROM WITHIN.

BUT THE COURAGE TO FACE THIS BEHEMOTH
COMES FROM TRUST IN GOD
IN HIS PRESENCE HERE AND NOW-
IN PRAYER AND SPIRITED CONVICTION!

FOR, REST ASSURED,
THE WILL OF GOD,
-ALMIGHTIER THAN ANY BEHEMOTH-
WILL BRING US THROUGH TO THE OTHER SIDE,
WHOLE AND ALIVE,
IN THE FAITH AND HOPE WHICH COMES FROM COURAGE-
A COURAGE *WILLING* TO EMBRACE ONES CROSS FOR LOVE. +

+BOYS IN SIN BECOME MEN IN REPENTANCE,
WILLING TO TACKLE THE CROSS FOR LOVE.

FOR MERCY BRINGS STRENGTH IN NEWNESS OF LIFE,
AND NEWNESS IN LIFE BRINGS COURAGE-
STRONG ENOUGH TO SACRIFICE EVERYTHING…
EVERYTHING FOR THE MERCIFUL *ONE*.

ALL SUFFERINGS AND LOSSES,
BATTLES WITH PRINCIPALITIES, WARS WITH POWERS,
NONE DETER THE COURAGE OF THE FORGIVEN ONES.

FOR IN THE MIDST OF THE WAR *ALREADY WON,*
THE FORGIVEN IS EMPOWERED
IN THE GRACE OF THE CRUCIFIED AND RISEN SON,
VICTOR IN THE WAR, OVER THE GREATEST OF OUR ENEMIES,
IN THE SNAKESKIN AUTHOR OF OUR SIN AND OUR DEATH. +

+THE DEMON LURKS IN THE HOUND OF HUNGRY CRITICISM,
SEEKING TO DEVOUR CHARITY ATTRACTIVE AND TRUE.

BUT CHARITY ATTRACTIVE AND TRUE, NEVER COWERS TO CRITICISM,
FOR THE LIGHT WHICH IT SHEDS ON THE PRESENCE OF THE LORD
SCATTERS DEMONS IN CRITICISM,
REVEALING THEM AS MALISCIOUS AND JEALOUS CHILDREN IN LIES,
DEAD TO LOVE, IN THE HELL OF ENVY!

AND CHARITY, WHICH HEALS AND HOPES,
ILLUMINATES FAITH IN LOVE,
DRIVING DEMONS OF CRITICISM AND ENVY
TO THE PERIPHERY OF ONES REALITY,
TO STARVE IN THE DESERT OF VIRTUE
IN THE SANDS OF PURIFYING GRACE-
WANDERING DESOLATE PLACES
WITH THE PRINCE OF PETTY JEALOUSY-
HE WHO FAILED IN HIS CRITIQUE OF THE LORD. +

+**THOSE OF US** WITH ILLNESSES OF THE MIND
SEEK FOR THE HEALING TOUCH OF JESUS CHRIST.
THOSE OF US WITH DISEASE OF THE BODY
AND DIS-EASE IN ADDICTIONS,
SEEK FOR THE SALVE OF COMFORT
IN THE SALVATION OF WHOLENESS LOST-
IN THE HEALING TOUCH OF JESUS COMPASSIONATE.
THOSE OF US WITH ILLNESSES OF SPIRIT,
IN HATRED AND ENVY AND LUST,
SEEK FOR THE FIRE OF THE SPIRIT
AND THE PURGATION OF REPENTANCE
-IN CONVERSION AND HEALING-
FOUND IN THE TOUCH OF THE CRUCIFIED.
THOSE OF US DEAD IN MORTAL SIN,
AND THOSE OF US DYING SLOWLY AND VENIALLY,
SEEK FOR THE GRACE OF HOLY SHAME,
AND THE CONSOLATION OF HOLY CONTRITION,
AND RECONCILIATION IN THE BLOOD OF THE LAMB-
WHO ROSE IN THE FULLY HEALED TRANSFORMATION OF HUMANITY-
IN THE WHOLENESS OF DIVINE LOVE,
AND THE GRACIOUSNESS OF THE SPIRIT OF GOD. +

+I AM UNDER CONSTANT ATTACK.
MY MIND BEATS ME WITH THOUGHTS OF PAST FAILURE.
MY HEART HOUNDS ME WITH SENTIMENTS OF LOST LOVE.
MY SPIRIT BERATES ME IN GUILT AND SHAME OF PAST SIN.
MY SOUL EXHAUSTS ME IN THE ILLUSIVE PURSUIT OF PERFECTION.

YET MY FAITH SAVES ME-
IN HE WHO IS GREATER THAN I.

AND MY HOPE (IN HIM) REFRESHES ME-
IN THE CHOICE TO CHOOSE FOR THE BETTER.

AND *HIS* LOVE RENEWS ME IN SIN WASHED AWAY...
AND IN THE STRENGTH OF MY NEW HUMILITY,
WHERE HE CONQUERS MY WEAKNESS IN PRIDE! +

+VULNERABILITY DEFINES MY SELF PERCEPTION.
WEAKNESS IS THE STATE OF MY WILL.
WOUNDED IS THE CONDITION OF MY SPIRIT.
FLOUNDERING IS THE FACT OF MY FAITH.
LIMP CRAWLS FORWARD MY HOPE.
SMOLDERING IS THE FAINT FIRE OF MY LOVE.

DEAR MERCIFUL FATHER,
FORGIVE ME,
REVIVE ME,
RENEW ME!
CRUCIFY ME IN THE PASCHAL FIRE OF YOUR SON.
THEN RAISE ME IN THE GOLDEN REFINEMENT
OF EASTER PERFECTION
IN THE SPIRIT OF YOUR RESURRECTED LOVE! +

+**HE** OFFERED HIS BACK
FOR THE TYRANTS OF THE FLESH,
SO THAT WE COULD TURN OUR BACK TO THE ENTICEMENT OF SIN.
HE BORE THE SPIT AND THE FIST,
SO THAT WE COULD REVEAL THE FACE OF MERCY.
HE BORE THE NAILS AND THE SPEAR OF IGNOMINY,
SO THAT WE COULD SHARE THE PASCHAL TREASURE
OF RESURRECTION UNTO EVERLASTING LIFE. +

+THIS PUFF OF WIND WE CALL THE WORLD
IS A DEMANDING TASKMASTER.
NOT THE TREES AND THE WIND AND PEOPLE THEMSELVES,
BUT THE WORLD OF SYSTEMS
AND POWERS AND COMPETITIONS AND MARKETS
AND LORDS AND RULERS AND SECRET DARK INSPIRATIONS.

THIS WORLD DEMANDS ADHERENCE AND ZEALOUS SERVITUDE
IN THE CHAINS OF IDOLATRY AND PERVERSITY
AND GREED AND CELEBRITY AND UTILITARIAN MOXY.

ONLY IN THE POWER OF THE CRUCIFIED
-UPON HIS CROSS-
DOES COUNTER CULTURALISM FLOW WITH LOVE.

PURPOSE AND PERSEVERANCE
TRUMP PRIDE AND POPULARITY
FOR THE DISCIPLE
WHO LIVES IN THE WORLD
WITHIN THE LIFE OF CHRIST. +

+*IT SEEMS* AS THOUGH SOME HEBREWS LIKE ME,
HAVING OBSERVED THE PASSOVER, HAVE NOT BEEN PASSED OVER.
IT SEEMS THAT THE BLOOD OF THE LAMB,
ON THE DOORPOSTS OF MY HEART,
HAS NOT KEPT THE ANGEL OF DEATH FROM VISITING ME.
IT SEEMS THAT THE PLAGUE OF GOD'S WRATH
HAS VISITED MY HOME.
AND I CAN'T SEEM TO FIND A MOSES TO HELP ME. +

+KNOWING ON THE EVER OF HIS PASSION
"THAT THE FATHER HAD PUT EVERYTHING INTO HIS HANDS"
JESUS EXEMPLIFIED
THE POWER, THE MAJESTY, AND THE PURPOSE
OF THE SERVANT KING OF GOD.
FOR THE LORD REIGNED DOWN THE THUNDEROUS POWER OF MERCY
WHICH FLOWS FROM PURITY AND HUMILITY AND FAITH,
-THE CONDUITS OFEARTH SHATTERING POWER-
IN LOVING SERVICE TO THE MISSION OF MERCY
FOUND IN LIFE THROUGH BAPTISM IN THE CROSS. +

+AS A COWARDLY CUB,
I MUST BELIEVE IN THE EVERLASTING LOVE OF THE LION!

AS COWARDLY CUBS,
LET US GROW IN THE COURAGE OF THE SPIRIT OF THE LION
AND SHOUT: "HIS LOVE IS EVERLASTING."

AS CUBS OF THE CROSS,
MAY WE RELY SOLELY ON THE CRUCIFIED LAMB-
WHOSE METAMORPHOSIS IN THE SPIRIT
LION*IZED* MAN FOREVER! +

+IF I WERE CRUCIFIED BY MAN,
WOULD I SERVE HIM ON THE THIRD DAY?

IF I WERE SLAIN BY SINNERS,
WOULD I TEACH THEM TO FISH?

IF I WERE ABANDONED, BETRAYED, AND DENIED THREE TIMES,
WOULD I DINE IN THE JOY OF THEIR PRESENCE?

IF I WERE BEATEN, PEIRCED, AND HUNG FOR DEAD,
WOULD I OFFER "MY PEACE BE WITH YOU?"

ONLY IN CHRIST MAY WE BE TRULY CHRISTIAN! +

+FAITH IN CHRIST
IS A LIVING, BREATHING PORTRAIT OF THE GOSPEL JESUS.

THOUGH IMPERFECT IN IMITATION,
THE SPIRIT OF CHRIST ANIMATES THE DISCIPLE
IN A SLOW AND STEADY TRANSFORMATION
WHICH PREPARES THE DISCIPLE
FOR LIFE'S INEVITABLE PASSION,
AND FAITH'S HOPED FOR RESURRECTION.

LIKE CHANGES IN SEASONS, AND MORNING FOG FADING AWAY,
FAITH AND HOPE SLOWLY REVEAL
THE WONDERFUL WORK OF GOD'S GRACE...
LOVE TRANSFORMING BELOVED IN THE IMAGE OF *THE BELOVED*! +

+IN THE SIX WINGS OF SERAPHIM FLIGHT,
I RUN FROM DISASTER IN THE SINS I SO LOVE TO COMMIT.

IN THE SANCTUARY OF GOD'S HOLY TEMPLE,
I SEARCH MY SOUL FOR AN OUNCE OF REPENTANCE,
AND BESEECH MY SPIRIT TO LAMENT MY FALL,
ACCUSING MY MIND OF FOLLY, MY HEART OF DECEIT,
AND MY WILL OF UNHOLY COWARDICE.

AND I BRIDLE MY BODY,
DRIVING MYSELF TO MY KNEES,
DROWNING MY FACE IN SHAMEFUL TEARS,
WHILE BEATING MY PRIDEFUL BREAST DOWN.

AND THE LORD,
THE HOLY ONE IN THREE,
SENDS HIS SPIRIT TO CONVICT MY CONSCIENCE,
HIS SON TO PURGE MY SIN IN BLOOD,
AND IN ALMIGHTY FATHERHOOD,
HE FORGIVES MY SIN PERFECTLY,
IN THE ANGUISH OF TRUE CONTRITION,
CRUCIFORM CONTRITION,
WHICH RISES FORGIVEN IN THE JOY OF BEING LOVED. +

+OVERCOME ME O LORD.
OVERCOME MY ANGER AND RAGE
AND HURT AND ENVY AND LUST,
OVERCOME MY LACK OF TRUST IN YOU.
OVERCOME ME IN A WORLD SO EMPTY.
OVERCOME ME IN A HEART SO DRY OF HOPE-
A HEART SO HARD TO COMPASSION.
OVERCOME ME FOR ME,
IF NOT FOR ME, FOR MY WIFE
AND MY LITTLE GIRL.
OVERCOME ME IN COURAGE-
IN COURAGE TO LIVE RIGHT,
IN COMPASSION TO FORGIVE AND LIVE,
IN COMPOSURE TO TRUST IN YOU, TO PRAY TO YOU,
TO RELY ON YOU, TO LIVE IN YOU,
WHEN ALL ELSE LEADS ME TO DIE. +

+CHRIST DESIRES OBEDIENCE
TO THE LETTER OF THE LAW,
IN THE SPIRIT OF THE LAW OF LOVE.

FOR CHRIST OBEYED HIS FATHER IN HEAVEN
IN THE LETTER OF THE LAW OF THE FLESH
-AS HE DIED ON THE CROSS,
SUFFERING THE PAIN OF HUMAN NATURE-
IN THE SPIRIT OF THE LAW OF AGAPE LOVE.

FOR GRACE EMPOWERS NATURE
TO FOLLOW COMMANDMENTS IN BOTH TIME AND SPACE.

YET GRACE EMPOWERS OUR SPIRIT
TO SERVE GOD JOYFULLY,
NOT AS SLAVE TO THE LAW,
BUT BECOMING THE LAW ITSELF,
IN THE WILL OF THE FATHER,
IN THE SACRIFICE OF THE SON OF GOD,
IN THE SPIRIT OF FREEDOM IN TRUTH,
AS IMAGES OF GOD ONCE FALLEN,
FOREVER REDEEMED,
IN THE LAW OF UNENDING LOVE. +

+**DESPITE** DEVASTATION,
ENTRUST YOUR FALLEN LOT
IN THE SINGLE TRUE HOPE OF THE MERCIFUL JESUS.
JUST AN OUNCE OF CHRIST THRUST TRUST,
WILL YEILD ABUNDANT TREASURE
IN THE SILVER OF HOPE AND THE VIRTUES GOLDEN.
TRUST EMPOWERS THE MIND, BEATIFIES THE TONGUE,
SOFTENS THE HEART, AND STRENGTHENS THE SOUL,
IN THE FAITH FROM THE FATHER, HOPE IN THE SON,
AND LOVE IN THE HOLY SPIRIT.
FOR GOD IS THE ROCK OF PROTECTION
FOR THOSE WHO BELIEVE IN DARKNESS, HOPE IN HOPELESS TIMES,
AND LOVE IN THE FACE OF HATE.
THUS, GOD IS LOVE, AND LOVE OF GOD
INFUSES THE BELOVED DISCIPLE IN THE LIFE OF THE BELOVED SON,
AS LOVE ABSORBS LOVE IN LOVE. +

THE GARDEN

"IN THE DAYS OF HIS FLESH, JESUS OFFERED UP PRAYERS AND SUPPLICATIONS, WITH LOUD CRIES AND TEARS' (HEBREWS 5:7). JESUS CRIES OUT TO GOD IN PRAYER, SHARING THE HUMAN EMOTIONS OF ANGUISH AND DISTRESS. AS W.L. LANE PUTS IT: 'THE REFERENCE TO 'CRIES AND TEARS' DESCRIBES PRAYER IN A SETTING OF CRISIS.' PERHAPS THE EXPERIENCE OF GETHSEMANE IS IN VIEW: WHERE JESUS ENTERS THE DARKNESS OF AGONY AND 'BEGAN TO BE GREATLY DISTRESSED AND TROUBLED' (MARK 14:33). IN A GARDEN ADAM AND EVE BEGAN THEIR STRUGGLE WITH THE SERPANT; IN ANOTHER GARDEN CHRIST WRESTLES WITH THE POWERS OF DARKNESS. INDEED THE HOUR OF HIS PASSION IS THE CULMINATION OF THREE YEARS OF CONFLICT WITH NEGATIVE FORCES, ONLY OVERCOME BY THE POWER OF PRAYER (SEE MARK 9; 29)."

ANDREW D. MAYES
SPIRITUALITY OF STRUGGLE

"FATHER, LET THIS CHALICE PASS FROM ME...AND HIS SWEAT BECAME AS IT WERE DROPS OF BLOOD. FATHER, IF IT BE POSSIBLE...' WHATEVER ELSE HOLINESS MAY MEAN, IT CANNOT MEAN THAT WE ARE EXPECTED TO TAKE EVERY PAIN, EVERY SORROW, AS THOUGH IT WERE NO PAIN OR SORROW AT ALL. 'MY SOUL IS SORROWFUL UNTO DEATH...'"

"WHAT ELSE DOES HOLINESS MEAN: 'NEVERTHELESS,' HE GOES ON, 'NOT MY WILL BUT THINE BE DONE.' HOLINESS IS NOT A QUESTION OF WHAT WE FEEL, IT IS A QUESTION OF WHAT WE WILL. 'THY WILL BE DONE.'"

GERALD VANN, O.P.
FROM FR BENEDICT J. GROESCHEL'S . TEARS OF GOD

+LITTLE BIRD AM I,
FLY TO THE SHELTER
OF THE ALTAR OF THE LORD.

LITTLE BIRD IS ME,
FLY TO THE ARMS OF THE LOVING FATHER.

MAKE THE ASCENT
WITH LITTLE WINGS,
BOUYED BY GRACE,
WHICH IS PLACED IN THE SONG OF THE BIRD AS PRAISE.

FLY THROUGH SORROW,
EXPECT BLESSING! PRAY LITTLE BIRD, PRAY!

FOR THE NEST
OF BLESSED SALVATION
AWAITS THE FAITHFUL LITTLE BIRD. +

+CELEBRATE TODAY!
FOR THE MERCY OF GOD HAS FREED US FROM
"SHOULDERING THE BURDEN,"
AND CARRYING THE FULL BASKET OF GUILT, FEAR AND DESPAIR.

FOR CHRIST SHOULDERED THE BURDEN,
CARRYING THE CROSS OF OUR REDEMPTION
ON *HIS* BRUISED SHOULDERS, WOUNDED IN *OUR* SIN.

AND THE BASKET OF GUILT, OF FEAR AND DESPAIR,
-THE VERY CUP OF THE WRATH OF GOD-
CHRIST DRANK MERCIFULLY,
CARRYING *IT* TO DEATH IN *HIS* DEATH
TO RISE IN THE NEWNESS OF MAN,
INNOCENT, JOYFUL, AND FULL OF HOPE,
KNOWING THE FULL EXTENT OF GOD'S MERCIFUL LOVE-
FOUND IN THE SON OF GOD, THE MESSIAH,
HE WHO SUFFERED UNFATHOMABLY IN LOVE
FOR OUR FREEDOM AND OUR LIFE.
WHAT CAN WE SAY, KNEELING HUMBLY IN SELF KNOWLEDGE?
ONE CAN ONLY SAY: "PRAISE THE LORD FOR HE IS GOOD!" +

+I PRAY FOR THE RENEWAL OF THE EARTH,
AND A SMALL FLOWER BLOOMS.

I CRY FOR JUSTICE IN OUR NATION,
AND REPENTANCE IS PLACED IN MY HEART.

I YEARN FOR JOY AND PEACE AND HARMONY IN MY HOME
AND THERE STANDS MY WIFE AND MY DAUGHTER,
IN THE LIGHT OF GOD'S SPIRIT,
AND GRACE BECKONS A KIND COMPLIMENT,
A LOVING EMBRACE,
A FORGIVING HEART,
AND THE RENEWAL OF PRIORITY-
WHERE CHARITY BEGINS AT HOME. +

+THE BLOOD OF THE CROSS
PERPETUATES
IN THE BODY AND THE BLOOD OF OUR LORD
IN THE EUCHARIST,
FLOWING IN THE BLOOD OF THE MARTYRS,
SPREADING IN THE WOUNDS OF OUR SACRIFICE,
FROM OUR CROSS,
CO-MINGLING IN THE HOLY SPIRIT OF GOD'S LOVE,
UNITING WITH CHRIST IN HIS PERFECT SACRIFICE,
OFFERED TO THE FATHER,
AS PRAISE AND GLORY
IN THE FATHER'S GREATEST GLORY,
OUR SANCTITY,
WHICH BLEEDS FOR LOVE
AS SEED FOR SALVATION. +

+THE ROCK OF AGES IS MY FORTRESS AND MY STRENGTH.
GOD ALONE PROTECTS ME.
GOD ALONE SAVES ME.
GOD ALONE RESCUES ME, FROM EVIL WITHIN AND EVIL WITHOUT.
FOR THIS, GOD ALONE DESERVES MY ADORATION AND PRAISE!
GOD ALONE IS MY HOPE IN DARKNESS.
GOD ALONE KNOWS MY STRUGGLE.
GOD ALONE HOLDS MY VICTORY SECURE.
FOR GOD ALONE IS MY HAPPINESS AND MY HEAVEN. +

+IN THE DARKNESS OF NIGHT
THE LAMP OF THE PROPHETS
AND THE FIERY TORCH OF APOSTOLIC WITNESS
LEAD US TO A PLACE OF PEACEFUL HOPE
AND VIGILANT FAITH
IN ANTICIPATION OF THE SUBLIME,
WHERE THE SUBLIME COMES NEAR,
IN THE GRACE OF FORGIVENESS AND RECONCILIATION
WITH GOD AND NEIGHBOR,
IN THE VERY COMMUNION OF FATHER AND SON IN THE SPIRIT
THROUGH THE AMEN OF THE DISCIPLE
IN THE PARTICIPATION OF FAITH
WHERE THE BODY AND BLOOD
OF THE SON OF THE LIVING GOD
INCORPORATE
THE SUFFERING, THE PRAYER, AND THE PRAISE
OF THE BODY FAITHFUL
WITHIN THE PERFECT SACRIFICE
PERPETUATED UNTO ALL TIME
IN THE SPIRIT WHO BRINGS FORTH GLORY
TO GOD THE FATHER IN HEAVEN. +

+THE LOVELY LISTENING OF THE DISCIPLE
IS SANCTIFICATION
AND TRANSFORMATION
IN THE ALMIGHTY WORD OF GOD.

FOR FAITHFUL AND HOPEFUL DOCILITY,
IN RECEPTIVITY,
EMPOWERS THE DISCIPLE IN DIVINE GRACE
FROM WITHIN THE WORD OF GOD,
WHICH TRANSFORMS SINNER TO SAINT
IN PASCHAL STAGES OF STRUGGLE AND ACCEPTANCE,
EMPOWERED IN THE VICTORIOUS SUFFERING OF JESUS CHRIST,
RISEN AND PERFECTED ON THE CROSS OF HIS CHOICE
FOR THE LOVE OF HIS FATHER,
IN COMPASSION FOR ALL HIS BROTHERS AND SISTERS
FORMERLY LOST IN SIN,
NOW SAVED
IN PURGATIVE AND REDEMPTIVE MERCY. +

+IN THE MANY, WE LOSE OUR SALVATION!
IN *THE ONE* WE GAIN EVERYTHING!

FOR THE PATH TO HEAVEN
IS A PATH WALKED
WITH EMPTY HANDS,
OPEN ARMS,
AND A HEART AND MIND
WILLINGLY DEFEATED
IN SELF-EMANCIPATION;
ALL THE WHILE HUMBLY OPEN
AND FAITHFULLY HUNGRY
IN MEEKNESS AND HOPE,
EVER SEEKING FOR THE ONE TRUE REALITY-
THE ONE TRUE REALITY WHICH FULFILLS!
THAT REALITY BEING THE LOVE OF GOD. +

+HIDING FROM CHRIST IS LIVING IN FOOLISH DENIAL.

FOR HOW CAN THE WETNESS HIDE FROM THE WATER,
OR THE BREEZE HIDE FROM THE AIR ITSELF?

OUR LIFE CAN NEVER BE OUR ENEMY.
OUR HOPE CAN NEVER BE OUR DESPAIR...
UNLESS WE CHOOSE TO LOSE IT.

FEAR OF GOODNESS IS FOOLISH.
FEAR OF LOVE IS INSANITY. +

+I HAVE KILLED...
COMMITTED ADULTERY...
STOLEN...
DISHONORED MY MOTHER AND MY FATHER.
IF NOT OVERTLY,
IN FLESHLY MOVEMENT,
MANY TIMES IN INTENT OF WILL!
IF YOU ARE THE PECULIAR ANOMOLY IN HUMANITY...
INNOCENT OF THE ABOVE CHARGES,
HAVE YOU SOLD ALL YOU HAVE AND FOLLOWED THE CHRIST,
ALL FOR THE GLORY OF GOD? +

+MY SONG TO THE LORD
IS BUT BROKEN VERSE
IN SIN AND SORROW AND HURT.

MY SONG TO MY SAVIOR
IS BUT WARPED MELODY
IN FEAR AND PRIDE AND ANGER.

MY SONG IN THE SPIRIT OF GOD'S MERCY
IS EVER RENEWED
-DAY BY DAY-
IN GRACED REPENTANCE
AND INSPIRED DIALOGUE
WITH THE FATHER, AND THE SON,
WHO LOVE MY SONG,
IN EVERY NOTE WHICH IS ME. +

+WEARY AS WE ARE,
WE ARE EMPOWERED-SPIRITUALLY-
TO SING PRAISE AND THANKSGIVING FOR OUR SAVIOR.

FOR HIS STRENGTH IS OUR FAITH AND HOPE,
PERSEVERANCE IN MINDFULNESS OF HIS FAITHFUL LOVE.

VIGILANT, PERSEVERING, MINDFUL OF HIS LOVE,
WE MARCH FORTH, ABSORBING PERSECUTORY BLOWS,
ENDURING IN FAITH, CARRYING THE CROSS,
TOWARD THE TOMB,
PROCLAIMING THE LOVE OF THE RESURRECTION TO COME! +

+**WE** CROSS OUR T'S AND DOT OUR I'S,
BUT OUR MESSAGE IS VOID OF LOVE.
AND WE COMPLAIN WHEN THE LORD DRAWS US STRAIGHT...
FROM WITHIN *OUR* CROOKED LINES.
BUT TRUTH BE TOLD, WE SWEAT OVER OUTER PUNCTUATION,
BUT OUR INNER VOCABULARY LACKS SPIRIT.
FOR THE LORD WHO LOOSENS TIGHT WORDED ASCETICISM
AND STRETCHES THE PARYLIZING PARENTHESIS OF SELFISH PIETY,
INSPIRES *PURE* POETRY AND PROSE
IN COMPASSION AND MERCY AND LIFE. +

+IN THE DARKNESS OF MY WOUNDEDNESS,
THROUGH THE SMOKE OF BURNED BRIDGES IN MY SIN,
I SEEK FOR THE MERCY OF GOD.

WITHOUT LIGHT,
IN DOUBT AND FEAR,
A GENTLE SPIRIT IGNITES A SPARK WITHIN.

AND BLESSED REVERENCE,
AND CONTRITE SADNESS,
COME GUSHING IN.

THOUGH SUFFERING REMAINS,
MY PAIN IS NOW HOPE FILLED!

AND DARKNESS GIVES WAY TO THE LIGHT OF THE RISING SON! +

+AS IGNORANCE IS DESCRIBED AS BLISS, SIN IS DESPAIR!
FOR SIN IS AN ACT OF THE WILL.
DEFIANCE OF TRUTH,
DEFIANCE OF LOVE,
DEFIANCE OF TRANSCENDENCE
SIN IS AN INFORMED NO!
YET IGNORANCE IS FACTORED IN OUR WEAKNESS!
AND THANK GOD,
REPENTANCE IS GRACED WISDOM FROM ABOVE.

FOR TRUE BLISS IS NOT FOUND IN THE IGNORANCE OF MAN…
BUT IN THE MERCIFUL WISDOM OF GOD. +

+ HYPOCRICY IS THE FEAR OF REVEALING WHO WE REALLY ARE.
FOR SELF REVELATION IS SELF DISSAPOINTMENT,
AND POSSIBLE SOCIAL FALL.
BUT GOD ALONE KNOWS OUR WAYS,
AND DESIRES OUR HONEST WALK.
FOR FEAR OF MAN IS FALL INDEED.
BUT FEAR OF GOD IS *RISE* IN NEED.
FOR LIFE IN THE PROVIDENCE AND BENEVOLENCE OF HIS MERCY-
WHICH CREATES ANEW FROM THE HEART OF LOVE,
ETERNALLY HOLDS, EVER SO DEARLY, OUR SALVATION+

+I PRAY AND PRAY AND PRAY AND PRAY AND PRAY…
AND PERFECT TIME PASSES…
PERFECT PURGATIVE TIME PASSES…
NEVER PASSING, HOWEVER, IS THE LOVE OF GOD…
AND WHEN THY WILL PERFECTLY WISHES…
MY PRAYER IS ANSWERED PERFECTLY.

I THEN SEE AND HEAR AND FEEL AND KNOW
THAT ALL I DO AND SAY AND THINK
AND HOPE FOR
ARE IN THE PRESENCE OF ANGELS AND SAINTS
AND THE EYE OF SUCH A BENEVOLENT GOD.

FOR I PRAYED,
AND YOU GAVE ME FAITH,
AND I PRAYED,
AND YOU FORTIFIED MY HOPE,
AND I PRAYED,
AND YOU KEPT ME VIGILANT IN YOUR MERCY,
UNTIL THE DAY I OPENED MY EYES
AND SAW YOUR ANSWER EVER PRESENT IN LOVE.

AND NOW I PRAY, IN BRIGHTNESS DAY AND DARKNESS OF NIGHT,
CONFIDENT OF PERFECT FIDELITY
IN THE ONE WHO TRULY LOVES. +

+LORD, I HAVE PRAYED HARD FOR MONTHS-
WITHOUT CONSOLATION OR JOY.
BUT IF YOU INSIST, I WILL PRAY SOME MORE.
AND ONE PRAYER MORE,
JUST ONE MORE THAN DESPAIR,
AND PEACE AND JOY AND CONSOLATION CAME!
THIS CONVICTED MY CONSCIENCE!
GUILT AND SHAME FLOODED MY FAITHLESS SOUL.
POOR AM I! UNTRUSTING OF THE LORD I AM!
AND THE LORD SUMMONED ME,
TO PREACH OF PERSEVERANCE AND TRUST
WHEN ALL ELSE SAYS OTHERWISE.
AND IN WEAKNESS OVERCOME WITH GRACE,
I HAVE COMPLIED TO THIS DAY! +

+LOST YOUR WAY?
KNEEL REPENT, LAY PROSTRATE AND PRAY!
FOR SNAKES AND FRUIT AND GOLDEN CALVES
ARE A HARBINGERS WAY
OF RELAYING THE MESSAGE
OF A HEART AND A MIND GONE ASTRAY!

AND SORROW AND SUFFERING
AND HEART FELT LONGING,
ARE A SURE SIGN
THAT THE FATHER
THROUGH HIS SON
IN THE PURGATIVE SPIRIT,
INTENDS TO STAY!

RHYME

FOR THE FLAGELLATION
AND THE THORNS
AND THE CROSS
ARE A SURE SIGN
OF THE RISEN *WAY*!

AND SADLY,
COMFORT AND SUCCESS,
AND EASE WITH THE WORLD
IS BUT HARBINGER
OF DARKNESS TO COME...
ON JUDGMENT DAY! +

+I HAVE HEARD THE WORD, BUT I HAVE NEVER LISTENED!
I HAVE VIEWED THE PRESENCE, BUT HAVE NOT WITNESSED HIM!
BUT IN STRUGGLES AND THE *SPITTLE* OF GRACED FAILURE,
I HAVE FALLEN-WEARILY-ON MY KNEES DEAF AND DUMB,
SEEKING SINCERELY FOR HEALING.

"EPHPHATHA"
SORROW AND SUFFERING, PRAYER AND SACRAMENT,
CONTRITION AND PENNANCE, REPARATION AND CHARITY,
FAITH AND HOPE, RELIGION AND THE SPIRIT,
AND SLOWLY, I LISTEN, AND I SEE,
THAT LOVE IS TRULY IN LOVE WITH ME. +

+TRIALS ARE TESTS TO BE ENDURED.
VICTORY IS IN FAITH SECURE THROUGHOUT ONES SUFFERING.

REWARD IS INCREASED SPIRITUAL STRENGTH
AND FAVOR IN GOD'S EYES
IN THE GLORY BROUGHT UPON HIM
IN HOLINESS TRIUMPHANT OVER TEMPTATION.

PATIENCE AND HOPE WILL ABOUND
IN A HEART PURIFIED IN FAITH
THROUGH THE FIRES OF TRIBULATION
AND THE CHARITABLE DESIGN
OF GOD'S WILL FOR YOUR LIFE.

FOR PATIENCE AND HOPE
REST ON FAITH FIRMLY EMBEDDED
ON THE ROCK OF COMPASSION
OF THE CRUCIFIED AND RISEN CHRIST,
THE STRENGTH OF THE FAITHFUL. +

+WHEN I PRAY FROM ANGER AND RIGHTEOUS INDIGNATION,
MY PRIDE AND MY SELFISHNESS DEMAND A SIGN!

BUT WHAT TRULY SURFACES
IN THIS QUASI-PRAYER
IS MY FEAR AND MY DOUBT AND MY DESPAIR.

FOR WHO AM I TO TEMPT THE LORD...
BUT CERTAINLY A SATAN!

AND PUSHING THE GIVER OF ALL GIFTS
GIVES ME NOTHING BUT THE ECHO OF MY OWN FOOLISHNESS.

FOR CHRIST MOVES AWAY
IN SEARCH OF AN OPEN HEART,
A COMPLIANT MIND,
A WILLING SPIRIT,
AND A HUMBLE SOUL,
SEEKING, ASKING AND KNOCKING
FOR GOD'S WILL ALONE. +

+WHEN STORMS COME,
AND TRIALS BESET THE VIRTUOUS MAN,
HE DOES NOT RUN, HE DOES NOT TAKE FLIGHT,
HE STANDS FIRM
IN FAITH AND HOPE,
IN A JUST AND MERCIFUL GOD.

FOR TRIALS AND TEMPTATIONS
COME NOT FROM GOD,
BUT FROM MAN.

AND EVILS FLOW FROM DEMONS WITHOUT,
AND FROM WITHIN THE HEARTS AND MINDS AND SPIRIT
OF THE FALLEN CHILDREN OF GOD.

FOR GOD IS LOVE,
AND GOD IS GOOD,
AND ALL GOD SENDS
IS HIS PRECIOUS GRACE
IN HIS HOLY SPIRIT,
OFFERED IN THE SUFFERING OF HIS ONLY BEGOTTEN SON. +

+THE PASCHAL PARADOX OF THE PRINCE OF PEACE
IS THE PURIFYING POVERTY,
IN THE DISPOSESSION OF THE WORLD,
TO THE GAIN OF ALL THINGS GOOD!

FOR THE GARDEN AND THE CROSS
IS TEMPORAL LOSS FOR THE WILLING PURPOSE OF ETERNAL GAIN.

AND DEATH TO SELF,
-VOLUNTARY IN THE HOLY SPIRIT-
OF BLESSED SPIRITUAL VIOLENCE,
IS LIFE IN CHRIST
IN THE VOLUNTARY GIFT OF HIMSELF,
IN THE BODY AND BLOOD OF THE MOST BLESSED SACRAMENT,
IN THE HOLY SPIRIT OF THE BLESSED CRUCIFIED VICTIM.

FOR LOSS IS GAIN, AS THE MOTH OF MAN'S PRIDE *GIVES WAY*
TO THE BUTTERFLY OF DIVINE LOVE. +

+REALITY TUGS AT THE MIND OF THE RATIONALIZING IDEALIST.
FOR REALITY CRIES SIN!
SUFFERING! PERSECUTION! PREJUDICE!
THEY ARE REAL!
THEY WON'T FADE WITH EVOLUTION OR EDUCATION!

BUT REALITY ALSO WHISPERS:
GOD IS REAL...
PROVIDENCE IS IN THE WIND...
POWER IS IN THE SUFFERING...
YOU ARE NOT ALONE...
SEEK THE TRUTH IN COMPASSION...
YOU WILL NOT BE DISAPPOINTED...
GOD IS BUT A PRAYER AWAY. +

+THE LORD NEVER CRUSHES OUR DREAMS,
NOR DOES HE PUT OUT OUR FIRE!

WHAT IS UNIQUE TO US,
SPECIAL TO US,
BEAUTIFUL AND DESIROUS FOR US,
IS, RATHER,
TRANSFORMED IN THE BLOOD OF CHRIST,
THE VERY SOURCE OF GOD'S LOVE FOR US.

WHO WE ARE AND WHAT WE DREAM
ARE THE VERY GIFTS OF GOD'S LOVE.
BEING HUMAN, HOWEVER, CAN TAINT THAT DREAM.
THE GRACE OF GOD SIMPLY PURIFIES THE ORIGINAL GIFT. +

+THE HOLINESS OF GOD IS UNCOMPROMISING!.
AND THAT MAY SEEM HARSH.
FOR WE ARE A COMPROMISING PEOPLE.

BUT OUR FAITH
AND OUR HOPE
REST UPON THE UNCOMPROMISING MERCY OF THE LORD.
HE WHO DID NOT SPARE HIS SON,
IN THE UNCOMPROMISING LOVE
THAT SAVES US. +

+THE SAINT IS THE CLAY,
MANIPULATED,
WITHIN FREE WILL,
BY THE BENEFICENT HAND OF GOD,
THROUGH PARTICIPATION IN DIVINE CREATIVITY,
AS GOD BREATHES HIS SPIRIT AND GRACE
AND THE SAINT LIVES
IN COMMANDMENTS INCARNATE,
IN PURE FEAR AND TRUE LOVE EMBRACED,
 WHERE LIGHT AND LIFE
FROM CROSS AND SPIRIT
INVADE AND PERVADE AS GOLD AND HONEY,
SWEET IN SANCTITY AND GLORY! +

+MAY THE SPIRIT
WHO CUTS TO THE DEPTHS OF THE MARROW
UNLEASH THE RIGHTEOUS ANGER OF THE LORD
IN ME,
CLEANSING ME
OF PROFITEERING, COUNTERFEIT RELIGION,
GREED, LUST, ENVY,
AND THE SELF-DESTRUCTION OF HIS TEMPLE
IN VANITY AND ENMITY,
WHICH TURN HIS TEMPLE IN ME INTO A HOUSE OF IDOLATRY
WHERE GOD IS SHUNNED AND SELF IS WORSHIPPED.
TURN MY TABLES! TOSS MY RICHES!
RID ME OF ALL BEASTS!
MAY YOUR "ZEAL" FOR YOUR HOUSE DEVOUR ME! +

+THE DESERT PREPARES US
FOR A BETTER APPRECIATON OF THE OASIS.
PAIN AND SUFFERING PREPARE US
FOR THE GRACE
WHICH STRENGTHENS OUR FIDELITY
AND ENLIVENS OUR PRAISE AND THANKSGIVING.
GOD ALWAYS PREPARES US
IN HOLY THURSDAYS
FOR THE INEVITABLE GOOD FRIDAYS,
SO THAT OUR WAIT IN THE SILENCE OF SATURDAYS,
MAY BRING FORTH A MORE GLORIOUS EASTER SUNDAY. +

+THE MESSAGE OF THE CROSS ON CALVARY
CAN ONLY BE UNDERSTOOD
THROUGH *THE GARDEN OF GETHSEMANE*,
FOR ONLY IN THE ISOLATED SILENCE
OF REJECTION AND SUFFERING
MAY ONE HAVE THEIR OWN WISDOM DEFEATED,
THEIR OWN SELFISH PRAYERS REJECTED;
ONLY IN ISOLATED SILENCE
CAN ONE PERCEIVE THE LOSS OF ONES LIFE
AND THE GAIN OF ONES GOD
-ENVISIONED IN THE PRAYERFUL SUFFERING OF CHRIST-
AS THE WAY TO UNDERSTANDING, ACCEPTANCE, AND PEACE. +

+THE CROSSES AND *GETHSEMANE'S* OF LIFE
PURIFY THE SOUL,
ENHANCING MAN'S ABILITY TO PRAISE GOD WORTHILY.

FOR PRAISE IN GOOD TIMES *MAY* BE PRAISE OF ONESELF.
YET, TO THE DELIGHT OF THE SACRED HEART
AND THE SACRED WILL OF GOD,
PRAISE IN SUFFERING IS TRULY EUCHARISTIC. +

+CHRISTIANITY IS NOT PERFORMANCE ART,
BUT AN ACT OF SUBMISSION.
SEE THE PHARISEE AND THE TAX COLLECTOR.
CHRISTIANITY IS NOT ABOUT WHO FINISHES FIRST,
BUT WHO FINISHES.
SEE THE PRODIGAL SON.
CHRISTIANITY IS NOT ABOUT BUILDING LARGE TEMPLES,
BUT IN HUMBLY BEING BUILT INTO THE TEMPLE OF GOD'S SPIRIT.
SEE HEROD AND JOHN THE BAPTIST.
CHRISTIANITY IS NOT ABOUT HUMAN ART,
BUT SUBMITTING AS CANVAS TO THE WORK OF THE DIVINE ARTIST.
SEE THE IMMACULATE MARY.
CHRISTIANITY IS NOT ABOUT OUR TRIUMPHS!
RATHER, IT IS ABOUT GOD'S TRIUMPH,
IN OUR TRAGEDY!
SEE *THE GARDEN*,
THE CROSS,
AND THE EMPTY TOMB! +

+TO LIVE VICARIOUSLY THROUGH ONES NEIGHBOR,
IS TO LOSE APPRECIATION FOR WHAT ONE ALREADY HAS.

TO TIPTOE THROUGH THE OPINIONS OF ALL OF THOSE AROUND US,
IS TO WALK TOO SOFTLY TO BE FIRM ABOUT ANYTHING!

TO ALLOW ALL SORTS OF INJUSTICES
IN ORDER TO ATTAIN SOME MISGUIDED FORM OF PEACE
IS TO ATTAIN ONLY VICTIMHOOD IN A WAR ALREADY LOST.

TO SEE THE CUP HALF FULL,
TO HOLD TO CAPITOL **T** TRUTH,
AND TO FIGHT INJUSTICE FOR TRUE AND LASTING PEACE,
THIS IS TO LIVE **THY WILL BE DONE**
IN A RICH AND DIGNIFIED LIFE. +

+FOR ALL WHO STRUGGLE IN TEMPTATIONS AND DOUBT…
…AND ALL THOSE SCARRED WITH A LIFETIME OF SIN
AND HELL ALREADY VISITED…
BELIEVE IN GOD'S MERCY!
SEE THE CROSS.
HOPE IN GOD'S PROVIDENCE!
SEE CHRIST RISEN.
EMBRACE GOD'S PRESENT LOVE!
BE RECONCILED AND JOIN HIS COMMUNION.

FOR HIS SAINTS,
PETER AND PAUL,
WERE NOT MEN WITHOUT STRUGGLE,
NOR MEN UNAQUAINTED WITH SIN.
RATHER,
THEY WERE DYING TO SELF
IN THE MOST SWEET PASSION OF CHRIST,
EMBRACING PURGATION, EXPRESSING REDEMPTION,
MANIFESTING HOLINESS, FREELY, WILLINGLY,
GRACED IN THE LOVING WILL OF GOD,
THE GRACE WHICH PERFECTED THEIR FRAIL NATURE,
GAINING VICTORY, DAILY, EXPRESSED IN STRUGGLES,
WON IN FAITH, HOPE,
AND LOVE. +

THE CROSS

"CRUCIFIED INWARDLY AND OUTWARDLY WITH CHRIST, YOU WILL LIVE IN THIS LIFE WITH FULLNESS AND SATISFACTION OF SOUL, AND POSSESS YOUR SOUL IN PATIENCE (LK. 21:19)."
ST JOHN OF THE CROSS
THE COLLECTED WORKS OF ST JOHN OF THE CROSS

"IN OUR POOR PRESENT LIFE, LET US DRINK TO THE LAST DROP FROM THE CHALICE OF PAIN. WHAT DOES IT MATTER TO SUFFER FOR TEN, TWENTY, FIFTY YEARS, IF AFTERWARD THERE IS HEAVEN FOREVER, FOREVER…FOREVER!
AND ABOVE ALL-EVEN BETTER THAN FOR THE SAKE OF THE REWARD, *PROPTER RETRIBUTIONEM*-WHAT DOES SUFFERING MATTER IF WE ACCEPT IT TO CONSOLE, TO PLEASE GOD OUR LORD, WITH A SPIRIT OF REPARATION, UNITED WITH HIM ON HIS CROSS-IN A WORD, IF WE SUFFER FOR LOVE?…
JOSEMARIA ESCRIVA
THE WAY

"SEE, MY PHILOTHEA, IT IS CERTAIN THAT ON THE TREE OF THE CROSS THE HEART OF JESUS, OUR BELOVED, BEHELD YOUR HEART AND LOVED IT."
ST FRANCIS DE SALES
INTRODUCTION TO THE DEVOUT LIFE

"WE SHOULD GLORY IN THE CROSS OF OUR LORD JESUS CHRIST, FOR HE IS OUR SALVATION, OUR LIFE AND OUR RESURRECTION, THROUGH HIM WE ARE SAVED AND MADE FREE (GAL. 6:14)."
AN ENTRANCE ANTIPHON OF THE EASTER SEASON

+NEVER LISTEN TO A NATURAL JUDGMENT,
WHICH CONDEMNS YOU WHILE YOU STILL LIVE!

WHETHER FROM WITHIN,
IN A DEMON BURROWED DEEP WITHIN OUR OWN HURT,
OR FROM WITHOUT,
JUDGMENT IS THE SOLE POSSESSION OF THE LORD!

CHRIST, OUR BLESSED SAVIOR,
DID NOT SUFFER SO GREAT A SUFFERING,
SHEDDING SO PRECIOUS HIS BLOOD,
AS FOR OUR SALVATION TO BE LOST IN THE CORRUPTION
OF SUCH A FINITE AND BROKEN JUDGMENT,
WHICH COMES FROM LOST AND BLIND SOULS. +

+TO SUFFER FOR THE LORD
IS TO JOIN SIMON OF CYRENE,
CARRYING THE INSTRUMENT OF THE LORD'S PASSION
FORWARD IN TIME,
FOR THE COMPLETION OF THE PERFECT SACRIFICE
ALREADY ACCOMPLISHED, YET NOT FULLY REALIZED,
IN THE HEARTS AND MINDS OF VAST STRUGGLING PILGRIMS,
HUNGRY FOR JUSTICE AND MERCY, YET BLIND AND LOST IN SIN,
SEEKING THE LIGHT OF WISDOM,
WHICH LIBERATES AND REDEEMS IN THE BLOOD OF THE LORD
FOUND IN THE SPIRIT OF GOD WITHIN HIS CHURCH,
WHERE SAINTS AND SINNERS STRUGGLE IN WORSHIP FOR SANCTITY
AND REACH OUT AS THE ARMS OF CHRIST TO FULFILL GOD'S DESIRE
AS THE MESSIAH OF MERCY. +

+POVERTY IS THE GIFT OF UNBURDENED HANDS.
BETTER TO BE NAILED TO THE CROSS!
SORROW AND HUNGER ARE GIFTS OF A RECEPTIVE BODY.
BETTER TO BE NAILED TO THE CROSS!
PERSECUTION AND SCORN ARE GIFTS OF A CHRIST ONLY SPIRIT.
BETTER TO BE NAILED TO THE CROSS!

THE GIFTS OF POVERTY, SORROW, HUNGER, AND PERSECUTION,
THESE ARE THE GIFTS OF THE CROSS.
AND ONLY THROUGH THE CROSS WILL ONE SEE RESURRECTION! +

+FOR THOSE WITH EARS TO HEAR:
THE WAY OF THE CHRIST
IS IN THE PASSION OF OUR DAILY CROSS.

THE MISSION OF THE MESSIAH,
FOR THE DISCIPLE OF TODAY,
IS FORGIVENESS SEVENTY TIMES SEVEN.

THE NAILS, THE CROWN OF THORNS,
AND THE LANCE WHICH PEIRCED THE CHRIST,
ALL WHICH BRING REDEMPTION TO THE WORLD,
ARE OURS FOR THE SHARING
IN THE LOVE GIVEN TO OUR ENEMY.

FOR EVERY LASH RECEIVED
AND EVERY NAIL TO PIERCE OUR FLESH,
THE IMAGE OF CHRIST IS REVEALED.

AND AS WE PERSEVERE IN CHARITY,
THROUGH WHATEVER MAY COME,
DETERMINED TO RISE AGAIN,
WE SHALL KISS THE CROSS,
OUR BLESSED CHARIOT,
WHICH DELIVERS US IN CHRIST
FOR ETERNAL BEATITUDE
IN THE VISION OF THE FATHER AND THE SON,
GLORIFIED IN THE SPIRIT OF THEIR LOVE,
IN THE COMPANY OF MARY
AND THE SAINTS AND THE ANGELS, FOREVER. +

+AS WE SIN, SO DO ALL THE CHILDREN OF GOD SIN IN THE WORLD.
FOR IGNORANCE IS NOT AN ISOLATED PHENOMENON.
WE ARE BORN IN IGNORANCE, BRED IN IGNORANCE,
STRUGGLING DAILY IN OUR OWN IGNORANCE,
AND IN THE IGNORANCE OF THE WORLD AROUND US.
ONLY IN THE WISDOM OF GOD, REVEALED IN CHRIST JESUS,
-INCARNATE AND FOREVER TRANSFORMATIVE OF ALL MANKIND-
ARE WE RETURNED TO GOD'S IMAGE, IN GRACED REPENTANCE,
FREEING US FROM IGNORANCE,
SAVING US IN THE WISDOM OF THE CROSS. +

+YOU LORD ARE MY TREASURE,
FAR TOO MAGNIFICENT FOR THE APPRECIATION
OF SUCH AN IMPOVERISHED BEGGAR LIKE ME.
THAT IS WHY I SIN!

YOU LORD ARE MY ROCK, MY SHELTER, MY SALVATION!
FOR YOUR MERCY NEVER GIVES UP ON IMPOVERISHMENT!
AND YOUR GRACE CONVERTS A BEGGAR
INTO THE WEALTHIEST OF REPENTANTS.

FOR THE CROSS *TRANSFORMS*
WILLING WEAKNESS INTO MIGHTY SALVATION! +

+I AM A CITIZEN,
SON,
BROTHER,
FATHER,
HUSBAND,
FRIEND,
NEIGHBOR,
WORKER,
MEMBER,
TEAMMATE,
MAN,
CHILD,
STUDENT,
DISCIPLE,
MINISTER,
LEADER,
SERVANT...
BUT MOST OF ALL,
I AM A SINNER.
AND THAT IS WHY I AM IN NEED OF A SAVIOR. +

+*S*ALVATION *IS N*OW, *N*EVER *E*VADE *R*EPENTANCE! +

+FAST IN REPENTANCE, FEAST IN GRACE.
FOR THE ONLY FOOD WHICH SATISFIES IS THE BREAD OF CHRIST,
BORN OF THE CROSS,
FOR OUR SALVATION. +

+THERE ARE MANY DEADLY BATTLES.
SOME TRAGIC BATTLES ARE SUDDEN AND UNEXPECTED.
OTHERS ARE BURDENSOME
WITH LONG AND DRAWN OUT SUFFERING.
SOME COME
WITH PEACE AND ACCEPTANCE.
OTHERS APPEAR
AS THE ULTIMATE BATTLE,
WITH THE COMBATANT LEAVING KICKING AND SCREAMING.
YET, THERE IS ONE BATTLE COMMON TO ALL.
THE BATTLE OVER ONESELF!
THIS BATTLE
IS A LIFELONG BATTLE
WON ONLY IN LOSS!
FOR THE *WORLDLY* VICTOR
IS SURELY THE HEAVENLY LOSER
IN THE VICTORY OF DEATH IN SIN.
BUT WORLDY LOSS
IS HEAVENLY GAIN
AS THE CROSS IS EMBRACED
AND THE WORLD IS LOST
IN THE DEATH TO SIN,
WHICH RISES AGAIN
IN THE VICTORY OF PASCHAL DEFEAT. +

+WHAT BITES US AS POISEN,
QUITE OFTEN PRODUCES AN ANTIDOTE.

AS PAIN AND SUFFERING ARE POISEN IN DEATH FROM SIN,
SO TOO ARE THEY ANTIDOTE IN PURGATION
THROUTH MORTIFICATION AND DETACHMENT
AND THE RESULTING GLORY OF VIRTUE.

AND THE CROSS
-THE VERY SYMBOL OF PERSECUTION
AND HUMILIATION AND GUILT-
HAS BEEN TRANSFORMED
IN THE PERFECT AND INNOCENT BLOOD OF THE CHRIST,
BECOMING OUR SALVIFIC ANTIDOTE
FOR ETERNAL LIFE. +

+JESUS IS THE ONLY TRULY HEAVENLY SON OF MAN.

FOR ALL OTHERS ARE BORN, TRULY,
AS SONS AND DAUGHTERS OF ADAM AND EVE.

YET, SOLELY THROUGH CHRIST'S CROSS,
WE ARE BAPTIZED ANEW,
AS SONS AND DAUGHTERS OF GOD.

LITTLE BROTHERS AND LITTLE SISTERS
OF THE HEAVENLY SON OF MAN. +

+TEARS OF JOY AT HIS BIRTH.
TEARS OF PAIN AT HIS DEATH.
SUCH RELIEF AT HIS FINDING.
SUCH ANGUISH AT HIS BURIAL.
SUCH AWE AT HIS ANNUNCIATION.
SUCH CONFUSION ON HOLY SATURDAY.

OUR LADY OF SORROWS,
IMMACULATELY CONCEIVED,
PURELY ASSUMED,
YOU KNOW OUR SUFFERING
AND HAVE SUFFERED SECOND ONLY TO CHRIST.

OH LADY COMPASSIONATE AND UNDERSTANDING,
PRAY FOR US IN OUR SUFFERING,
THAT WE MAY LEAN HEAVILY ON *YOUR SON'S CROSS*,
AND BE LIFTED UP IN HIS RISEN MERCY. +

+FEAR NOT THE BEAST WHO WORSHIPS MONEY AND POWER,
THEIR GOD IS FADING!
JEALOUSY OF THE RICH, ENVY OF THE POWERFUL,
IS THE FOOLISHNESS OF BEING JEALOUS AND ENVIOUS
OF A DYING BREED.
FOR WHO CAN BUY REDEMPTION;
AND WHAT IS THE PRICE OF TRUE INNER PEACE AND JOY?
FOR GREED IS IGNORANCE,
NEVER SCHOOLED
IN THE CLASSROOM OF THE CROSS. +

+THE WAY OF CHRIST, THE WAY OF THE SPIRIT,
THE WAY BACK TO THE FATHER,
IS THE WAY PAVED IN RETURN TO CHILDLIKE INNOCENCE.

PRAYING IN THE SPIRIT,
DESTROYING THE STRONGHOLD OF LIES INOUR HEART
AND DECEPTIONS IN OUR MIND,
CHRIST JESUS LEADS US BACK TO THE PURE IMAGE OF HIMSELF,
IMBEDDED IN OUR HEARTS FROM THE BEGINNING,
LOST IN ORIGINAL SIN,
AND REDEEMED IN THE PRICELESS BLOOD
OF THE LAMB OF THE GOD OF LOVE. +

+WHY IS THE PERRENIAL QUESTION.
WHY THE PAIN?
WHY THE SUFFERING?
WHY THE EVIL?
WHY THE HATE AND THE HURT AND THE SILENT RESPONSE?
WHY? WHY? WHY?

ONLY THE PASSION,
THE MISERABLE SUFFERING OF OUR LORD,
TOUCHES THE MISERY OF THE WORLD…
AND THROUGH A COMMON TOMB,
LINKS US TO HIS RESURRECTION
AND HIS ETERNAL LIFE. +

+IN GOOD TIMES,
THE PASSION OF THE CHRIST, AND OUR IMPENDING PASSION,
BRING CONFUSION AND FEAR AND UNCERTAINTY.

FOR THE GATES OF HEAVEN
ARE NEVER STORMED BY THE RICH AND THE COMFORTABLE;
RATHER, THE ANGELS SUCCUMB, SOLELY,
TO THE POWER OF GOD'S LOVE
FOUND IN THE POOR AND THE AFFLICTED.

FOR THE KEYS TO THE KINGDOM OF GOD
COME ONLY IN GRACED SUFFERING
AND GRACED FAITHFULNESS. +

+TRUE DISCIPLESHIP IN CHRIST
IS TAKING THE SPIT AND THE FIST
IN THE FACE OF INNOCENCE.

TRUE CHRISTIANITY
IS ACCEPTING THE FLAGELLATION OF IGNORANCE,
AND THE CROWN OF THORNS
IN MALISCIOUS ENVY.

CHRISTLIKE SANCTITY
IS OPENING ONES ARMS
TO A HAMMER WEILDING,
NAIL DRIVING,
VICTIM OF LIES,
INTENT ON KILLING CHRIST,
THE TRUTH UNBEKNOWNST TO HIM.

YET, TRUE DISCIPLESHIP SEEKS RESURRECTION AND LIFE! +

+THE ASCENT TO HEAVEN
IN THE PILGRIMS JOURNEY
IS FIRST A DESERT INTO SALVIFIC SUFFERING.

THE WAY OF THE SAINT
IS NOT MARKED WITH A HALO,
BUT WITH A CROWN OF THORNS.

THE WAY OF THE DISCIPLE IS NOT SHOWERED WITH FLOWERS,
BUT WITH FLAGELLATION AND FISTS.

THE WAY OF HOLINESS
IS NOT RESTING IN CONTEMPLATIVE COMFORT,
BUT IN CRUCIFORM AFFLICTION.

THIS IS THE ONLY *WAY*
TO RESURRECTION AND LIFE EVERLASTING. +

+LORD, HELP ME *TO LEARN* TO SUFFER FOR THE GOOD!
THEN ALL MY LIFE WILL TRULY BE JOY
IN THE PURPOSE OF TRUTH AND LOVE! +

+THE "LEAST OF THE APOSTLES,"
THE PERSECUTOR OF GOD'S CHURCH,
BORE FRUIT IN GRACE
TO WORK "HARDER THAN ANY OF THE OTHERS"
BEARING *A THORN* OF THE FLESH,
PREACHING TRUE TO THE APOSTOLIC TRADITION,
WITNESSING TO THE LOVE OF GOD AS MERCY,
TO A PAGAN WORLD DESPERATE IN DARKNESS.

AND IN RECEIVING A SINGULAR VISION, AND A DAUNTING MISSION,
THE APOSTLE TO THE GENTILES
WAS GRACED ABUNDANTLY IN THE SPIRIT,
WHILE PARTICIPATING UNIQUELY IN THE CROSS OF CHRIST.

FALLING TO THE GROUND IN CONVERSION,
HE WAS RAISED IN THE GOSPEL KERYGMA
IN COMMUNION WITH THE BODY HE ONCE PERSECUTED.

ONCE A TERROR TO THE PEOPLE, IN THE BENEVOLENCE OF GOD,
PAUL BECAME THEIR COURAGE IN A LIFE CRUCIFIED WITH CHRIST. +

+NO FOOD OF TEMPORAL ORIGIN CAN SPOIL THE SPIRIT OF MAN.
BUT THE DEMONIC DESERTS AND THE PERVERSE PASTRY
OF CARNAL INDULGENCE,
THIS WILL SURELY DEVOUR BOTH SPIRIT AND BODY FOREVER!
FOR THE FRUIT OF DIRT AND WATER
WILL BEAR ONLY FRUITS OF CREATION.
AND IN GOD'S WORD THIS IS GOOD.
BUT THE FRUIT OF DECEPTION AND DISOBEDIENCE
WILL BEAR ONLY FRUITS OF CONDEMNATION.
AND IN GOD'S WORD THIS IS DEATH.
FOR THE FOOD AND SUSTENANCE
IN TILLING THE SOIL OF GOD'S GREEN EARTH
IS THE LOT OF EVERY MAN!
BUT THE FOOD OF TRUTH IN HUMAN DIGNITY,
FOUND IN THE BREAD AND WINE OF SUFFERING,
THIS ALONE IS THE LOT OF THE FAITHFUL SERVANT,
THE LOT OF THOSE WHO WALK
THE STRAIGHT AND NARROW WAY
OF THE CRUCIFIED AND RISEN CHRIST. +

+DON'T BE SURPRISED WHEN YOU SEEK FOR MERCY
AND *OUR* FATHER TESTS YOUR RESOLVE.
FOR LOVE IS TRUTH
AND MERCY IS JUSTICE
AND FORGIVENESS SEEKS VIRTUE ANEW.
SO BEND YOUR KNEE
AND REVEAL YOUR SOUL
AND TAKE LOVES LASHES AS GRACE.
FOR THE SCARS
YOU BEAR,
WITNESS TO LOVE SO TRUE,
FOR LOVE BORE SCARS FIRST IN REDEEMING YOU.

SO PAIN DEALT OUT
IS PERFECTIONS PREREQUISITE
IN THE MYSTERY OF THE LOVE OF THE CROSS. +

+I AM RATHER FLAT AND HARD,
AND TOUGH TO INCORPORATE IN COMMUNITY
DUE TO MY LACK OF *LEAVENLY* LOVE.

BUT THANKS BE TO GOD
-THANKS TO THE THANK OFFERING OF GOD
IN THE EUCHARISTIC CHRIST-
I AM FILLED WITH THE SPIRIT,
SOFTENED IN COMPASSION,
AND BETTER ABLE TO PARTICIPATE
IN THE COMMUNION OF DISCIPLES
DUE TO THE RECEPTION
OF GOD'S *HEAVENLY* LOVE.

FOR THE SACRIFICE OF CHRIST,
IN THE BODY OF THE SAVIOR,
FROM THE BLOOD OF HIS CROSS,
DELIVERS LIFE ENHANCING LEAVEN
IN FAITH, HOPE AND LOVE. +

+THE VISION OF HEAVEN IS AN ABSTRACT TERM.
THE SUFFERING SANCTITY OF A FAITH FILLED SAINT,
THIS IS THE CONCRETE REALITY THAT CHANGES THE WORLD! +

+PEACE IS FOUND
IN LAW ABIDING LOVE!

JOY IS FOUND
IN A HEART AFIRE IN DIVINE ADORATION!

REVELATION IS THE WILLFUL REVEALING
OF LOVE AS MERCY!

TRUE HAPPINESS IS FOUND
IN REVELATION RECEIVED IN FAITH,
OBEDIENTLY LIVED OUT IN HOPE!

THANKSGIVING SPRINGS FORTH
FROM FAITH REWARDED
AND HOPE RENEWED
IN THE LOVE OF EMMANUEL.

SALVATION IS FOUND
IN HOLINESS' BATTLE WITH ONESELF-
IN HIM WHOSE CROSS IS VICTORY! +

+LENT IS MORE THAN FASTING,
MORE THAN PRAYERS,
MORE THAN ALMSGIVING.

LENT IS DETACHMENT OF THE HEART,
AND MORTIFICATION OF THE BODY
IN EARNEST SEARCHING FOR THE GREATER LIFE OF CHRIST.

LENT IS SMALL STEPS
IN WILLFUL SUFFERING,
JOYFUL SACRIFICE,
AND FAITHFUL CHARITY,
IN THE SHADOW OF THE CROSS,
WHERE TRUE LOVE IS WITNESSED,
AND TRUE LIFE RECEIVED,
IN THE FORTY DAYS OF THE CROSS, AND THE TOMB,
THE ONLY WAY TO RESURRECTION
AND THE EVERLASTING BEATIFIC LIFE. +

THE EMPTY TOMB

"WHEN THE SON ROSE FROM THE DEAD, THE WOMEN FOUND THE STONE ROLLED AWAY BY ANGELS. EVIDENTLY A RELEASE HAD TAKEN PLACE BETWEEN THE SEALED TOMB AND THE SCENE IN THE GARDEN. THIS WAS A FIRST SCHOOL IN THE IDEA OF RESURRECTION FOR SINNERS WHO ARE HARD OF UNDERSTANDING."
ADRIENNE VON SPEYR
THE MYSTERY OF DEATH

"IN THE INCARNATION, "I AM" BECAME "HE WAS" CONCEIVED OF THE HOLY SPIRIT AND BORN OF THE VIRGIN MARY. THEN, ON CALVARY, THE *I* WHO BECAME A *HE* BECAME AN *IT:* THE GOD WHO BECAME MAN BECAME A CORPSE."
PETER KREEFT
THE PHILOSOPHY OF JESUS

"WHEN WE EAT THIS BREAD AND DRINK THIS CUP, WE PROCLAIM YOUR DEATH, LORD JESUS, UNTIL YOU COME IN GLORY."
MEMORIAL ACCLAMATION

+AS I STRUGGLE TO MEET THE NEEDS OF THE DAY,
THE DEMONS OF WEAKNESS
AND PRIDE
AND FEAR
ATTACK MY ENERGY,
MY CREATIVITY,
MY PATIENCE AND
MY DEVOTION.

THESE DEMONS LIVE WITHIN ME,
IN THOUGHTS AND DESIRES AND ACTS.

BUT, IN ME, THEY ARE NOT *OF* ME-
FOR I AM A REDEEMED CHILD OF GOD.

FOR I LIVE IN CHRIST
AND STRUGGLE IN GRACE,
DYING TO THE DEMONS,
ONLY TO RISE IN THE SON. +

+SHED THE WORLD IN A SONG OF JOY!
EMBRACE LIFE IN THE CHORUS OF CREATION!
SING FATHER, SING SON, SING SPIRIT!
SING IN THE SON.
SING IN THE MOON!
SING IN THE EAST AND WEST!
SING IN THE NORTH OF MERCY AND GRACE.
SING SOUTH IN SALVATION COME NEAR.
SING TO THE SKY,
SING TO THE SEA,
SING TO THE OPEN FIELDS.
SING TO THE BIRDS,
AND ALL THE LAND HOLDS.
SING STRONG, SING BOLD, SING TRUE!
SING FOR YOUR LIFE,
SING TO YOUR DEATH,
SING TO JUDGMENT DAY.
BUT MOST OF ALL,
SING TO GOD'S MERCY-SING *IN* HIS LOVE-
SING OF HIS PROMISES TRUE. +

+MAY THE FATHER OF ALL MERCY KISS YOUR FACE.
MAY HE HOLD YOU DEAR.
MAY HIS SON BRING YOU LIGHT.
MAY HIS SPIRIT COMFORT YOU.
MAY THE LORD SHINE ON YOU IN DARKNESS.
MAY YOU RISE
AFTER A LONG SUFFERING
IN THE PEACE OF HIS CHRIST
IN THE SPIRIT OF HIS LOVE
FOR ETERNAL UNION IN HIS LIFE EVERLASTING. +

+THE SOURCE OF ALL LOVE
SEEKS FOR COMMUNION
IN THE CO-NATURALITY
OF OUR CHARITABLE HEART.

FOR THE ESSENCE OF GOD
TRANSCENDS OUR SENSES,
BUT HIS LOVE KEEPS US WITHIN HIS GRIP.

FOR HIS SPIRIT HOLDS US
WHEN OUR SENSE
HAS LOST ALL SIGHT OF HIM.

AND HIS SON,
IN REVEALING HIS FACE,
HAS SAVED US
IN THE LIFE OF TRANSCENDENT LOVE.

FOR THE APOSTLES
ATTEST TO LOVE
AS THE GATEWAY
TO THE SACRED HEART OF THE LORD.

THE GATEWAY
PREPARED FOR, INCARNATE,
PROTECTED IN PASSION,
REVEALED IN RESURRECTION,
AS *THE WAY*
OF TRANSCENDENT LOVE COME NEAR! +

+A GOOD MAN BAPTIZED THE GOD-MAN
IN THE BAPTISM OF WATER AND REPENTANCE.

BUT THE BAPTIZED
-ONE WITHOUT SIN-
HUMBLED HIMSELF IN A BAPTISM OF SOLIDARITY
WITH THE FALLEN CHILDREN OF HIS FATHER.

FROM THE WATERS OF HUMBLE SOLIDARITY
SPRUNG FORTH THE SAVIOR OF MAN!

AND THE HEAVENS PARTED,
THE DOVE DESCENDED,
AND THE FATHER BEAMED BRIGHT
IN THE GLORY OF HIS SON.

AND THE GOOD MAN DECREASED
AS THE GOD MAN INCREASED,
IN THE BAPTISM OF SPIRIT
AND THE FIRE OF AGAPE LOVE. +

+SITTING IN IMPROPRIETY,
DEALING IN SELFISH DEEDS,
THE GRACE OF THE LORD,
THE MERCY OF GOD,
AND THE LOVE OF THE SPIRIT
SUMMONED *ME*.

"FOLLOW ME." AND I DID!
AND MY LIFE, A COLLECTION OF FOOLISH MISTAKES,
WAS REDEEMED FROM WITHIN!

FOR I WAS THE SAME WEAK AND VULNERABLE FOOL.
YET GRACE MOVED ME IN LITTLE WAYS TOWARD CHRIST.

AND WHEN I FELL,
-MANY A TIME-
AND SCRIBES AND PHARISEES POINTED AT MY GUILT,
THE LORD, IN SPIRIT, SUMMONED MY REPENTANCE,
AND CALLED ME FROM DEATH TO LIFE. +

+"CHRIST HAS DIED, CHRIST HAS RISEN,
CHRIST WILL COME AGAIN."

AS OUR BELOVED HAVE DIED,
IN FAITH THEY WILL BE RISEN,
AND IN HOPE WE WILL SEE THEM AGAIN!

AS OUR DREAMS MAY DIE,
IN FAITH THEY MAY BE RISEN,
SO IN HOPE WE MAY SEE THEM AGAIN!

AS OUR RELATIVES HAVE DIED,
IN OUR CHILDREN THEIR LINEAGE IS RISEN,
AND IN GENERATIONS TO COME THEIR LEGACY LIVES AGAIN!

SO ALSO WE WILL DIE, AND WE PRAY TO BE RISEN,
IN LIFE AND LOVE AGAIN!

FOR LOVE HAS DIED FOR OUR LIFE,
AND HE HAS RISEN FOR OUR HOLINESS,
SO THAT PEACE AND JOY
WOULD REIGN AGAIN!

FOR FAITH VIEWS DEATH
IN HOPE OF RESURRECTION
WHERE LOVE WILL LIVE AGAIN! +

+PLAIN AND SIMPLE IS THE TRUTH:
GOD DOES NOT JUDGE MAN AS DOES MAN JUDGE HIS BROTHER.
FOR MAN SEEKS FOR OUTER ATTRACTIVENESS.
MAN SEEKS FOR OUTER SIGNS.
AND MAN JUDGES ON ACTION SANS INTENT.
FOR MAN CANNOT DELVE INTO THE HEART OF ANOTHER PERSON.
THUS, FLESH AND BLOOD ARE BUT AN OBSTACLE TO TRUTH!
BUT THE LORD GOD ALMIGHTY,
HE WHO CREATED MAN *EX NIHILO*,
HE ALONE JUDGES MAN BY HIS HEART,
IN THE SPIRIT OF THE CHRIST,
HE WHO KNOWS THE NATURE OF MAN-
THROUGH THE PERFECT TEST OF SUFFERING UNTO DEATH. +

+JESUS IS THE GREAT MAGNET OF HOPE
FOR A WOUNDED AND WEARY HUMANITY
SEEKING FOR PUROSE AND WHOLENESS AND JOY
-IN THE EMPTINESS OF LIFE-
LIVED ON THE OUTSKIRTS OF GOD.

FOR ONE SIMPLE AND PRESCIOUS TOUCH OF THE CHRIST
IS ABSOLUTE HEALING FOR THE SOUL
IN FAITH FIRM, HOPE HEAVENLY, AND LOVE SECURE!

AND DEMONS OF SKEPTICISM,
AND DESPAIR, AND MALICE, AND ENVY,
IN ATHIEST AND AGNOSTICISM AND GNOSTICISM,
FLEE FEARFULLY TO HELL,
MUTE IN THEIR POWER TO SPREAD THE SEED OF THEIR FATHER,
THE FATHER OF ALL LIES, THE DEVIL. +

+APOSTOLIC FAITH-PETER

APOSTOLIC HOPE-JAMES

APOSTOLIC LOVE-JOHN

APOSTOLIC TRADITION-ANDREW

APOSTOLIC SCRIPTURE-PHILIP

APOSTOLIC MAGISTERIUM-BARTHOLAMEW

APOSTOLIC DOCTORS-MATTHEW

APOSTOLIC SAINTS-JAMES

APOSTOLIC LITURGY-THADDEUS

APOSTOLIC SACRAMENTS-SIMON

THE MYSTERY OF GOD
IN HIS MERCY AND JUDGMENT
-JUDAS ISCARIOT.   +

+SADNESS STRIKES AT THE HEART OF THE DISCIPLE
WHO WITNESSES THE FALL OF A COMPANION IN CHRIST
TO THE MORTAL SWORD OF SIN.

HOW MUCH BETTER THAT THEY WOULD HAVE PERISHED
HOLY AND UNDEFILED IN THE DEATH OF THE BODY!

HOW MUCH BETTER THAT THEY WOULD REPENT
AND LIVE AGAIN
IN THE LOVE OF GOD, IN THE MERCY OF THE CRUCIFIED,
IN THE SPIRIT OF RESURRECTION AND LIFE!

HOW MUCH BETTER TO FIGHT
-SIDE BY SIDE-
FALLING AND THEN RISING IN THE GRACE FOUND FLOWING
IN THE WATER AND THE BLOOD
FROM THE SIDE OF OUR WARRIOR KING. +

+DISCIPLESHIP IN CHRIST
IS FAITHFUL RESPONSE
TO UNFATHOMABLE EUCHARISTIC GRACE,
WHERE THE WEAK WALK ALL ROADS
SEEKING ALL CREATURES, ESPECIALLY CHRIST'S ONE LOVE,
THE PINNACLE OF HIS DESIGN,
THE IMAGE AND LIKENESS OF HIS BEAUTY,
THE ONES WHO CARRY THE DIGNITY
OF LIKENESS IN HIS ONE BELOVED SON, THE HUMAN PERSON.
THIS PERSON IS TO RECEIVE THE GOOD NEWS
OF GOD'S MERCY IN JESUS CHRIST.
THE DISCIPLE UPON THE WELCOMING OF THIS PERSON,
IS TO RESTORE THEIR ORIGINAL DIGNITY
IN THE BAPTISM OF THE CROSS IN THE MOST HOLY TRINITY.
AND IF DEMONS SHALL LURK,
THE DISCIPLE, ARMED WITH FAITH AND HOPE,
SHALL SLAY THE SNAKE WITH LOVE!
IN THIS, THE WOUNDED WILL RECEIVE FAITH,
THE DESPAIRING HOPE,
AND THE DEAD, LIFE IN LOVE!
AND THE MESSIAH WILL WALK THE LAND VICTORIOUS,
IN THE MERCY OF GOD'S UNENDING LOVE. +

+LIFE IS SO HARD!
SO MANY DISTRACTIONS, SO MANY TEMPTATIONS,
SO MANY FAILURES, SO MUCH SUFFERING,
SO MANY IN NEED!

WHAT MAKE LIFE EVEN HARDER,
IS MY WEAKNESS IN FEAR AND IN HURT,
WHICH CAUSES TEMPTATIONS TOWARD SELFISHNESS,
AND RATIONALIZED NON-COMPASSION-
WHERE MY ARMS REMAIN FOLDED IN SELF INTEREST,
NOT REACHING FOR THE GENUINE NEEDS
FOUND WITHIN MY NEIGHBORS POVERTY.
AND THIS IS MY GREATEST POVERTY!

THUS, I PRAY FOR GRACE
IN COURAGE AND IN HEALING,
-MY GREATEST NEEDS-
IN THE CHARITABLE SPIRIT OF JESUS.
HE WHO OPENED HIS ARMS
IN PAIN AND SUFFERING UNTO DEATH,
FOR MY NEEDS IN THE GENUINE POVERTY OF MY SIN,
FOR THE PURPOSE OF PROCURING
THE HEALING GIFT OF COMPASSION
WHICH WILL OPEN MY ARMS
-IN THE SPIRIT OF CHRIST'S PASSION AND DEATH-
TO SMALL ACTS OF CHARITY. +

+BAPTISM IS BIRTH IN FAITH STRONGER THAN DOUBT;
CONFIRMATION IS ANNOINTING IN HOPE STRONGER THAN DESPAIR;
IN THE SPIRIT OF POWER IN SELF MASTERY,
IN THE BODY AND BLOOD OF LOVE,
IN CHARITY AND SELF DENIAL,
FOR THE PURPOSE OF VOCATION IN WITNESS TO CHRIST
IN PRAYER, ALMSGIVING, WORSHIP, LONGSUFFERING, PATIENCE,
FORGIVENESS, LABOR, PLAY, AND REST
ALONE, AND IN COMMUNION
IN VIRTUE OF VIRTUES GIVEN TO BE EXERCISED IN ERNESTNESS,
SOLELY, FOR THE GLORY OF GOD
IN DEVOUT APPRECIATION FOR THE GIFT OF REDEMPTION,
WON FOR US IN SUCH INTENSLY LOVING SUFFERING UNTO DEATH. +

REPENTANCE AND CONVERSION

"REPENT. BE CONVERTED. BEGIN AGAIN. THESE ARE THE THREE
STAGES OF THE SPIRITUAL LIFE."
GEORGES CHEVROT
THE PRODIGAL SON

"COME LORD, WORK UPON US, CALL US BACK, SET US ON FIRE AND
CLASP US CLOSE, BE FRAGRANT TO US, DRAW US TO THY
LOVELINESS: LET US LOVE, LET US RUN TO THEE."
ST AUGUSTINE
CONFESSIONS
BOOK VIII

"ABBA LOT WENT TO SEE ABBA JOSEPH AND SAID TO HIM: ABBA, AS
MUCH AS I AM ABLE I PRACTICE A SMALL RULE, A LITTLE FASTING,
SOME PRAYER AND MEDITATION, AND REMAIN QUIET AND AS MUCH
AS POSSIBLE I KEEP MY THOUGHTS CLEAN. WHAT ELSE SHOULD I DO?
THEN THE OLD MAN STOOD UP AND STRETCHED HIS HANDS
TOWARDS HEAVEN, AND HIS FINGERS BECAME LIKE TEN TORCHES OF
FLAME AND HE SAID TO HIM: IF YOU WISH, YOU CAN BECOME ALL
FLAME."
GREGORY MAYERS
LISTEN TO THE DESERT

+LOVE,
OF WHICH THERE IS BUT SPIRIT,
SEEKS FOR FLESH
-TO MOVE AND BREATHE AND RECREATE-
IN THE UNFORTUNATE REALM OF FALLEN MAN.

CARVED IN STONE,
THE OLD COVENANT,
-GOD'S LOVING BOUNDARY FOR RUNAWAY MAN-
ONLY THREATENED AND COERCED IN FEAR,
EXTERNAL OBLIGATION,
AND MINIMAL DEVOTION.

YET, WHEN SPIRIT MARRIED CHASTE FLESH,
BLOOD SPILLED FORTH IN PERPETUAL SACRIFICE
SO THAT THE NEW COVENANT
-IN BODY AND BLOOD, SOUL AND DIVINITY-
MIGHT SHAPE THE HUMAN HEART IN TRUE INTERNAL DEVOTION
-FOR EXTERNAL CHARITY-
FREELY GIVEN IN THANKSGIVING AND PRAISE
FOR THE SACRIFICE OF SALVATION SO COSTLY IN LOVE. +

+LOVE IS HERE!
IF ONLY WE REALIZE THAT IMPERFECTION SEEKS TO BE LOVED,
AND SEEKS TO SHARE LOVE,
IN OUR NEIGHBOR,
AND THE MAN OR WOMAN IN THE MIRROR.

FOR LOVE IS A FORCE UNDENIABLE,
AS EVERYONE SEEKS IT,
AND MANY OFFER IT-THOUGH IMPERFECTLY-
OFTEN STUMBLING AND CHASING AWAY
THE BELOVED WHOM THEY OFFER LOVE
OR THE OFFERER OF LOVE BELOVING.

ONLY IN THE LOVE OF GOD
DOES IMPERFECT LOVE REALIZE PERFECTION
IN THE PURGATIVE COMMUNION OF MYSTICAL EMBRACE
WHERE love BECOMES LOVE
AS THE BELOVED IS CONSUMED IN THE LOVER. +

+SHARE YOUR JUSTICE
OH LORD,
WITH THIS CRIMINAL HEART OF MINE.

BLESS THIS SINFUL SOUL,
WITH MERCIFUL AND FORGIVING RIGHTEOUSNESS.

THEN AS I WALK IN GRACE,
PRACTICING JUSTICE AND MERCY IN THE RIGHTEOUS SPIRIT,
THEN THEY SHALL SEE *YOUR* LIGHT WITHIN MY DARKNESS,
YOUR MERCY IN MY HOPE DESPITE PAST SIN,
YOUR LOVE IN MY SALVATION,
AND *YOUR* GRACE, MERCIFULLY OVERCOMING MY WEAKNESS.

FOR REPENTANCE IS THE KEY
TO THE TREASURE CHEST OF MERCY-
FOR "THE POOR AND FEEBLE" NEED ONLY CRY! +

 +SIN IS A LIE BOUGHT INTO.
SIN TEACHES US THAT WE ARE
UNAPROACHABLE,
UNDESIRABLE,
AND WORTHLESS.

SIN CAUSES US GUILT
-THOUGH THIS MAY LEAD TO REPENTANCE.
THIS GUILT BUILDS ANIMOSITY TOWARDS THOSE AROUND US-
AND CREATES A MONSTER WITHIN.

THE SINNER, HOWEVER, DESIRES MERCY.
MERCY WHICH REACHES OUT AND TOUCHES THE SINNER
IN RECONCILIATION-
RECONCILIATION, WHICH FLOWS FROM UNCONDITIONAL LOVE.

MERCY-CHRIST'S MERCY-
IS FOUND INCARNATE IN SACRAMENTS.
SACRAMENTS FOUND WITHIN HIS LIVING BODY, THE CHURCH.
THIS CHURCH IS FAITHFULLY ALIVE!
ALIVE IN THE GROWTH OF FORGIVENESS…
IN THE GRACE OF BEING FORGIVEN FIRST. +

+REPENT.
RENEWED, SING ANEW!
ALLELUIA!

MAKE YOUR LIFE, MUSIC TO THE VERY EAR OF GOD.
SING PRAISE, PLAYING TUNES OF THANKSGIVING
TO OUR LORD AND SAVIOR.

PLAY THE SYMPHONY OF HUMAN WEAKNESS,
ELEVATED TO THE HEAVENS IN THE GLORY OF GOD,
IN JESUS CHRIST OUR LORD!

FOR THE SONG IS WITHIN OUR HEARTS-
IN THE SPIRIT OF OUR REDEMPTION.
THUS, WE SING JOYFULLY IN FAITH AND HOPE
-GOSPEL BOUND-
IN THE LIFE AND THE PASSION
OF THE RISEN SON OF GOD. +

+I APPROACH THE WORD OF GOD
IN THE SACRAMENT OF RECONCILIATION,
GUILTY AND UNDESERVING OF GRACE;
I APPROACH THE WRITTEN WORD OF GOD,
THE WORD OF INTEGRITY,
ILLUMINATED IN MISERY THROUGH INFIDELITY;
I APPROACH THE REAL PRESENCE OF MY LORD AND SAVIOR
IN THE MOST HOLY EUCHARIST,
REVEALING HOW SMALL AND WEAK
AND DESPERATELY IN NEED OF MERCY I AM;
REVEALING MY RELATION TO THE GREAT *I AM*;
THE GOD WHO LOVES ME IN THE SPIRIT OF HIS BODY,
WHOM I AM GRACEFULLY PART OF,
DESPITE MY WEAKNESSES,
YET BECASUSE OF HIS STRENGTH,
DESPITE MY FAILURES,
YET BECAUSE OF HIS FIDELITY,
DESPITE MY HARDENED HEART,
YET BECAUSE OF HIS SACRED HEART,
IN MY REPENTANCE,
THROUGH HIS GRACE, HIS MERCY AND HIS LOVE. +

+SADDENED BY PAST FAILURES,
RIDDEN WITH GUILT FROM PAST SIN,
WOUNDED IN WARS AS BOTH VICTIM AND OPRESSOR,
DASHED IN DESPAIR IN DREAMS UNFULFILLED...
EMPTINESS BEST DESCRIBES THE STATE OF MY HEART,
THE DRIFTING OF MY SPIRIT,
AND THE MALAISE OF MY SOUL.

MY LIFE SUFFERS ME!

BALANCE AND WHOLENESS
STARVES FOR VIRTUE,
WHILE DROWNING IN VICE.

GOD OF THE COSMOS,
KING OF ALL KINGS,
SAVIOR OF THE FAITHFUL,
HEAL MY PAST IN FORGIVENESS,
MY PRESENT IN FAITH AND HOPE,
AND LOVE ME TANGIBLY
IN MY WEAKNESS,
DRAWING ME IN LOVE TO LOVE THROUGH LOVE. +

+EMPTY OF POCKET
AND DEEP IN DEBT,
I CALL UPON THE LORD
-DAY AFTER DAY-
SEEKING FOR MERCY,
DESIROUS OF GRACE,
WANTING FOR LABOR,
TO ONCE AGAIN BECOME THE MAN OF MY HOUSEHOLD.
YET,
-FILLED WITH STRUGGLE IN THE WAFFLING OF PRAYER AND
DESPAIR-
DAY TURNS TO NIGHT,
AS HOPE FADES FOR A MORE PROMISING TOMORROW.
AS TIME IS MY WITNESS,
PRAYER AND DESPAIR PERSEVERING,
I STRUGGLE ON,
HOPING FOR GOD'S TIME IN DELIVERANCE. +

+ "THE TIME HAS COME, HE SAID, AND THE KINGDOM OF GOD IS
CLOSE AT HAND. *REPENT*, AND BELIEVE THE GOOD NEWS."

THE ONLY PROPER REPLY
WOULD BE TO FALL FROM MY CHAIR IN SHOCK,
REPENTANT,
CONTRITE,
CUT DEEP TO THE MARROW IN GUILT FROM SIN,
IN SORROW FOR HURTING THE LORD,
IN SADNESS FOR WASTED YEARS,
IN HURT FOR HARM CAUSED...
IN JOY FOR GOD'S FORGIVENESS!
IN FAITH RENEWED IN DIVINE PROMISES FULFILLED!
IN HOPE REFRESHED IN BREATHE AND STEP RESTORED!
IN LOVE, FOR LOVE RECEIVED FIRST!
IN LIGHT,
FOR LIGHT WHICH ABOLISHED THE ABYSS OF SIN AND DEATH!
AND FOR LIFE,
LIFE ETERNAL INTERNALIZED IN THE PERPETUAL PRESENCE
OF THE SAVIOR OF MAN,
FOUND *ESPECIALLY* IN THE EUCHARISTIC JESUS. +

+DAILY I FALL IN THE PIT OF DESPAIR,
FORGETTING MERCY,
ONLY TO SEE WHAT I CHOOSE TO SEE
IN PRIDE AND FEAR AND WEAKNESS.
YET UPON FALLING,
AND FEELING THE FILTH OF MY CHOICES,
I CRY TO MY SAVIOR
WHO SAVES ME INCESSANTLY IN ABUNDANT MERCY.
WHEN WILL I EVER LEARN? FOR YOUR GRACE AMAZES ME!
YOUR MERCY, A FLOOD TOO GRANDE TO ENGULF!
THUS, I DESIRE TO BE YOUR FAITHFUL DISCIPLE-
BUT YOUR HOLINESS SEEMS TOO GREAT FOR THIS BROKEN VESSEL.
SO, CRYING TO THE HEAVENS,
IN PRAISE (AND PETITION) AND THANKSGIVING,
I WALK AMONG THE COMMUNION OF YOUR LOVE,
PRAYING FOR STRENGTH,
REPENTING OF WEAKNESS,
AND HOPING FOR YOUR WILL BE DONE IN ME. +

+OUR FRIEND IS SO HEAVY.
BUT WE MUST *CARRY* ON!
FOR WE SEE THE HOUSE OF HIS SALVATION;
YET ARRIVING LATE, THE CROWD BLOCKS *OUR* WAY.
WE MUST BRING HIM TO THE HOPE OF ISRAEL!
THE ROOF!
THE ROOF!
WE WILL GO THROUGH THE ROOF!

AND THE CROWD SCREAMS AND SHOUTS
AS THE HOPE OF ALL SALVATION
SMILES AND WAVES OUR FRIEND DOWN.

FOR WITH A WORD AND A TOUCH,
OUR EFFORTS BEAR FORTH GLORIOUS FRUIT,
IN THE HEALING OF OUR MOTHER'S SON.

FOR AS HE *WALKS* AWAY,
IN THE COMPANY OF HIS BROTHERS,
HIS SOUL SHINES CLEAN AND PURE,
IN THE FORGIVENESS OF SUCH AN UNFORGETTABLE MAN. +

+THINK ABOUT IT.
TO THE EYES OF PERFECTION,
AND THE HEART OF TRUE LOVE,
WE ARE *NOT YET* SPARKLING SPECIMENS OF JEWELED CHARITY.

UNBEKNOWNST TO OUR SUPERFICIAL AND PREJUDICIAL VISION,
WE BEAR MANY WARTS, MANY SCARS, AND MANY IMPERFECTIONS
IN BODY, MIND, SPIRIT AND SOUL.

BUT TO THE VISION OF DIVINE MERCY,
WITHIN OUR REPENTANCE,
AND FROM HIS FORGIVENESS,
WE RADIATE GRACED BEAUTY!

IF, THEREFORE,
DIVINE CHARITY BESTOWS BEAUTY
IN FORGIVENESS AND COMPASSION,
SHOULDN'T WE? +

+WE DIG FOR TRUTH,
AND PLUMMET THE DEPTHS OF THE SEA FOR ANSWERS.
WE SEARCH THE SKIES
AND PROBE THE GALAXY FOR KNOWLEDGE.
WE DIVIDE THE CELL
AND SPLICE THE GENE IN HOPE OF FINDING LIFE'S SECRETS.
WE RE-READ HIS-TORY'S WORKS,
REDEFINING WHAT WAS,
WHILE PREDICTING WHAT WILL BE.

YET, WE SPEND PRESCIOUS LITTLE TIME
ON WHO WE ARE, AND WHY WE ARE HERE,
AND WHERE WE ARE GOING,
AND WHAT WE ARE MEANT TO BE.

FOR IN FINDING FACTS,
WE SEARCH FOR THE WHAT
AND FORGET THE *WHO.*

AND IN NEVER SURVEYING THE CANVAS
FOR ITS MESSAGE,
BUT RATHER THE PARTICULARS OF ITS MATTER,
WE MISS THE ARTIST OF ALL WE SEE.

AND THIS, TO OUR DESPAIR,
IS HOPE FOR REPENTANCE
AND SALVATION
IN THEE. +

+IN THE MIDST OF OUR COMA,
A FLASH OF INFINITE LIGHTNING INVADED OUR DOMAIN.
WITH UNCOMPROMISING TRUTH,
HE BINDED OUR LOT TO THE PATH FROM EARTH TO HEAVEN.
YET LIFE AND DEATH AND CHOICE REMAINED!
FOR IN CLOUD AND WIND AND MERCY'S MIGHT,
THE LIGHTNING LORD PARTED ALL EVIL,
DROWNING ALL SIN IN HIS BLOOD,
OPENING A VISTA TO THE STARS,
WHERE SAINTS SUFFER FOR SALVATION,
AND THE HEAVENS SWELL WITH LOVE. +

+IF YOU MUST…
LET ME SEE WHAT I DON'T WANT TO SEE, BUT NEED TO SEE…
LET ME TASTE BITTER AND SOUR REALITY IN MY SIN…
LET ME TOUCH THE WOUNDS I HAVE INFLICTED…

BUT IF YOU WILL…
LET ME SMELL THE SWEET FRAGRANCE OF YOUR MERCY…

THEN…
GRACE INCARNATE WILL WALK
-HUMBLY AND REPENTANTLY-
ALONG THE PATH OF SANCTITY IN *THE WAY* OF THE LORD-
HE WHO REVEALS TRUE MAN-IN DIVINE MERCY-TO MAN. +

+FOR SAFETY AND COMFORT AND STANDARD OF LIVING
-AS FAR AS THE WORLD IS CONCERNED-
MANY A DISCIPLE HAVE GONE THE WAY OF THE PAGAN,
SO AS TO ASSIMILATE INTO ANOTHER SOCIETY.

BUT SOONER OR LATER THE CONFORMING CHILD REALIZES
THAT THEIR TRUE RELIGION MUST GO!

IN A SOCIETY WHICH BECOMES ITS OWN DEITY,
THERE IS NO ROOM FOR COMPETING GODS!
ISRAEL MUST CHOOSE TO STAND…OR TO FALL!
ISRAEL MUST *REPENT* AND SEEK FOR STRENGTH!
FOR INEVITABLY, ISRAEL MUST FACE ITS ACCUSOR!

FROM THIS COMES THE MARTYR,
THE TRUE TYPE BEFORE,
AND THE FRUIT BEYOND,
THE CROSS OF UNCOMPROMISING TRUTH. +

+I AM WEAK
AND PRONE TO FALL,
BUT MY ABBA
IS PATIENT,
LOVING,
AND ALWAYS THERE TO PICK ME UP, GUIDE ME,
AND SET ME ON *HIS WAY.* +

+RIGHTEOUS ANGER IS WITHIN ME,
AND ALL AROUND ME IN THE APOSTACY OF HUMAN LIVING!

AS PERSECUTED,
I REMEMBER THE CROSS AND THE RESURRECTION.

AS PERSECUTOR,
I REMEMBER THE GOOD THEIF!

SAVE ME, FROM CRUEL SINNERS!
SAVE OTHERS, FROM MY CRUEL SIN!

HOW BLIND WE ARE, OPRESSOR AND OPRESSED.
SALVATION SEEKS ONLY THE REPENTANT.

HENCE FORTH,
RIGHTEOUS ANGER SHALL ONLY BE
FOR THE UNREPENTANT. +

+I AM POOR AND BLIND AND UNSOCIABLE.
YET, I AM PROUD AND CURIOUS AND DESIROUS OF LIFE.

HENCE, WHEN THE BREEZE OF THE SPIRIT
BLOWS MY WAY,
I BREATHE IN DEEPLY AND DESPERATELY!

BUT MANY SCORN MY INSPIRATION,
FOR TO THEM I DO NOT QUALIFY.

BUT GRACEFULLY, I BREATHE IN ALL THE DEEPER!
AND AS I BREATHE,
THE BREEZE CHALLENGES ME TO BREATHE AGAIN!
FOR TO BREATHE THE BREATH OF LIFE,
IS TO BELIEVE AND TO BREATHE AGAIN.

THUS,
BELEIVING AND BREATHING,
IN AND OUT,
IN THE BREEZE OF LIFE,
I BREATHE OF LIFE AND LOVE ETERNAL. +

+HOW DO I PRAISE IN THE MIDST OF AFFLICTION?
HOW DO I PRAISE IN BURNING ADDICTION?
HOW DO I PRAISE IN REJECTION AND PERSECUTION?

HOW DO I PRAISE ON THE SIDE OF THE ROAD,
WITH PASSING PRIEST AND LEAVING LEVITE,
PRONOUNCING ME DEAD?

HOW DO I PRAISE FAR FROM MY FATHER'S HOUSE,
HUNGRY AND DESTITUTE,
BEGGING TO EAT THE PIGS SLOP,
WANTING TO WEAR THE GARB OF A LOWLY SERVANT?

HOW DO I PRAISE IN THE MIDST OF DARKNESS,
ALL ALONE AND FACING DEATH?

BY CRYING IN FAITH FROM WITHIN THE ABYSS
OF A DEADENED SOUL:
IN SELF INFLICTED SIN,
AND WOUNDS ACQUIRED IN LIFE'S BATTLE,
IN THE HOPE OF SOMEONE GREATER,
SOMEONE DIFFERENT,
SOMEONE COMPASSIONATE,
SOMEONE MERCIFUL,
SOMEONE TRUE,
SOMEONE GOD! +

AMERICA REPENT!

+AS THE KING RETURNED TO THE GREAT CITY,
THE GREAT CITY OF COMMERCE AND ART,
THE GREAT CITY OF ARCHITECTURE AND INGENUITY,
THE GREAT CITY OF WEALTH AND DIVERSITY,
THE GREAT CITY OF CULTURE AND LEISURE,
THE GREAT CITY OF FREEDOM AND OPPORTUNITY,
HE WEPT.

FOR IN ALL ITS RICHES,
AND GLORY,
THE CITY HAD FORGOTTEN OF HIM. +

THE SACRAMENT OF RECONCILIATION

"EVEN THOSE WHO WISH TO LOVE FAIL OFTEN TO DO SO, OR ELSE LOVE MOST IMPERFECTLY. WE SIN, AND, EVEN WHEN WE ARE NOT SINNING, WE BLUNDER REPEATEDLY. IN THE SACRAMENT OF PENANCE, JESUS PARDONS OUR SINSAND STRAIGHTENS OUR PATHS. TO JUDGE BY THE EVIDENCE, MANY CATHOLICS TODAY HAVE CONCLUDED THAT, FOR THE MOST PART, THEY CAN DO WITHOUT THE SACRAMENT OF PENANCE. THEY ARE WRONG TO THINK SO, AND ALMOST CERTAINLY THEY LOVE LESS WELL BECAUSE OF THEIR MISTAKE."
RUSSELL SHAW
WHY WE NEED CONFESSION

"THE ATTITUDE OF PENANCE, THE PRACTICE OF PENANCE, THE HABITS OF PENANCE, THE SACRAMENT OF PENANCE: ALL OF THESE SERVE AS REMINDERS OF WHO WE ARE. WE ARE CHILDREN OF A LOVING FATHER, A LAVISHLY WEALTHY FATHER; BUT WE ARE LIVING FAR FROM HOME, IN SHAMEFUL CONDITIONS. OUR DAILY EXAMINATION OF CONSCIENCE AND OUR WEEKLY OR MONTHLY CONFESSION WILL HELP US TO KEEP OUR STORY STRAIGHT-AND MAKE STRAIGHT OUR WAY HOMEWARD."
SCOTT HAHN
LORD, HAVE MERCY

"CONTRITION AND CONFESSION ARE SO BEAUTIFUL AND HAVE SO GOOD AN ODOR THAT THEY WIPE AWAY THE UGLINESS OF SIN AND PURIFY ITS STENCH."
ST FRANCIS DE SALES-INTRODUCTION TO THE DEVOUT LIFE

+IN THE NAME OF THE FATHER,
WHO WAS AND IS ALWAYS WILLING TO OFFER
THE VERY ESSENCE OF HIS LIFE
IN THE SON WHOM HE LOVES,
FOR THE SAKE OF MAN;
AND OF THE SON,
WHO DISCARDED HIS HEAVENLY PRIVILEDGE
TO BECOME A SERVANT AND A SLAVE,
TAKING ON THE GUILT AND THE PENALTY
OF ALL MEN,
THOUGH HE WAS PURE AND INNOCENT,
FOR THE LOVE OF FATHER, BROTHER AND SISTER;
AND OF THE HOLY SPIRIT,
WHO VIVIFIES THE CHURCH
IN THE COMMUNION OF FAITH, HOPE AND CHARITY,
FORGING SAINTS IN SANCTITY
AND BREATHING LIFE INTO THE BODY OF THE MESSIAH-
UNTIL ALL NATIONS HAVE SEEN THE LIGHT
AND HEARD THE WORD
AND ARE OFFERED THE MERCY
WHICH NEVER ENDS.
AMEN. +

+THREE TIMES DENIED,
THREE TIMES THE LORD GRACED PETER
WITH RECONCILIATION AND VOCATION.
BUT THIS GRACE SIGNALED THE UNCHANGING TRUTH
OF TRUE CHRISTIAN DISCIPLESHIP.
A DEATH TO SELF,
OBEDIENCE ON A NARROW AND ROCKY PATH,
CRUCIFIXION BY THE WORLD, AND A PATIENT LONGSUFFERING
IN ACQUIESENCE TO THE SILENT MYSTERY
OF GOD'S WILL IN GOD'S GOOD TIME.

OH! AND I FORGOT ONE THING:
ETERNAL LIFE, BEGINNING IN THE IMMEDIACY OF *REPENTANCE*,
BRINGING PEACE, JOY, FAITH, HOPE, AND MERCIFUL LOVE
TO GREAT TO DESCRIVE IN WORDS,
ONLY TO BE UNDERSTOOD IN THE HEART OF DISCIPLESHIP
IN JESUS THE WORD OF TRUTH!   +

+GOD ALMIGHTY RESIDES IN HEAVEN.
HEAVEN IS WHERE THERE IS LOVE.
LOVE IS FOUND SOLELY IN CHRIST.
CHRIST IS TRULY PRESENT IN THE EUCHARIST.

REPENTANCE AND RECONCILIATION
PREPARE THE HEART FOR THE LORD.

REPENT! RECEIVE!
BRING HEAVEN TO EARTH! LIVE HEAVEN! +

+PEACE IS ITS OWN REWARD!
FOR THE MAN WHO RAISES NOT HIS FIST IN REVENGE,
BUT OPENS HIS ARMS AND SOFTENS HIS LIPS
IN FORGIVENESS AND RECONCILIATION
STANDS FIRM, UNCOMPROMISINGLY,
IN THE TRUTH OF THE ABUNDANT MERCY
OF JESUS THE MESSIAH.

FOR CHRIST,
MOCKED, BEATEN, AND NAILED IMMOBILE,
TO A MERCILESS TORTURE TREE,
NEVER RAISED HIS MIGHTY FIST IN REVENGE,
BUT WILLINGLY OPENED HIS ARMS
TO THE NAILS OF SIN,
OFFERING HIS PEACE AS OUR REWARD IN FAITH. +

+THE HEART AND THE MIND AND THE SOUL
OF MY NEIGHBOR IS BUT MYSTERY TO ME...
AND THE SUREST OF KNOWLEDGE TO GOD.
THEREFORE, TO JUDGE MY NEIGHBOR IS TO ASSUME DIVINITY,
IN ABSURDITY, THROUGH STUPIDITY,
JUDGING FROM MY HEART AND MY MIND AND MY SOUL,
WHICH I DO NOT UNDERSTAND MYSELF!
LET LOVE AND MERCY JUDGE!
FOR IGNORANCE JUDGING IGNORANCE IS DEATH.
BUT PERFECT LOVE AND PURE LIFE HIMSELF,
WILL ONLY TRANSFORM TAINTED NATURE
IN THE FORGIVING GRACE,
WHICH SEEKS TO REDEEM! +

+STRONG AND SMART AND BRAVE...THAT IS WHO I AM!
WELL, SIN HAS A WAY OF DESTROYING DELUSIONS OF GRANDUER.
YET GOD *WILL* STEP IN,
IN REPENTANCE AND SACRAMENT AND PRAYER,
CREATING IN ME,
A NEW HEART THAT IS STRONG,
A NEW MIND THAT IS WISE,
AND A NEW LIFE THAT IS COURAGEOUS
IN THE COMPASSION OF THE MERCIFUL CHRIST.   +

+GOD IS JUDGE AND JURY,
AND PROSECUTION AND EXECUTION...AND REDEMPTION!
THERE IS NO ESCAPE FROM THE WILL OF GOD.
HOWEVER THIS MAY SEEM AN IMPRISONMENT,
MAN IS NEVER FREER THAN IN REPENTANCE
AND RECONCILIATION
AND LOVING OBEDIENCE
IN RELATIONSHIP WITH THE ALMIGHTY GOD
OF ALL THAT EXISTS!
FOR GOD IS ALL POWER!
AND GOD IS JUSTICE THROUGH AND THROUGH.
BUT THE TRUEST ESSENCE OF HIS POWER
IS FOUND IN THE SIGN OF CHRIST'S CROSS...
FOR HIS ESSENCE IS IN MERCY, AS HE HIMSELF IS LOVE. +

+IN CONFESSION,
I HAVE BEEN SET FREE FROM THE EVIL TASKMASTERS
OF MY SPRITUAL EGYPTIAN BONDAGE.
AS MY MOSES, CHRIST LEADS ME TO FREEDOM IN THE SPIRIT,
IN APPOINTED DESERT PENANCE,
IN FLEETING ATTACKS OF THE PHARAOH
OF DOUBT, GUILT AND SHAME,
AND IN THE CHARIOTEERS OF THE ROMANCE OF MY PAST SIN,
WHICH EVER PURSUES ME.
BUT GOD THE FATHER PARTS THE WATERS OF LIFE
-IN SANCTIFYING GRACE-
DROWNING THE STRENGTH OF THE DESTROYERS ARMY,
IN THE SPIRIT OF VIRTUE INFUSED.
WHERE HIS SON LEADS ME ON TOWARD THE PROMISED LAN
IN THE CUP OF REDEMPTION AND THE BREAD OF LIFE. +

+THE SOWER OF GOOD SEED
WILL SEND HIS ANGELS WITH THE FIRE OF JUSTICE
AND THE UNQUENCHABLE BLAZE OF HIS MERCY.

BURNING WITHIN THE FIRE OF JUSTICE
WILL BE THOSE WHO *FREELY* CHOSE TO FORSAKE THE LORD.
THERE THEY WILL BURN IN THEIR FREEDOM,
"WEEPING AND GRINDING" THEIR TEETH.

BURNING IN THE FIRE OF MERCY,
WILL BE THOSE, IMPERFECT YET DESIROUS OF GOD'S LOVE,
WILLING TO LOSE ALL THAT HINDERS CHARITY,
PRAISING GOD WITHIN THE FLAME,
BEING PERFECTED IN PURGATIVE EMANCIPATION,
SEEING HEAVEN EVER SO CLOSE,
WHILE BEING PREPARED FOR THE HEAVENLY BANQUET OF JOY,
WHERE CHRIST AND FULFILLMENT AND HAPPINESS
WILL NEVER END. +

+KING DAVID COMMITTED ADULTERY WITH ANOTHER MAN'S WIFE,
AND THEN SENT HIM OUT TO A CERTAIN DEATH.

YET DAVID, COMMITTING AUDACIOUS SIN,
STILL PRESSED FORWARD IN REPENTANCE-
CONFIDENT IN GOD'S MERCY.

I HAVE ALSO HAD THE AUDACITY TO SIN BOLDLY.
AND ALSO, I HAVE REPENTED TIME AND AGAIN,
HOPING IN THE MERCY OF GOD.

BUT IN WEAKNESS AND IN DEEP HURT,
WHEN THE DARK CLOUDS OF TURMOIL APPEARED,
I HAVE ABANDONED MERCY IN DESPAIR AND VILE PLEASURE.

FOR MERCY DOES NOT ALWAYS GUARANTEE A SUNNY DAY.
ONLY THE STRENGTH TO SHINE FROM WITHIN,
IN THE SON WHO FILLS REPENTANCE WITH CHARITY
-SO VERY MUCH NEEDED IN A DARKENED WORLD-
BRINGING LIGHT TO THE WORLD
IN THE NEW LIFE OF MERCY. +

+SHAME IS MY GARMENT,
WORN IN PERSONAL CHOICE,
THROUGH ACTIONS AND OMISSIONS COMMITTED FREELY,
IN MY WILL AND MY DESIRE.

FOR I HAVE HEARD THE PROPHETS, I HAVE READ THE LAW,
AND I HAVE BEEN GIVEN THE COMMANDMENTS;
MY MIND AND MY HEART,
ALONG WITH MY CONSCIENCE AND MY WILL
CARRY SUFFIENT FORMATION IN THE TRUTH AND THE INTEGRITY
OF THE MERCIFUL AND JUST GOD.

THAT IS WHY MY GUILT IS SO GREAT!
THAT IS WHY MY SHAME IS SO STRONG!

THAT IS WHY MY REPENTANCE SEEKS FOR THE MERCIFUL ONE,
UNFATHOMABLY FORGIVING! +

+I AM A TAX COLLECTOR, A TRAITOR AND A THEIF.
ON THE OUTSKIRTS OF *COMMUNIO,* I STEAL AND DEAL AND HIDE.
ASHAMED AND DESPARING, I LOATHE MY OWN SELF.
YET, THE PRINCE AND KING AND LORD SUMMONS ME!
FORGIVEN AND INVESTED, I AM THE DISCIPLE OF THE GREAT I AM!

CONFOUNDING THE SELF-RIGHTEOUS,
THIS TAINTED EX-TRAITOR SHOUTS FOR JOY
IN THAT PARODOX OF RECREATING FORGIVENESS...
FROM OUTHOUSE TO PENTHOUSE,
FROM MUDHUT TO MANSION,
ALL IN DIVINE MERCY! +

+AS A DISCIPLE OFA HOLY DISCIPLE I FAST FOR THE LORD.
AS A SERVANT OF THE CHURCH I FAST FOR THE CHRIST.
AS A CHILD OF GOD,
A MEMBER OF CHRIST'S BODY,
BRIDE TO THE HOLY GROOM,
I FEAST AT THE BANQUET OF LOVE.
FALLEN I REPENT, WEAKENED I FAST,
FORGIVEN I GIVE PRAISE AND THANKS,
RECONCILED, I COMMUNE IN HOLY AND REDEMPTIVE LOVE. +

+SIN IS MY WARDROBE. SIN IS MY SAD STYLE!
I AM AN OFFENDER OF DIVINE LOVE.
I AM GUILTY AS CHARGED! BORN AND SELF-BRED IN MALICE.
YET, SACRED IS YOUR HEART, REDEEMING IS YOUR LOVE.
ABUNDANT IS YOUR MERCY, YOUR FORGIVENESS MY HOPE.
REMEMBER NOT MY SIN, RENEW ME. CREATE ME ANEW!
THEN, MY LIFE WILL BE TRUE WORSHIP AND PRAISE,
IN REDEMPTION, BORN OF LOVE. +

+THE INCARNATION ALLOWS THE GRACE TO REPENT OF ONES SIN,
TO SEEK THE FORGIVENESS OF ONES BROTHER AND SISTER,
TO DO PENANCE AND MAKE REPARATION,
FROM WITHIN GOD'S MERCY,
IN THE PRESENCE OF GOD'S JUSTICE,
IN FEARFUL AND TREMBLING HOLINESS,
IN THE FAITH WHICH BRINGS FORTH HOPE,
FROM CHARITY FIRST RECEIVED,
EXPRESSED AS FORGIVENESS GIVEN
AND MERCY EXTENDED
IN THE SANCTITY WHICH IS BORN
IN THE SACRAMENT OF PASCHAL FORGIVENESS EMBRACED. +

+I CONFESS TO THE RESTORER OF RESPLENDENT SIGHT,
TO THE ONE WHO GRACES SYMPHONY TO THE DEAF,
TO THE LORD WHO PLACES A SONG ON THE LIPS OF THE MUTE,
WHO PLACES VIBRANCY IN A FORMERLY DEAD HEART,
WHO PLACES COMPASSIONATE FAITH
AND ZEALOUS HOPE IN A FORMERLY LUKEWARM SOUL,
AND THE COURAGE AND CONVICTION
TO LIVE IN THE FREEDOM OF GOD'S LAW,
ALIVE IN CHRIST,
TO A FORMER SLAVE,
AND AN ADDICT TO THE VARIED SHACKLES OF THE LIAR
AND AUTHOR OF ALL SIN.

I CONFESS
TO THE GOD OF INEXHAUSTABLE,
UNFATHOMABLE,
OMNIPOTENT,
AND BEATIFIC MERCY. +

+ALMIGHTY GOD,
MOST SUBLIME, MOST GLORIOUS, MOST MAJESTIC...
THOUGH I MARVEL AT YOUR CREATIVE POWER,
I HUNGER, MOST OF ALL,
TO FEEL YOUR MERCIFUL TENDER-HEARTEDNESS!

PLEASE DISPLAY YOUR MERCY,
-IN THE SACRAMENT OF YOUR FORGIVENESS-
DESPITE MY INJUSTICES, MY FAITHLESSNESS,
AND MY LACK OF FIDELITY.

FOR YOU ARE JUSTICE
AND FAITHFULNESS,
AND FIDELITY YOURSELF!

BUT YOU ARE DESIRED, MOST OF ALL,
BY SINNERS LIKE ME,
FOR WHO YOU ARE AS MERCY! +

+THE FATHER
IS THE AUTHOR
OF ALL TRUE SCIENCE
AND ALL SOUND PHILOSOPHY!

YET OUR FATHER
IS MOST OF ALL
LOVING POET!

FOR HE LOVES
MANKIND,
EACH AND EVERY CHILD,
BORN OF HIS LOVING CREATION,
ADOPTED IN THE BLOOD AND SUFFERING
OF HIS ONE TRUE SON,
IN THE SPIRIT OF LOVE,
EXPRESSED BIBLICALLY, LITURGICALLY, EXISTENTIALLY,
AS THE POETRY OF RECONCILIATION
IN THE UNFATHOMABLE AND INEXHAUSTABLE TREASURE
OF THE MERCY OF HIS LOVE. +

THE MOST HOLY EUCHARIST

"AT THE LAST SUPPER, ON THE NIGHT WHEN HE WAS BETRAYED, OUR SAVIOR INSTITUTED THE EUCHARISTIC SACRIFICE OF HIS BODY AND BLOOD. HE DID THIS IN ORDER TO PERPETUATE THE SACRIFICE OF THE CROSS THROUGHOUT THE CENTURIES UNTIL HE SHOULD COME AGAIN, AND SO TO ENTRUST TO HIS BELOVED SPOUSE, THE CHURCH, A MEMORIAL OF HIS DEATH AND RESURRECTION: A SACRAMENT OF LOVE, A SIGN OF UNITY, A BOND OF CHARITY, A PASCHAL BANQUET IN WHICH CHRIST IS EATEN, THE MIND IS FILLED WITH GRACE, AND A PLEDGE OF FUTURE GLORY IS GIVEN TO US."
SACROSANCTUM CONCILIUM
THE SIXTEEN DOCUMENTS OF VATICAN II

"WHAT MIRACLES! WHO SHOULD EVER HAVE IMAGINED SUCH! ... IF THE ANGELS COULD BE JEALOUS OF MEN, THEY WOULD BE SO FOR ONE REASON: HOLY COMMUNION."
ST MAXIMILIAN KOLBE

"THE EUCHARIST INVOLVES MORE THAN JUST RECEIVING; IT ALSO INVOLVES SATISFYING THE HUNGER OF CHRIST. HE SAYS 'COME TO ME.' HE IS HUNGRY FOR SOULS. NOWHERE DOES THE GOSPEL SAY: 'GO AWAY,' BUT ALWAYS 'COME TO ME.'"
MOTHER TERESA OF CALCUTTA

+I CALL YOU 'MASTER' AND THEN I SEEK A SIGN.
WHAT A DEVILISH AND UNFAITHFUL MAN I AM!
FOR I SEEK SIGNS AND WONDERS
TO SOOTHE MY FEAR,
TO ASSAIL MY DOUBT,
AND TO REMEDY MY GUILT AND SHAME.

BUT ALL ALONG
I HAVE BEEN GIVEN THE SIGN OF JONAH
ALL THROUGHOUT MY LIFE!

FOR HOW MANY DAYS AND NIGHTS
IN THE BELLY OF THE BEAST OF SIN
HAVE I NOT SLEPT
-AND WEPT-
ONLY TO BE REDEEMED IN MERCY ON GOD'S THIRD DAY.

AS NINEVAH PERCEIVED GOD'S TRUTH IN JONAH,
AND THE QUEEN OF THE SOUTH IN SOLOMON,
MAY THE GRACE OF GOD
SOFTEN MY HEART TO THE EVER-PRESENT MERCY
OF OUR EUCHARISTIC LORD AND SAVIOR JESUS CHRIST. +

+ONE IS THE NUMBER
OF OUR FAITH AND OUR HOPE.
ONE IS THE TYPE OF OUR BAPTISM.
ONE IS THE LOVE, *AGAPE* LOVE,
SELF-SACRIFICIAL LOVE,
IN WHICH THE ONE SUFFERED
AND BLED THE BLOOD OF LIFE FOR US.

FROM ONE FATHER IN ONE SPIRIT
WE ARE TO LOVE
-DESPITE MANY WEAKNESSES-
IN THE ONE BODY FROM THE ONE BLOOD
OF THE ONE SAVIOR
IN THE ONE COMMUNION OF THE MANY CHILDREN
WHO BECAME ADOPTED AND MARRIED AS ONE,
IN THE ONE LOVE OF THE THREE PERSONS
OF THE ONE ALMIGHTY GOD. +

+FROM FIVE BARLEY LOAVES AND TWO FISH
CAME DOUBT *OVERCOME*
BY THE GREATEST OF MIRACLES.

BUT ONE DAY IS BUT A SPECK OF SAND
ON THE SHORELINE OF THE GREATEST MIRACLE
EVER *BEING* PERFORMED!

FOR EACH AND EVERY DAY,
ON EACH AND EVERY CONTINENT,
IN EACH AND EVERY HOUR,
MEN AND WOMEN GATHER,
OFFERING THEIR MEAGER BARLEY LOAVES AND FISH,
TO THE LORD OF HOSTS,
WHO FILLS THEIR BELLIES WITH HOSTS
IN THE COMMUNION BREAD,
IN THE SPIRIT OF THE COMMUNION OF GOD AND MAN,
IN THE BREAD AND WINE BECOME BODY AND BLOOD
OF THE SAVIOR OF ALL MANKIND. +

+AS MOSES WON FAVOUR IN THE EYES OF GOD,
CALLING UPON THE MERCY OF THE LORD
FOR THE FORGIVENESS OF SINS,
SO TOO,
SO MUCH MORE DOES THE FAVOUR OF THE LORD
REST UPON THE CHRIST.

SO MUCH MORE DOES CHRIST MEDIATE GRACE UPON GRACE,
FACE TO FACE WITH HIS FATHER, OUR FATHER,
FOR THE FORGIVENESS OF OUR SINS
AND THE ETERNAL SALVATION OF OUR SOUL.

WE TOO ARE FAVOURED IN THE EYES OF THE LORD,
IN THE SPIRIT OF THE COMMUNION
OF THOSE WHO SHARE
IN THE BODY AND BLOOD
OF THE REDEEMER.
SO TOO, ARE WE CALLED TO DISPENSE GOD'S MERCY-
FOR THE SALVATION OF ALL MEN AND WOMEN,
CREATED IN LOVE. +

+OUR LIFE IS TO BE A CONSTANT PILGRIMAGE
TOWARD THE EUCHARIST,
OUR SOURCE
OF LIFE AND COMMUNION WITH GOD
AND WITH OUR FELLOW PILGRIM.

TOWARD THE EUCHARIST
WE MUST MARCH TOGETHER,
REPENTANT FOR OUR SINS
AND FORGIVING OF OTHERS
IN THE PROMISED MERCY OF GOD.

AS WE GATHER TOGETHER,
AS CHILDREN IN THE SPIRIT,
ENTERING INTO THE LIFE OF JESUS,
CHRIST JESUS ENTERS OUR VERY SOUL
AND OFFERS OUR VERY BEST
-ALONG WITH HIS PERPETUAL AND PERFECT SACRIFICE-
TO THE FATHER IN THE SPIRIT OF LOVE.

FROM THE EUCHARIST
WE BECOME THE VERY MERCY OF GOD IN CHRIST,
AND IN FAITH, HOPE AND CHARITY,
WE CLIMB THE MOUNTAIN OF GRACED SANCTITY
-WITH THE SPIRIT IN OUR HEART AND THE CROSS ON OUR BACK-
KNOWING FULLY WELL
THAT THE GOD OF MERCY
WILL BRING US TO *THE SUMMIT* OF HIS LOVE. +

+YOU GIVE...*I TAKE...* AND I COMPLAIN!
YOU FREE ME FROM MY SLAVERY IN PRIDE AND GREED AND LUST,
AND BAPTIZE ME IN THE PARTED WATERS OF FAITH AND HOPE-
IN THE MERCIFUL LOVE OF THE CRUCIFIED AND RISEN ONE.

AND, MY DESERT TREK, THROUGH THE WASTELAND OF MY CHOICES,
LEADS ME, IN FEAR, AND SIN,
TO BLAME YOU WITHIN MY PURGATIVE SUFFERING!
YET, IN MY WEAKNESS AND FOOLISH PRIDE,
YOU BUILD ME UP IN PERFECT LOVE ON THE MANNA OF THE CHRIST,
AND LEAD ME TO THE PROMISED LAND OF MY SALVATION. +

+OUR DAILY BREAD IS WHAT WE TRULY NEED,
AND WHAT WE ARE GIVEN TO SHARE WITH OUR BRETHREN.

IN THIS WAY,
AS THE MANNA FROM HEAVEN WAS BOTH SUSTENANCE AND TEST,
WHAT WE TRULY NEED IS WHAT WE MUST SHARE WITH THE POOR.

FOR IN THE END, ARE WE NOT ALL BROTHERS AND SISTERS,
SO ALIKE IN NATURE?

AND,
IS NOT OUR SUPERNATURAL ELDER BROTHER, CHRIST JESUS,
PRESENT BOTH IN THE POOR AND AS OUR DAILY BREAD? +

+I CRY OF INJUSTICE!
MY INJUSTICE, AND THE INJUSTICE OF OTHERS.
I CRY OF THE SILENCE OF GOD!
MY SILENCE, AND THE SILENCE OF THE APPARENT GODLY.

FOR THE BODY OF THE LORD SEEMS, AT TIMES,
TO TROD THE PATH OF THE PAGAN.
AND THE HEAD SUFFERS IN THE SILENT HOST.

I CRY IN FAITH,
IN HOPE OF MERCY
FROM WITHIN GOD'S MIGHTY
PASSIVE EUCHARISTIC CONSISTENCY.

FOR MYSTERY AND PARADOX SHINE
-ILLUMINATING DIFFERENTIAL ESSENCES-
ON THIS IMPATIENT, INCONSISTENT,
AND IMPETUOUS PROVOCATUER. +

+OH MAGDALA IN ME, WHERE IS THE CHRIST?
RUN TO PETER AND THE BELOVED!
SEEK THE SWIFT COMPASSION OF THE CHURCH BELOVED,
SEEK THE AUTHORITY AND WITNESS OF THE KEEPER OF THE KEYS.
THERE, YOU SHALL FIND NOT ONLY THE CLOTH OF WITNESS,
BUT THE BODY AND BLOOD, SOUL AND DIVINITY
OF CHRIST PRESENT AMONG US! +

+ALL OUR JUDGES ARE IN-JUDICIAL.
ALL OUR POLITICIANS IMPOLITE.
ALL OUR LEADERS BAND A WAGON.
ALL KINGS AND QUEENS ARE MASKED IN FRIGHT.
BUT THERE IS ONE RULER WHO JUDGES IN JUSTICE.
ONE LORD TENDER AND SWEET.
ON LEADER WHO LEADS BY EXAMPLE.
ONE KING, WORTH KNEELING AT HIS FEET.

FOR INJUSTICE AND CRUELTY AND FALSITY AND FEAR,
MARK THE FLESHLY LORD.
YET JUSTICE AND COMPASSION AND COURAGE AND LOVE
WEILD A HEAVENLY SWORD.

FOR LORDLY MAN MUST BE ABHORED.   *RHYME*

BUT THE LORD AS LORD,
WEILDING HIS MERCIFUL SWORD,
PEIRCING OUR SIDE
IN LOVE NEVER DENIED, IN WATER AND BLOOD,
AND PROTECTION FROM SINS FLOOD,
-FROM THE CROSS AND THE HOST-
MEETS US INTIMATELY IN THE COMMUNION
AND THE SPIRIT OF HIS LOVE,
WHERE REDEMPTION IS APPLIED. +

+TO ENTER THE SACRAMENT OF RECONCILIATION,
THE SACRAMENT OF CONFESSION,
THE SACRAMENT OF PENANCE,
THIS MAY SEEM AS DAUNTING AS ENTERING A FIRE!
YES! AS OUR SIN WEIGHS HEAVY ON OUR SOUL,
THE ENTRANCE TO FORGIVENESS SEEMS TO US A BURNING ABODE.
YET UPON ENTRANCE,
THAT BLAZING FIRE, WHICH PURGES THE SOUL,
AND FREES THE SPIRIT, IS THE SPIRIT OF THE FIRE OF GOD'S LOVE,
IGNITED IN THE PERFECT SACRIFICE
OF THE SON OF GOD ON CALVARY.
AND THIS LOVE IS PERPETUATED IN THE MERCY OF GOD
IN THE DAILY PRESENCE OF DIVINE FORGIVENESS HIMSELF,
IN JESUS CHRIST OUR LORD. +

+THE SEED OF TRUE CHRISTIAN COMMUNION IS TRUST IN CHRIST.
THIS TRUST IS PLANTED AND WATERED
BY THE CONTINUING AND UNBROKEN WITNESS OF THE APOSTLES.
FROM THIS A TREE APPEARS,
AND IT GROWS IN THE HOLY SPIRIT;
AND THIS IS THE HOLY TREE OF GOLGOTHA.
AND THIS TREE,
BEARING ONE PERRENIAL FRUIT,
THE TRUE AGAPE SACRIFICE
-FOR THE FORGIVENESS OF SIN
AND THE REDEMPTION OF MAN-
IS FOUND IN THE PRECIOUS BODY AND BLOOD
OF OUR EUCHARISTIC LORD AND SAVIOR,
JESUS THE CHRIST. +

+WE ARE NOT FORGOTTEN!
WE ARE NOT ONLY CHOSEN, BUT CALLED TO BE GOD'S SAINTS!
CLOTHED IN THE GRACE OF THE RISEN LORD,
WE ARE STRENGTHENED IN THE HOLY SPIRIT,
EMPOWERED IN GIFTS OF VIRTUE
TO FORGIVE AS WE HAVE BEEN FORGIVEN,
AND TO LOVE AS WE HAVE BEEN LOVED FIRST.

IN THE COMMUNION OF THE RISEN LORD,
IN THE SPIRIT WHICH FEEDS US
ON THE SAVIORS BODY AND BLOOD,
WE FIND PEACE
-IN THANKSGIVING AND PRAISE-
AND WALK IN FEAR AND TREMBLING,
RENEWING THE EARTH...IN FAITH, HOPE, AND LOVE. +

+GOD IS LOVE!
GOD *IS* LOVE.

GOD IS LOVE IS WITH US.
GOD IS LOVE IS WITHIN US!

GOD IS LOVE DRAWS US INTO HIM.
GOD IS LOVE...
AND WE BECOME LOVE THROUGH HIM. +

+ANIMAL SACRIFICE WAS THE DISDAIN
OF THE DIVINE DESIRE.
HUMAN SACRIFICE WAS THE DIVINE DESIRE,
TO SAVE MAN FROM DISDAIN.
FOR RITUALS AND OBSERVANCES
AND OFFERINGS AND GIFTS,
GIVEN WITHOUT CHARITY,
ONLY CAME TO OFFEND THE HOLINESS
OF THE MERCIFUL ONE.

YET,
IN THE PERFECT OFFERING
OF THE SPOTLESS LAMB OF GOD,
THE LIFE OF THE MAN AND THE WOMAN
OF FAITH AND DEVOTION
NOW REACH HEAVEN AS SANCTIFIED INCENSE
IN THE SACRIFICE
OF THE BODY AND BLOOD OF THE LORD,
PERPETUATED AS SACRAMENT
FOR OUR BENEFIT
FOR THE OFFERING OF OUR LIFE
AS HOLOCAUST
IN THE HOLINESS FOUND IN PASCHAL PARTICIPATION
IN THE CROSS OF THE CHRIST. +

+IN POVERTY THROUGH WORLDLY OPRESSION,
IN OBSCURITY IN THE NAZARETH OF OUR NOTHINGNESS,
THE ANGEL OF EPIPHANY APPEARS IN OUR MIDST
-IN REPENTANCE AND CONFESSION AND CONTRITION-
IN HOLY RECEPTION OF THE EUCHARIST,
IN HEARING THE WORD OF GOD,
IN HUMBLE AND OBEDIENT SUFFERING,
IN SELF SACRIFICE FOR THE POOR-
AS WE ARE SUMMONED TO BEND OUR KNEE, QUIET OUR MIND,
HARNESS OUR PASSIONS, AND SUPRESS OUR WILL,
AS THE SPIRIT OF GOD ENTERS OUR SOUL
AND GIVES BIRTH TO CHRIST OUR LORD AS LOVE.
AS MARY DID.
SO MUST WE.
EUCHARISTIC HANDMAIDS WE MUST BECOME! +

+DRY AND CRACKED AND PEELING OF VITALITY,
I DECAY WITHIN IN SPIRITLESS DESPAIR.
FOR I HAVE BOUGHT INTO A LIE!

I HAVE BEEN SPOON FED GOD'S DIVINE HATRED,
MY SOLE HUMAN PREDICAMENT,
AND A FUTURE THAT ONLY PROMISES A GRAVE.

BUT DIVINE PRECIPITATION
-IN GRACED AWARENESS OF LIFE ITSELF AS GIFT-
HAS REVIVED AND RENEWED THE INTEGRITY OF MY SPIRIT.

AND FAITH IN PURPOSE RESURFACES,
AS HOPE IN MERCY ABOUNDS,
IN LOVE WHICH SENSES LOVE'S TRUE PRESENCE! +

+*BEFORE* THE FALL
AND THE EXODUS
AND THE EXILE
AND THE BIRTH OF THE REDEEMER, YOU KNEW ME.
BEFORE THE SERMON ON THE MOUNT,
AND THE FEEDING OF THOUSANDS
WITH BUT FEW LOAVES AND LITTLE FISH,
YOU KNEW MY HUNGER.
BEFORE THE CROWN OF THORNS,
AND THE FLAGELLATION,
AND THE TERRIBLE BLESSED CROSS,
YOU SAW MY SIN AND PLANNED MY REDEMPTION.
BEFORE THE STONE WAS EVER ROLLED AWAY,
AND THE SPIRIT AWOKE THE SON,
YOU DESIRED MY PRESENCE-
THROUGH HIS PERPETUAL AND ATONING TRUE PRESENCE-
FOREVER! +

+THE INTERSECTION OF OUR FAITH AND GOD'S WILL
IS THE LIFE OF CHRIST.
FOR WHERE HUMANITY AND DIVINITY INTERSECT IS IN JESUS,
BOTH MAN OF NAZARETH, FAITHFUL, AND SON OF GOD, DIVINE.
WE ENTER THIS INTERSECTION IN PRAYER AND GOOD DEED...
ESPECIALLY IN THE SUBLIMITY OF THE EUCHARISTIC CELABRATION. +

+IN THE ARMS OF THE SHEPHERD
LIES THE SHEEP WHO LACK NOTHING.
HE WALKS, I FOLLOW.
HALLOWED GROUND-
HALLOWED STREAMS-
THE PATH OF LIFE.

HIS WAY
MY HOLINESS-
MY SALVATION-
GOD'S GLORY!

IN DARKNESS, I FEAR NOT,
IN INFUSED COURAGE THROUGH PURGATIVE CARESS.

FROM WATER AND SPIRIT,
IN BREAD AND WINE,
YOU FEED ME AND ANOINT ME
ON YOUR WAY.

IN SPIRIT AND GRACE
YOU NEVER RELENT,
FOR MY PLACE IS PREPARED,
MY HOME AWAITS,
MY LOT SECURED,
IN FAITH AND HOPE,
IN THE LOVE WHICH IS HEAVEN,
THE FIRE OF YOUR HEART,
SACRED AND SECURE. +

+ON THE PEAK OF HOLINESS, ON THE MOUNT OF PROVIDENCE,
AWAITS THE SUMPTUOUS BANQUET, WHERE BREAD AND WINE
BECOME BODY AND BLOOD, SOUL AND DIVINITY,
WHERE OUR SPIRITUAL SENSES SHARPEN TO A NEAR PERFECT POINT
-IN FAITH AND HOPE- WHICH TRULY HOLDS DEAR
THE MERCIFUL NEARNESS OF THE TRUE PRESENCE
OF THE SON OF GOD
IN CHRIST JESUS OUR LORD,
WITHIN THE MOST BLESSED SACRAMENT OF THE EUCHARIST,
BREAD OF LIFE!   +

+MY PRAISE,
MY WORSHIP,
MY THANKSGIVING,
ARE UTTERLY POOR, AND FEEBLE, AND BLIND,
TO YOUR AMAZING GLORY!

BUT I LIVE
IN FAITH AND HOPE
WITH A TOUCH OF CHARITY
IN THE RICHES,
AND STRENGTH,
AND LIGHT
OF YOUR AMAZING GRACE!

BEYOND THE TRANSFIGURATION,
THE BODY AND BLOOD OF THE CHRIST
STOOD BEFORE ST PETER,
AND THIS WAS HIS FAITH! +

+TRUST, LIVE, AND RECEIVE THE GRACE
TO BE THAT UNIQUE PERSON,
THAT UNIQUE EXPRESSION OF CHRIST,
THAT SHINING STAR IN THE HEAVENLY BODY,
THAT IMAGE OF BEAUTY,
WHO IS OUR GOD.

TRUST IN PROVIDENCE!
IN THE STORM, ALWAYS SEEK FOR NEW HORIZON,
CALL TO THE MORNING STAR, AS SHE POINTS LOVINGLY,
TO THE SIGN OF HER RISING SON!

FIGHT FOR VIRTUE.
RUN! WITH JOY FROM VICE.
FOR THIS, GOD SMILES!

SEEK SAFETY IN THE ROCK, SEEK COMMUNION IN THE CHURCH,
SEEK SOLACE AND TRUTH IN THE WORD,
SEEK NOURISHMENT AND LIFE IN HIS BODY AND BLOOD,
SEEK FOR HIM, HE LOVES YOU, DESIRES YOU, AND HOLDS YOU DEAR
TO HIS SACRED AND EUCHARISTIC HEART. +

THE SEVEN GIFTS OF GRACE

"IF ANYONE SAYS THAT THE SACRAMENTS OF THE NEW LAW WERE NOT ALL INSTITUTED BY OUR LORD JESUS CHRIST, OR THAT THERE ARE MORE OR LESS THAN SEVEN, NAMELY, BAPTISM, CONFIRMATION, EUCHARIST, PENANCE, EXTREME UNCTION, ORDER AND MATRIMONY, OR THAT ANY ONE OF THESE SEVEN IS NOT TRULY AND INTRINSICALLY A SACRAMENT, LET HIM BE ANATHEMA."
THE CANONS AND DECREES OF THE COUNCIL OF TRENT
TRANSLATED BY REVERAND H.J. SCHROEDER

"FROM THE FOREGOING WE REALIZE THAT THERE ARE TWO CAUSES OF GRACE IN THE SACRAMENTS: CHRIST AND THE SACRAMENTS THEMSELVES. HE IS, OF COURSE, THE PRINCIPAL CAUSE, FOR HE IS THE SOURCE OF GRACE, WHICH FLOWS TO US FROM THE SYMBOLIC REPRESENTATION OF HIS ACTS. BUT THE SACRAMENTS, TOO, CAUSE GRACE BECAUSE THEY ARE THE INSTRUMENTS, WHICH CHRIST USES, AND WHICH, AS INSTRUMENTS, CAUSE AND GIVE GRACE WHEN THEY ARE ENACTED. OF COURSE, IF THE RECIPIENT IS NOT RIGHTLY DISPOSED TO RECEIVE THE SACRAMENT, GRACE IS NOT GIVEN. EVERY SACRAMENT IS AN ENCOUNTER WITH GOD THAT IS THE RESULT OF GOD'S ACT AND OURS."
TRANSFORMED BY GRACE
DOM WULSTAN MORK, O.S.B.

+OUR INTEGRITY, OUR FIDELITY IN FAITH,
COMES FROM CHRIST OUR LORD.

WITH CHRIST IN OUR HEART,
AND OUR LIVES IN HIS HANDS
-EUCHARISTICALLY-
WE MAY UTTER 'AMEN.'

AND WE MAY KNOW THIS,
FOR THE FATHER ASSURES US
IN THE GIFT WHICH AFFIRMS AND STRENGTHENS FAITH...
THE COMFORTER,
THE COUNSELOR,
THE PARACLETE,
THE HOLY SPIRIT OF OUR GOD. +

+THE MERCY OF GOD
IS LARGE ENOUGH AND EVER HUNGRY ENOUGH
TO DEVOUR THE SINS OF THE REPENTANT SOUL.
NO SIN IS UNFORGIVABLE
IN THE FACE OF TRUE CONTRITION,
OFFERED HUMBLY IN THE SACRAMENT OF RECONCILIATION.

FOR EVEN JUDAS,
IF HE CHOSE NOT THE ROPE,
CONTRITE OF HEART,
WOULD HAVE MET THE UNFATHOMABLE, TRANSCENDENT,
AND AMAZING GRACE OF THE MERCIFUL ONE,
IN WHOM ALL SINS ARE FORGIVEN. +

+RECONCILIATION BEGINS WITH A SIMPLE PLEA
FROM THE BOTTOM OF ONES HEART.
IT CRIES FOR THE MERCY OF GOD
FOR DROWNING ONESELF FOOLISHLY, PRIDEFULLY, SHAMEFULLY,
IN THE SELF DESTRUCTIVE MUCK
OF WORDS, ACTIONS AND OMISSIONS,
WHICH SPURNED THE ONE WHO LOVES US MOST.
NOW IS THE TIME FOR RECONCILIATION!
NOW IS THE TIME TO ACCEPT THE GOD
OF UNFATHOMABLE MERCY. +

+THERE IS NO SUMPTUOUS CARCASS!
IT ALL STARTS AND ENDS WITH THE EUCHARIST.
THE EUCHARIST IS BREAD OF ANGELS,
AND WINE OF EVERLASTING LIFE.

FOR THE EUCHARIST IS CHRIST, BODY AND BLOOD!
THE NOURISHMENT OF GOD HIMSELF,
WORD OF GOD,
PERFECT MAN.
FOOD THAT PERFECTS!

LIKEWISE,
WE ARE THE BODY OF CHRIST,
WE ARE THE FAITHFUL, THE CHURCH OF THE APOSTLES,
AND WE MUST REMAIN ABUNDANTLY HEALTHY
IN AND THROUGH THE GRACE OF GOD,
BUILT UP ON THE NEW MANNA OF CHRIST...
ONLY THEN CAN WE FEED A DESPERATE AND STARVING WORLD. +

+RAINBOWS REMIND US OF GOD'S LOVE FOR CREATION,
MANIFESTED MOST POWERFULLY
IN THE INCARNATION OF THE WORD MADE FLESH.

THE WORLD, IN CHRIST,
IS THE PLACE OF REPENTANCE,
THE PLACE OF REDEMPTION,
THE LOCATION OF HIS CHURCH,
THE LIVING TEMPLE OF COMMUNION
IN THE GOD OF MERCY AND HIS BELOVED CHILDREN.

RAINBOWS REMIND US OF THE LIVING WATERS OF CHRIST,
THE FLOOD OF GRACE,
NAILED TO THE CROSS,
PEIRCED FOR OUR SALVATION,
IN THE BAPTISM OF PASCHAL PARTICIPATION,
IN HIS LIFE, DEATH AND RESURRECTION. +

+LORD, I HOPE THOSE SEVENTY TIMES SEVEN FORGIVENESSES
ARE A DAILY GIFT,
BECAUSE I PASSED THAT NUMBER A LONG TIME AGO! +

+AS THE SPIRIT HOVERED OVER THE WATER,
AND THE FLOOD CLEANSED THE EARTH,
THE ROCK OF GOD HAS ALWAYS PROVIDED
LIVING WATER
IN THE DESERT SOJOURN.
FOR THE LORD WHO PARTS THE SEA,
IS THE LORD WHO WAS PIERCED FOR OUR TRANSGRESSIONS.
AND HIS LOVE WHICH FLOWED
IN TWIN STREAMS OF WATER AND BLOOD
LIVES IN THE SACRAMENTS OF HIS GRACE AND HIS LIFE. +

+BAPTISM IS MORE THAN THE CHRISTIAN CLOAK OF LIFE.
IT IS THE EMBRACE RECEIVED AS A CHOSEN CHILD
FROM THE LOVE WHICH DID NOT SPARE EVEN HIS BELOVED SON;
TO ACQUIT OUR GUILT,
AN ACQUITAL THAT CAN NEVER BE REMANDED, EVEN BY GOD;
TO REPRESENT OUR PLEAS
EVEN AT THE RIGHT HAND OF THE FATHER,
EVEN IN THE BODY AND BLOOD OF HIS SON
IN THE SPIRIT OF RESURRECTED LIFE
WITHIN THE COMMUNION OF THE CHILDREN FAITHFUL, HOPEFUL,
LIVING WITHIN CHARITY EXTENDED
IN THE PROMISES OF THE ESCHATON OF GLORY-
MANIFEST IN THE OPEN ARMS OF THE DYING AND RISEN SAVIOR,
SEEN THROUGH THE VISION OF EUCHARISTIC FAITH. +

+LIFE IS IN THE SPIRIT!
THE HOLY SPIRIT IS THE SWEET SPIRIT OF LIBERATION,
OF COURAGE, IN THE *CONFIRMATION* OF OUR FAITH.
LIFE IS IN THE SPIRIT!
IT IS THE SPIRIT WHICH INSPIRES HOPE
IN THE JOYFUL 'ABBA, FATHER!'
LIFE IS IN THE SPIRIT!
THE SPIRIT OF GOD IS WITHIN US WHEN WE WORK AS ONE
-AS BROTHERS AND SISTERS OF CHRIST-
HUMBLY SUBMITTING TO THE CROSS
-REPENTANT AND DEPENDANT ON GOD'S MERCY-
KNOWING IN FAITH THAT THE CROSS PREPARES US
FOR SALVATION IN RESURRECTION AND LIFE.
LIFE IS IN THE SPIRIT! +

+HOURLY, DAILY, ANNUALLY,
THE FAITHFUL MESSAGE OF THE APOSTLE IS SHARED
-IN PRAYER AND ACT AND WORD-
REACHING THROUGH ALL CREATION,
ANNOUNCING THE PRESENCE AND THE PROMISE
-BOTH FULFILLED AND YET TO COME-
OF THE SALVIFIC PARADOX
OF THE COMING OF THE LORD OF THE UNIVERSE,
NOT AS KING,
BUT AS BRIDEGROOM AND HERO,
AS THE ONE TRUE UNCONDITIONAL LOVER. +

+FROM THE FATHER, THROUGH THE SON,
IN THE SPIRIT,
ST PETER HAS PASSED THE TORCH OF FAITH,
-IN WORD AND TRADITION-
THE VERY LIGHT OF CHRIST,
OUR SALVATION,
ON TO THE SUCCEEDING BISHOPS OF ROME.

IN TURN, BISHOPS, WITH PRIESTS, DEACONS, RELIGIOUS, AND LAITY,
HAVE ALSO PASSED THE TORCH OF FAITH,
FANNING THE FLAMES OF GRACE
IN INCARNATE SACRAMENTAL WAYS.

FOR OUR FAITH IS A FIRE WHICH BURNS IN THE SPIRIT
AS APOSTOLIC, SACRAMENTAL, AND IN COMMUNION.

AND WE KNOW THIS TRUE,
SINCE WE ARE REVEALED IN HIS-TORY,
IN WORD AND SPIRIT
AS THE BODY OF THE INCARNATE MESSIAH. +

+IT IS NEVER TOO LATE TO REALIZE THE RICHES,
GIVEN *FROM THY BOUNTY,*
IN THE PRECIOUS FORM OF MY WIFE. +

+CHRIST HAS PLACED HIS CONFIDENCE IN HIS BRIDE,
WHOM HE HAS BOUGHT WITH HIS BLOOD,
WELL BEYOND "THE PRICE OF PEARLS." +

+A GOOD AND HONORABLE MAN
DESIRES TO BE THAT VINE,
WHICH SHOOTS FORTH BRANCHES-LOVINGLY-
IN WIFE AND CHILD,
FAMILY AND FRIEND,
UNTO ETERNITY.

BUT THAT GOOD AND HONORABLE MAN
MUST FIRST BE A HUMBLE AND GRACIOUS BRANCH,
IN LOVING OBEDIENCE
TO THE ONE TRUE, GOOD, AND HONORABLE MAN,
THE VINE, THE CHRIST.

IN DOING SO,
HE WILL DERIVE THE GRACE
TO TRANSFORM FROM BRANCH TO VINE IN SANCTITY. +

+THE SACRAMENTAL LIFE
-INDEBTED TO FAITH, ENLIVENED IN PRAYER-
IS THE SOURCE OF GRACED STRENGTH
FOR CLIMBING THE HEIGHTS,
WHICH HAVE ONLY BEEN CONQUERED BY THE SAVIOR OF MAN...
IN SCALING THE HEIGHTS OF PERFECTION
IN HUMAN SANCTITY
WHICH ALWAYS RELIES ON THE POWER OF CHRIST'S DIVINITY
AND THE MANIFEST PERFECTION OF HIS HUMANITY,
RISEN AND GLORIFIED
THROUGH THE CRUCIBLE OF FAITHFUL SUFFERING. +

+TO ADORE THE EUCHARIST
IS TO GAZE IN APPRECIATION ON GRACE RECEIVED,
AND IN TURN TO RECEIVE HIM, AND MANIFEST HIM,
WITH EVER INCREASING DEVOTION.

FOR TIME SPENT WITH THE LORD
IN AN INTERCOURSE OF SPIRITUAL INTIMACY, SHARING EVERYTHING,
DEEPENING DESIRE FOR THE OTHER,
CHARGES COMMUNION,
AND FANS THE FLAMES OF LOVE
IN THE INDWELLING SACRAMENT BECOME SPIRIT. +

+CONFIRMED IN THE SPIRIT,
I AM TO EVANGELIZE, RECONCILE, ILLUMINATE, LIBERATE, FORGIVE,
AND FIGHT FOR JUSTICE
TO AND FROM MY SOURCE OF STRENGTH
-IN CHRIST LIKE GOSPEL VIRTUE-
IN THE SEED OF LOVE AS MERCY,
PLANTED DEEP WITHIN MY SOUL
IN THE EUCHARISTIC LORD,
AND HIS SPIRIT-THE CONQUERER OF THE WORLD. +

+JOSEPH, MOST HUMBLE SERVANT OF THE LORD,
YOUR LOVE FOR MARY
WAS SURPASSED ONLY
BY YOUR HUMBLE LOVE FOR THE LORD.

HOW COURAGEOUS WAS YOUR WILL
IN STEPPING ASIDE
FOR THE BETROTHAL OF YOUR BRIDE IN THE SPIRIT;
TRUSTING, FROM A DREAM
THE EVER-FAITHFUL AND BENEVOLENT GOD. +

+VERACITY
  OPENING
  CHARISMS
  ATTUNED
  TO
  INCARNATE
  OPTIONS
  NOW! +

+HAPPY MARRIAGE IS FULLNESS OF LIFE!
A FAITHFUL WIFE IS A HUSBANDS PEACE.
A LOYAL WIFE IS THE SPIRIT MANIFEST IN ENOBLED FLESH.
IN THE FAITHFULNESS TO EACH OTHER,
BORN OF HOPE IN GOD, WHETHER IN BOUNTY OR FAMINE,
LOVE WILL PERSEVERE THROUGH TIME.
FOR MARRIAGE IS THE SPIRITUAL MIRROR OF GOD'S LOVE FOR MAN
IN THE BRIDEGROOM WHO IS CHRIST,
AND HIS BELOVED BRIDE THE CHURCH,
WHERE THE CROSS BEARS OUT HIS LOVE. +

+THE DISEASED AND THE SICK
ARE LIKE SHEEP WITHOUT A SHEPHERD.

THE DISEASED ARE WROUGHT WITH MALADY AND DILEMMA-
PHYSICAL, MENTAL, EMOTIONAL AND SPIRITUAL.

THE SICK SUFFER THE REALITIES OF LIFE,
THE FEAR OF DEATH,
AND THE UNCERTAINTY THEREAFTER.

"THE HARVEST IS RICH, BUT THE LABORERS ARE FEW..."
BUT WHO AMONG US IS NOT SICK,
AND WHO IS NOT DIS-EASED?

"...SO ASK THE LORD OF THE HARVEST
TO SEND LABORERS TO HIS HARVEST."

FOR THE SHEPHERD WILL PROVIDE FOR HIS SHEEP. +

+THE SPOUSE OF THE SPOUSE OF THE HOLY SPIRIT
WAS A COMPASSIONATE,
COURAGEOUS
AND CONSCIENTIOUS HUSBAND
TO THE MOTHER OF OUR LORD,
THE BLESSED VIRGIN MARY.

MAY I BE BLESSED TO IMITATE ST JOSEPH
AS COURAGEOUS,
COMPASSIONATE,
AND CONSCIENTIOUS HUSBAND.

THE FATHER OF JESUS, FOSTER FATHER,
TO THE SON OF THE HEAVENLY FATHER,
ALWAYS READY-AT AN AWAKENING MOMENT-
TO FULFILL THE WILL OF GOD,
MAY ST JOSEPH'S FATHERHOOD OF DEVOUT DISCIPLESHIP
IN CARING FOR THE SAVIOR-BOY
AND HIS BLESSED VIRGIN WIFE
INSPIRE ME TO BE THE FATHER OF MY CHILD
IN HUMBLE OBEDIENCE TO THE WILL OF THE FATHER IN HEAVEN. +

+THE APOSTLE IS CHOSEN BY THE FATHER,
ANOINTED WITH THE SPIRIT,
DIRECTED IN THE SON,
TO SEEK FOR THE WILL OF GOD,
TO CONVERT IN THE GOSPEL,
TO REDEEM IN THE BODY AND BLOOD OF CHRIST,
TO TEACH AND PREACH AND PROPHESY,
AS PROPHET, PRIEST AND KING
IN NEW LIFE IN THE BAPTISM OF THE CROSS,
IN SALVATION IN THE BLOOD OF THE LAMB,
AND IN HEAVEN AWAITING IN A LIFE OF GRACED HOLINESS,
WHICH ANTICIPATES WITH HOPE
THE RESURRECTION OF CHARITY THROUGH FAITH IN CHRIST. +

+SO FEW PRIESTS, SUCH DWINDLING RELIGIOUS...
SO MUCH SUFFERING,
SUCH GROWS THE HUNGER FOR SACRAMENTAL GRACE!
YET I AM BUT A MAN!
I AM FINITE AND WEAK AND SELFISH.
I AM CERTAINLY NOT THE SAVIOR!
AND MOST CERTAINLY I NEED SALVATION!
WHAT MUST I DO?

AS THE SUFFERING AND HUNGER GROW,
AS THE HARVEST SPREADS LIKE WILD FIRE,
WHERE ARE THE LABORERS,
THE ANOINTED VESSELS OF SACRAMENTAL GRACE?

THEY ARE HERE AMONGST US!
THEY ARE YOUNG MEN AND WOMEN,
LITTLE BOYS AND LITTLE GIRLS,
NOT YET TAINTED WITH THE PESSEMISTIC SPIRIT,
NOT YET RUINED BY WORLDLY SKEPTICIMS AND DESPAIR.
THEY ARE OUR NEIGHBORS, OUR SONS AND OUR DAUGHTERS.
AND WE MUST RAISE THEM IN THE FAITH.
EXEMPLIFYING CHARITY WHILE POINTING TO THE BEAUTY
OF THE POPE, THE BISHOP, THE PRIEST,
THE DEACON, AND THE RELIGIOUS,
AND WE MUST PRAY FOR THE WILL OF GOD IN THEIR LIVES,
AND THE GENTLENESS OF SPIRIT, SO AS NOT TO BE AN OBSTACLE. +

+TWELVE MEN.
ONE MISSION.
MUCH FAITH.
SOME DOUBT.
MUCH GRACE.
SOME CONFUSION.

ONE DENIES.
ONE RUNS AWAY NAKED.
TEN DESERT.
ONE REMAINS WITH COURAGEOUS WOMEN.
ONE BETRAYS.

ONE REPENTS.
ELEVEN HIDE.
ONE DESPAIRS...AND DIES.
ONE DOUBTS.

ONE IS COMMISSIONED.
ELEVEN ARE FORGIVEN.
THE SPIRIT GIVES THEM ALL MIGHT!

A TWELFTH IS ADDED.
A THIRTEENTH IS TRANSFORMED-FROM ZEALOT TO SAINT!

THE LAYING ON OF HANDS,
THE TURN OF THE CENTURIES,
THE LINE OF THE TWELVE CONTINUES TO THIS DAY. +

+I LAY ON THE SIDE OF THE ROAD
A BLOODY AND IGNOMINOUS MESS!
THE PERPETRATORS MOCK ME AS THEY RUN!
PASSERS BY SEEM TO SEE NO LIFE!
I NEED A SAVIOR!
AS STRANGE AS IT SEEMS, SO CLOSE TO DEATH,
MY SPIRIT SEEKS TO PRAISE AND GLORIFY GOD
IN THE MIDST OF LIFE'S WORST TURMOIL.
FOR FLESH MAY LIE DYING, BUT THE SPIRIT REACHES DEEP WITHIN,
BREATHING FAITH AND HOPE IN THE OIL OF CHURCH COMPASSION,
AND LOVE ETERNAL IN THE SWEET CARESS OF VIATICUM. +

PRAYER

"WE OFTEN HEAR IN SERMONS, AND READ IN PIOUS BOOKS, OF THE NECESSITY OF AVOIDING BAD COMPANY, OF HATING SIN, OF FORGIVING INJURIES, AND OF BEING RECONCILED TO OUR ENEMIES; BUT SELDOM ARE WE TAUGHT THIS GREAT TRUTH, OR, IF IT IS SOMETIMES SPOKEN OF, IT IS RARELY DONE IN A MANNER CALCULATED TO LEAVE UPON OUR MINDS A LASTING IMPRESSION OF ITS GREAT IMPORTANCE OR NECESSITY. NOW THIS IMPORTANT TRUTH IS, THAT ACCORDING TO THE ORDINARY COURSE OF DIVINE PROVIDENCE, MAN CANNOT BE SAVED WITHOUT PRAYER."
FATHER MICHAEL MUELLER, C.SS.R.
PRAYER/THE KEY TO SALVATION

"LISTEN CAREFULLY, MY SON, TO THE MASTER'S INSTRUCTIONS, AND ATTEND TO THEM WITH THE EAR OF YOUR HEART. THIS IS ADVICE FROM A FATHER WHO LOVES YOU; WELCOME IT, AND FAITHFULLY PUT IT INTO PRACTICE. THE LABOR OF OBEDIENCE WILL BRING YOU BACK TO HIM FROM WHOM YOU HAD DRIFTED THROUGH THE SLOTH OF DISOBEDIENCE. THIS MESSAGE OF MINE IS FOR YOU, THEN, IF YOU ARE READY TO GIVE UP YOUR OWN WILL, ONCE AND FOR ALL, AND ARMED WITH THE STRONG AND NOBLE WEAPONS OF OBEDIENCE TO DO BATTLE FOR THE TRUE KING, CHRIST THE LORD."
PROLOGUE
THE RULE OF ST BENEDICT

"PRAYER FOR ME, IS SIMPLY A RAISING OF THE HEART, A SIMPLE GLANCE TOWARDS HEAVEN, AN EXPRESSION OF LOVE AND GRATITUDE."
THE LITTLE WAY OF ST THERESE OF LISIEUX
INTO THE ARMS OF LOVE

+I EXPLODE WITH ANXIETY,
IRRITATED FROM WITHIN TO THE POINT OF SCREAMING.

I HAVE CHOSEN NOT TO TAKE THE LONG TREK IN FAITH,
AND NOW I AM HAVING SECOND THOUGHTS ABOUT MY DECISION.

I AM SEEMINGLY ALONE,
OBVIOUSLY POOR,
AND PROBABLY DESTITUTE.

MY PRAYER IS A MIXTURE OF FATIGUE,
DESPAIR,
AND MUFFLED SPEECH.

I DO NOT WANT TO DIE!
BUT I FEEL DEATH ALL AROUND ME.

WHEN WILL DAYBREAK COME?
WHEN WILL THIS DARK CLOUD VANISH?
WHEN WILL I HAVE A DAY IN THE SON? +

+THE DISCIPLE,
A POOR SINNER BY NATURE,
MUST RELY, SOLELY,
THROUGH PRAYER AND SACRAMENT,
ON THE HOLY SPIRIT OF THE LOVE
BETWEEN THE FATHER AND THE SON,
FOR THE GRACE TO FULFILL THE GREAT COMMANDMENT
OF THE LORD JESUS CHRIST,
SO THAT IN DOING SO,
THE DISCIPLE MAY BE SANCTIFIED
IN THE GRACE BESTOWED UPON THEM,
SOLELY, BY THE WILL OF THE FATHER,
SHARED, IN THE FREE AND REDEMPTIVE GIFT OF LOVE,
ACTUALIZED AND FOREVER EXPRESSED
IN THE CROSS
AND IN THE EUCHARIST
OF OUR CRUCIFIED
AND RISEN LORD,
JESUS THE CHRIST. +

+WHAT OF THE EMPTY DAYS?
WHAT OF THE TIMES WHEN PEOPLE ARE CRUEL
AND I AM A TARGET?
WHAT OF THE DAYS WHEN I AM EXHAUSTED,
AND THE LIST OF RESPONSIBILITIES IS AS LARGE AS AN OAK?
WHAT OF THE TIMES WHEN I PRAY FOR FAITH,
AND I CRY FOR HOPE,
AND NARY IS A DROP OF LOVE FELT IN THE AIR?

WHAT OF THE CROSS?
"ELOI ELOI LLAMA SABACHTANI"
WHAT OF THE CRUCIFIED?
WHAT AM I TO THINK OF IT ALL? +

+IN CHAINS I PRAY, IN BONDS I CRY,
AS PRISONER MY FAITH AND HOPE PLEAD FOR CLEMENCY,
IN LIFE AND LOVE,
WHICH MATTERS NOT IN CIRCUMSTANCE OR IN ABUNDANCE
OR IN STATURE OR IN COMFORT,
BUT FLOWS FROM THE RIVER OF MERCY
IN WATER AND BLOOD,
IN BAPTISM AND FAITH,
IN ADOPTION AND DIVINE FILIATION,
WHERE I GO TO THE MOUNTAINTOP OF FAITH
IN THE COMMUNION OF HOPE
TO DRINK IN THE BLOOD OF LIFE IN EVERLASTING LOVE,
FOUND IN THE PERFECT SACRIFICE
OF MY ELDER BROTHER CHRIST,
WHICH DIVINIZES MY VERY SOUL
TO ENTER THE HEAVEN OF MOTHER MARY,
AND BROTHER AND SISTER SAINT,
BROTHER AND SISTER WHO LIVE WITH ME *NOW!* +

+ALMIGHTY GOD! MASTER ARTIST, BENEVOLENT CREATOR!
    SUSTAINER OF ALL LIFE, LOVER OF ALL CREATION!
JUDGE AND REDEEMER,
FATHER OF ALL MERCY,
BROTHER OF ALL GRACE, SPIRIT OF ALL LIFE.
PRAISE BE GOD!
HOW LITTLE DO MY WORDS DO JUSTICE TO YOUR GLORY! +

+THE DEMON LURKS IN THE SLEEPING CHAMBER
OF THE MARRIAGE WITHOUT PRAYER.

FOR IN THE LORD ALONE,
LOVE BETWEEN HUSBAND AND WIFE
BECOMES LOVE BETWEEN CHRIST AND HIS BRIDE,
THE CHURCH.

AS MYSTERY WITHIN MYSTERY
IS EXPRESSED
-IN PRAYERFUL UNION-
LOVE BEGETS LOVE IN FAITH,
AS TWO BECOME ONE
IN THE GOD
OF THREE PERSONS IN ONE LOVE.

BLESSED IS THE PRAYERFUL MARRIAGE!
WITHIN THE TRINITY IS BEHELD THEIR LOVE. +

+*R*IGHTEOUS
 *O*BEDIENCE
 *S*ERVING
 *A*LL
 *R*ELIGIOUS
 *Y*EARNINGS +

+THE LIFE OF A SAINT-
FILLED WITH FAITH, AGAINST ALL DOUBT,
ENLIVENED IN HOPE, ABOVE ALL HOPELESSNESS;
RELYING ON THE RARIFIED AIR OF THE GRACE OF GOD
FOR THE CHRISTIAN RESPIRATION IN AND OUT IN CHARITY;
THIS LIFE IS NOT VOID OF PERIL.

BUT WHETHER SUNSHINE OR STORM,
COMFORT OR POVERTY, MALICE OR MAGNANIMITY OF NEIGHBOR,
THE PRAYER OF THE SAINT IS CARRIED IN CERTAINTY
BY THE MIGHTY, FAITHFUL AND SWIFT HANDS
OF THE ANGEL OF GOD.
HIS ONLY DESTINATION,
THE FOOT OF THE ONE IN WHOM ALL PRAYER IS ANSWERED. +

+ALL THE NOISE, ALL THE CHATTER, ALL THE NERVOUS ENERGY
EXPANDED IN THE IRRELEVANT, THE TEMPORAL, AND THE
PROFANE...
ALL AT THE COST OF LOSING SWEET SILENCE.
SILENCE IS THOUGHT.
SILENCE IS LISTENING.
SILENCE IS SEEING.
SILENCE IS REST.
SILENCE IS HUMILITY IN MOTION.

SILENCE IS THE SEED OF PRAYER
AND THE SOUND OF THE SPIRIT,
ACTIVE IN OUR HEART.   +

+PRAYER IS DISCONNECT FROM IMMEDIATE GRATIFICATION.
PRAYER IS THE PARADOX OF SELF ABSORPTION
GLEEFULLY GREETING SELF DENIAL.
FOR GETHSEMANE IS PRAYER FOR THYSELF, STRUGGLING,
YET ACQUIESING TO "THY WILL BE DONE."
FOR PRAYER IS IMMEDIATE NEED,
AND IMPENDING DISASTER,
MEETING GRACE
-IN THE HOLY SPIRIT OF ALL PROVIDENCE AND BENEVOLANCE-
IN BECOMING MORE AND MORE A SAINT
IN PATIENCE, AND PERSEVERANCE, AND LONGSUFFERING,
AND WISDOM,
WHICH FORTIFIES FAITH AND HOPE
IN THE LOVE PROVEN ON THE CROSS,
VICTORIOUS IN RESURRECTION,
PRESENT IN SPIRIT AND SACRAMENT,
ALIVE IN CHARITY AND PRAYER,
ABLE TO CONQUER ALL OBSTACLES,
ONE DAY AT A TIME. +

+PRAISE HAS *POWER*. CERTAIN UTTERANCES ARE GRATUITOUS AND
DIGNIFYING FOR HUMANITY. *ALLELUIA! OUR FATHER WHO ART IN
HEAVEN...JESUS IS LORD!* NOT MERE WORDS, BUT COMMUNICATION
WITH THE DIVINE. THERE IS POWER IN PRAISE! THERE IS CULPABILITY
IN MISUSE. NOT MERE WORDS: SEEK, REVEAL AND SHARE THE POWER
OF PRAISE. *ALLELUIA!* +

+AS I PRAY FOR GRACE FROM THEE,
THEY SEE NO HOPE, NO CHANCE FOR ME...
BUT PALTRY AS MY VIRTUE IS,
YOU SHINE BRILLIANT GRACE
FROM THE SUFFERING THAT WAS HIS...
FOR THEY ARE RIGHT TO CONSIDER ME POOR,
BUT IN REPENTANCE AND MERCY
I WEAR SIN NO MORE...
SO WORD AND SNEER NO LONGER HARM,
FOR **WORD** COME NEAR IS MY HEARTS CHARM...
FOR IN FAITH AND HOPE I SINK NOT LOW,
FOR ALMIGHTY LOVE DEALS MALICE
ITS DEATH BLOW! +

+LACKING IN WISDOM,
SIMPLE IN CONTENT,
HUMBLE IN GOAL,
HEAR MY PRAYER FOR THE SAKE OF ITS SINCERITY!

FOR THE SAKE OF YOUR GLORY
AND THE SALVATION OF YOUR CHILDREN,
GUIDE MY STEPS.
LEAD ME IN *THE WAY* OF YOUR PEACE.

IN YOUR MOST HOLY SPIRIT,
STEER MY EYES AND MY EARS
AND MY HEART AND MY FEET
CLEAR OF THE DECEIVER,
AND DECEPTION,
AND THE WILLINGLY DECEIVED.

LET MY LIFE LEAD TO BEATIFICE PEACE. +

+THE DIVINE PHYSICIAN
SEEKS FOR THE WEAK PULSE
OF THE NEAR DEAD.
AND HE FINDS IT
IN GUILT
AND SHAME...
AND THE FAINTEST CRY FOR HELP. +

+HOW WONDERFUL YOU ARE!
FOR IN BETRAYAL, ON THE EVE OF SEVERE PERSECUTION,
AND HUMILIATION,
YOU BURST FORTH IN LOVE INCARNATE,
MANIFEST IN BREAD AND WINE
TURNED BODY AND BLOOD,
OFFERING UNFETTERED THANKSGIVING,
JOYFULLY ILLUMINATING FORGIVENESS
FOR THE GREATEST SIN YET TO BE COMMITTED...
THE DARKNESS OF CRUCIFIXION-
THAT WHICH YOU EMBRACED FOR THE SALVATION OF MANY
IN THE LIGHT WHICH SHONE FROM THE ROLLING ROCK
IN FRONT OF THE EMPTYING TOMB.   +

+PRAY I DO!
AND ALL THAT *THE MAN* ON HIS CRUCIFIX SEEMS TO DO
IS HANG THERE...DEAD.
NO SIGNS OF LIFE, NO MOVEMENT, NOTHING...
IN BOTH OF US!
YET SOMETHING INSIDE OF ME
KEEPS ME MOVING TOWARD THAT HANGING MAN...
AND HIS PROMISES. +

+THE RELATIVIST, THE SKEPTIC, THE SECULARIST,
HAVE BUILT MANY LEVY'S TO DAM UP THE RIVER EVANGELIST.

YET THIS RIVER DOES NOT FLOW FROM THE SEA
OF MERE HUMAN AMBITION.
IF SO, THE LEVY MIGHT NEVER BREAK.

BUT THE TRUE RIVER EVANGELIST
DRAWS IMMENSE POWER,
IMMENSE HYDRO-POWER,
FROM THE LIVING WATER OF PRAYER,
DRAWING FROM THE INFINITE OCEAN
OF GOD'S ABUNDANT MERCY. +

+THE CRUCIFIX IS THE SYMBOL, WHICH HOLDS FAITH INTACT,
WHILE DESPAIR DARKENS THE SOUL TO A LOVING GOD. +

+PRAISE THE LORD IN REPENTANCE AND CONTRITION, IN
CONFESSION AND PENANCE.
THE POWER OF GOD IS FOUND IN PRAISE!

FOR GOD IS OUR SAVIOR, OUR PROTECTOR,
OUR PROVIDER, AND OUR LOVING FATHER!

FATHER GOD, YOU PURGATE FOR A SEASON,
YOU PRUNE FOR A DAY,
YET YOU NEVER ABANDON US,
AND YOU FEED US AND CLOTHE US IN CHRIST,
RENEWING US DAY BY DAY
IN YOUR LOVING SPIRIT.

FOR THIS I THANK YOU, FOR THIS I GIVE YOU PRAISE! +

+PRAYERFUL PATIENCE
IS THE KEY TO THE TREASURE CHEST
IN PASCHAL MYSTERY.

FOR MARY OF MAGDALA SUFFERED SEVEN DEMONS,
THE FULLNESS OF ANGUISH,
TO BE THE FIRST TO WITNESS THE RISEN SAVIOR!

IT IS OFTEN SAID THAT GOD WORKS IN MYSTERIOUS WAYS.
FOR GOOD FRIDAY
AND HOLY SATURDAY
SEEMED AND ETERNITY TO THE DISCIPLES!

LIKEWISE,
SUFFERING AND PERSECUTION
ARE BURDENS WHICH SEEM TO DRAG TIME
TO A CRAWL IN THE CHALLENGE FOR HOPE.

YET EASTER REVEALED THE RISEN SAVIOR;
AND THE PAIN OF SEVEN DEMONS
SEEMED SO SCANT A PRICE TO PAY FOR ONE LORD! +

+PRAYER IS THE RELATIONSHIP OF THE PRAYER,
AND THE PRAYED TO-FAITHFULLY, HOPEFULLY, IN LOVE. +

ADVENT

"GOD, KNOWING HIMSELF WITH INFINITE KNOWING POWER, GENERATES IN THE DIVINE MIND AN IDEA OF HIMSELF. WE ALL HAVE AN IDEA OF OURSELVES IN OUR MIND, NOT ALWAYS A VERY ACCURATE IDEA, EVEN OUR DEAREST FRIENDS MIGHT LAUGH IF THEY COULD KNOW THE IDEA WE HAVE OF OURSELVES. BUT GOD'S IDEA OF HIMSELF IS TOTALLY ACCURATE, TOTALLY ADEQUATE. THERE IS NOTHING IN HIMSELF THAT IS NOT IN THE IDEA THAT HE ETERNALLY GENERATES OF HIMSELF; AND WHEREAS OUR IDEA IS MERELY SOMETHING, HIS IS SOMEONE AS HE HIMSELF IS SOMEONE, GOD AS HE IS GOD. AND THIS SECOND SOMEONE WITHIN THE GODHEAD IS ETERNAL AS HE IS ETERNAL-THERE NEVER WAS A MOMENT WHEN GOD DID NOT THUS SEE HIMSELF IMAGED IN HIS SON, THERE ARE NO MOMENTS IN ETERNITY.
THUS THE SON WHOM MARY CONCEIVED IN HER WOMB, THE SON WHO RECEIVED HUMAN NATURE IN HER WOMB, POSSESSED THE DIVINE NATURE ETERNALLY."
FRANK SHEED
TO KNOW CHRIST JESUS

"WE KNOW LITTLE OF HIS EARLY LIFE, ONLY THAT HE WAS BORN IN BETHLEHEM, CONCEIVED THROUGH THE POWER OF THE SPIRIT IN THE WOMB OF MARY, A YOUNG WOMAN OF NAZARETH. SHE WAS FULL OF GRACE AND OF BEAUTY, FULL OF THE HOLY SPIRIT, HIDDEN WOMAN, SILENT WOMAN, YEARNING WOMAN, IN LOVE WITH GOD AND WITH THE WORD OF GOD, TRULY ONE OF THE *ANAWIM*, THE POOR OF ADONAI. SHE THIRSTED FOR THE KINGDOM...IT WAS TO HER THAT AN ANGEL, GABRIEL, WAS SENT...IN HER LOVE AND LITTLENESS AND YEARNING SHE ACCEPTED: 'BEHOLD I AM THE HANDMAID OF THE LORD. LET IT BE DONE TO ME ACCORDING TO YOUR WORD.'"
JEAN VANIER
JESUS, THE GIFT OF LOVE

+CHRISTMAS IS FAMILY, HOLY POOR AND DEVOUT.
CHRISTMAS IS SHEPHERDS AND ANGELS SCURRYING ABOUT.
CHRISTMAS IS MARY PONDERING SO DEEP.
CHRISTMAS IS TRANSFORMED SHEPHERDS LEADING THEIR SHEEP.
CHRISTMAS IS THE FEW INSPIRED SO BOLD,
BELEIVING AND HOPING IN WHAT THEY'VE BEEN TOLD.
CHRISTMAS IS DAILY IN BURDEN AND CHORE.
CHRISTMAS IS LOVE'S BABE KNOCKING AT OUR HEARTS DOOR. +

+*CHRISTMAS* AND THE *CROSS*
ARE UNITED
IN THE PASSION OF CHRIST.

+ZECHARIAH IS A SIGN OF HOPE
FOR ALL WHO DOUBT THE WORD OF GOD.
STRUCK DUMB IN DOUBT,
HE WAS FORGIVEN
-MERCIFULLY-
IN REPENTANCE,
AND "WAS FILLED WITH THE HOLY SPIRIT,"
PROCLAIMING BOLDLY OF THE PROPHETIC BLESSING
OF VOCATION FROM GOD,
FLOWING FROM HIS SEED. +

+CHRISTMAS, REAL CHRISTMAS,
ADVENT, TRUE ADVENT,
IS GOD EMPOWERING A NEW YEAR!

CHRISTMAS IS
-TRULY UNDERSTOOD-
GOD AMONG US, GOD WITH US, GOD FOR US, GOD IN US.
AND ADVENT
-TRULY UNDERSTOOD-
IS TRUTH SO POWERFUL
AS TO ACTUALLY CHANGE US IN CHRIST-
FOR THE BETTER,
FOREVER.
CHANGE IN CHRIST-
BECOMING CHRIST-LIKE-
NOW *THAT* IS THE GIFT OF CHRISTMAS. +

+HE WAS BORN IN A CAVE,
WHICH WAS COLD AND FULL OF ANIMALS-
VOID OF HUMAN COMFORT.

HE WAS BURIED IN A ROCK,
WHICH WAS STONY COLD AND MORBIDLY DARK,
VOID OF LIFE, VOID OF GRACE.

YET, PRIOR TO THE CAVE,
HE SOARED THE HEIGHTS OF HEAVEN
AS WORD OF GOD;
AND AFTER LYING LIFELESS,
DENIED IN THE ROCK,
HE ROSE IN THE SPIRIT OF THE FATHER'S LOVE
AS REDEEMING WORD OF GOD,
PRINCE OF PASSIONED SALVATION,
MAN PERFECTED IN SUFFERING AND OBEDIENCE,
-GOD IN MERCY AND LOVE-
OUR REDEEMER, OUR EXEMPLAR, OUR HOPE, AND OUR LIFE. +

+AS JOSEPH,
SEEN YET UNHEARD,
WE ARE TO PROTECT THE CHRIST IN OUR CHILD.

LIKE MARY,
IMMACULATELY HUMBLE, YET VIRILE IN FAITH,
WE ARE TO NOURISH THE CHRIST IN OUR CHILD,
PATIENTLY BEARING THEIR SUFFERINGS
IN PERSEVERING COMPASSION.

AND LIKE SIMEON AND ANNA,
WE MUST AWAIT THE STIRRINGS OF THE SPIRIT WITHIN,
AND ON GOD'S GOOD TIME,
SHARE THE BEAUTY AND TRUTH OF CHRIST
-IN OUR CHILD-FOR THE WITNESS OF GOD IMMANUEL. +

+THE INCARNATION INFUSES GOD'S COVENANT IN OUR FLESH...
THE SACRED HEART PUMPS FRESH LIFE TO HIS BODY...
THE SPIRIT DWELLS WITHIN US...FOR GOD BECAME MAN SO THAT
MAN MIGHT DWELL IN GOD. +

+MY NEW YEARS RESOLUTION IS TO MAKE NO RESOLUTION!
RATHER, I PRAY THAT GOD ALMIGHTY,
EVER LOVING AND ALL MERCIFUL,
WILL CONTINUE TO GRACE ME, *FORWARD*,
TOWARD HIS GOAL FOR ME.

HALF A CENTURY OLD, AND I'M STILL A MYSTERY TO MYSELF.
ONLY THE LORD KNOWS WHO I AM, AND WHAT I TRULY NEED.

AND I TRUST THAT HE WILL DELIVER ON HIS PROMISES,
AS HE IS THE EVER FAITHFUL LORD. MY LORD!   +

+**PRAY** TO THE PRIMORDIAL CHRISTIAN THEOLOGIAN.
PRAY TO MARY THE MOTHER OF GOD.
THEOTOKOS.
PRAY TO THE INTIMATE BRIDE OF THE SPIRIT.
PRAY TO THE ONE WHO INSPIRES DIVINE ACTION.
PRAY TO THE EVER FAITHFUL BEARER OF CHRIST,
FROM BIRTH IN SWADDLING CLOTHES,
TO DEATH IN SACRED LINEN.
PRAY TO MARY IMMACULATELY CONCEIVED.
ASSUMED TO HEAVEN, EVER PRESENT BESIDE HER SON,
PIERCED TO KNOW OUR NEEDS. +

+THE MAGI SEARCHED THE HORIZON WITH OPEN MINDS AND
INQUISITIVE HEARTS.
THE KING, HIS HIGH PRIESTS, AND THE SCRIBES, HOWEVER,
WERE TOO BUSY ADMIRING THEIR OWN HANDIWORK TO NOTICE THE
CREATIVE ACTIONS OF THEIR GOD.
THE SHEPHERDS, LOWLY AND POOR, RECEIVED THE REVELATION-
STARVED FOR BY THE RICH AND THE POWERFUL,
FOR CENTURY UPON CENTURY-WITH REVERANCE AND AWE.
THE BABE IN THE MANGER, GOD'S REVELATION OF LOVE,
FOUND BY THE OPEN INQUISITORS
AND THE POOR AND HUMBLE SHEPHERDS,
WAS MISSED BY THE PROUD AND THE OCCUPIED.
CHRISTMAS IS AN EVERDAY EVENT.
MAYBE, JUST MAYBE, I WILL SEEK AND SHEPHERD
THE GIFT OF GOD'S GRACE IN THIS DAY,
WHEN CHRIST IS BORN IN ME. +

+JESUS IS FULLY MAN!
THEREFORE,
NO PAIN,
NO SUFFERING,
NO PERSECUTION ENDURED,
NO TEMPTATION EXPERIENCED,
SURPASSES THE UNDERSTANDING OF OUR LOVING MEDIATOR.

JESUS IS THE SON OF GOD!
GOD INCARNATE!
THE ETERNAL WORD!
THEREFORE,
NO PAIN,
NO SUFFERING,
NO PERSECUTION ENDURED,
NO TEMPTATION WRESTLED WITH,
NO SIN REPENTED OF,
CAN SEPARATE US FROM HIS LOVE AS MERCY,
SINCE HE IS OUR COMPASSIONATE LORD
AND MERCIFUL SAVIOR! +

+THE TRUTH OF THE MERCY OF THE LORD
IS THAT HIS TRANSCENDENT
AND ALMIGHTY POWER TO HEAL
WAS EQUALED
BY THE BEAUTY OF HIS DESIRE
TO TOUCH THE UNTOUCHABLE
AND REVEAL GOD'S LOVE FOR ALL. +

+BUT DUST IS MAN-
WITHOUT THE BREATHE OF GOD.
FOR CHRIST,
FROM SPIRIT
TO BLESSED AND VIRGIN WOMB,
DESCENDED UPON MAN IN UNSPEAKABLE MERCY...
AND ASCENDED WITH MAN
IN INDESCRIBABLE GLORY;
ELEVATING MAN
TO THE STATUS
OF BELOVED CHILD OF GOD. +

LENT

"ALTHOUGH I HAVE OFTEN ABANDONED YOU, O LORD, YOU HAVE NEVER ABANDONED ME. YOUR HAND OF LOVE IS ALWAYS OUTSTRETCHED TOWARDS ME, EVEN WHEN I STUBBORNLY LOOK THE OTHER WAY. AND YOUR GENTLE VOICE CONSTANTLY CALLS ME, EVEN WHEN I OBSTINATELY REFUSE TO LISTEN."
ST TERESA OF AVILA

"JESUS CRUCIFIED IS MY MODEL."
ST BERNADETTE SOUBIROUS

"NOTHING SHORT OF RELIGION WILL INSPIRE SELF-DETACHMENT. A MAN WILL REFUSE FOR THE SAKE OF HIMSELF AS A FINITE HUMAN ANIMAL TO UNDERGO THE DISCIPLINE TO WHICH HE WILL GLADLY SUBMIT, ONCE HE IS BROUGHT INTO CONSCIOUS RELATION WITH GOD. THIS IS THE *CRUX OF THE ENTIRE PROBLEM.* SEPARATE A MAN FROM HIS SPIRITUAL NATURE, LET HIM TALK OF HIMSELF MERELY AS A PHYSICAL ORGANISM, AND HIS RESPECT FOR HIMSELF WILL NOT BE SUCH AS TO INDUCE HIM TO MAKE A SACRIFICE FOR ANYTHING THAT HE CONSIDERS ESSENTIAL TO HIS MATERIAL WELL BEING OR ENJOYMENT. ONCE HE FACES GOD AND BECOMES AWARE OF THE DIVINE NATURE OF HIS PERSONALITY, HE WILL RECOGNIZE THAT MORE IS INVOLVED THAN WHAT CONSTITUTES HIS PHYSICAL BEING. HE WILL DO FOR HIMSELF AS RELATED TO GOD WHAT HE WOULD NOT DREAM OF DOING OTHERWISE."
ROM LANDAU
SEX, LIFE AND FAITH

"THE CROSS WILL NOT CRUSH YOU; IF ITS WEIGHT MAKES YOU STAGGER, ITS POWER WILL ALSO SUSTAIN YOU."
ST PIO OF PIETRELCINA

+TO REPENT IN THE DESERT OF FAITH,
SOLELY ON *GRACED* LOCUST AND HONEY
IS TO BECOME GREAT IN POVERTY.

BUT TO BECOME GREAT IN THE SPIRIT OF GOD
ONE MUST BE THE WILLING SERVANT,
THE HUMBLE HANDMAID,
BLIND IN FLESH,
YET ILLUMINATED IN SPIRIT
TO THE WILL OF THE LOVING GOD.

VIOLENCE IS THE WAY TO INNER PEACE!
THE CRUCIFIXION BEGINS WITHIN!
HEAVEN IS WON IN GRACED COOPERATION,
SUFFERED IN HUMBLE LOVE.

FOR THE CROSS IS A FIRE WHICH BURNS TO PERFECTION,
RESURRECTION THE REWARD OF LOVE.   +

+AS WE GROW IN GRACE,
WE MUST SEEK FOR DESERT SOLACE.

BEFORE THE COMING OF OUR RISEN LORD,
WE MUST SUBSIST ON LOCUST AND WILD HONEY,
PROCLAIMING AND RECLAIMING REPENTANCE WITHIN!

BUT THERE MUST COME A TIME
-AFTER MOUNTAINS ARE LAID LOW,
AND A HIGHWAY FOR THE LORD IS PAVED-
WHERE CHRIST APPEARS,
CLEANSING OUR LEPROSY,
CURING OUR BLINDNESS,
HEALING OUR DIS-EASE AND AFFLICTION,
TIME FOR CHRIST TO APPEAR WITHIN
AS LORD AND SAVIOR OF ALL!   +

+LORD, YOU WANT MY HEART. BUT MY HEART IS PERVERTED; IT
CANNOT BE TRUSTED. BY MY MASTER, WRITE YOUR LAW ON MY
HEART. TEACH ME TO LOVE YOUR RULE, YOUR TOUCH, YOUR
PRESENCE, YOUR DISCIPLINE, AND YOUR MERCY. +

+AS I TRAVEL THE BUMPY ROAD OF FAILURE,
AND THE ROCK STREWN PATH OF POVERTY AND OBSCURITY,
I PRAY FOR STRENGTH AND FOR TRUSTIN GOD'S GRACE
THROUGH GOD'S MERCY
-IN THE DRYNESS OF PRAYER, THE DARKNESS OF TRIBULATION,
AND THE COLDNESS OF THE WORLD-
FOR FAITH TO BELIEVE IN PROVIDENCE,
AND FOR HOPE TO SEEK AND FIND PURPOSE
IN A LIFE WHERE PAIN AND SUFFERING
OBSCURE A SENSE OF LOVE. +

+I AM VULNERABLE IN THIS DARK VALLEY,
A TARGET FOR LIGHTNING, FOOD FOR THE PREDATOR.

I NEED A STRONG ROCK,
AND A FORGIVING FORTRESS FOR MY SAFETY.

I AM A PEASANT IN A RICH LAND,
AND A FORIEGNER IN AN UNFRIENDLY COUNTRY.

HOPE HUNGERS FOR FAITH'S SAVIOR.
I WORSHIP IN THE FEAR AND TREMBLING OF A PRODIGAL DRIFTER.
WELCOME ME HOME LORD, PLEASE WELCOME ME HOME. +

+**LENT** IS THE OPENING OF ONES EYES
IN THE REVELATORY SPIRIT
OF ONES WRETCHEDNESS IN SIN
AND ONES UTTER NEED FOR A MERCIFUL SAVIOR.
LENT IS ALSO THE SEASON OF APPROPRIATE GUILT,
IN SEEING ONES SIN AS ABSOLUTE DISDAIN
FOR THE SACRIFICE IF UNCONDITIONAL LOVE.
LENT, HOWEVER, IS MORE THAN US!
LENT IS BLESSED AWAKENING IN THE GREATEST LOVE,
WITNESSED ON THE CROSS OF CHRIST,
LOVE WHICH CONQUERS PAIN AND DEATH,
TRANSFORMING THEM INTO INSTRUMENTS OF PERFECTION,
AS TOOLS OF DETACHMENT FROM PURVEYORS OF SIN,
LIBERATING US IN PEACE AND JOY AND HAPPINESS,
ETERNALLY REALIZED IN COMMUNION
WITH THE CHARITY OF CHRIST. +

+LENT IS BLESSED HUNGER, SWEET TEARS,
AND LOVELY LAMENTATIONS,
LAID DOWN HUMBLY AND CONTRITELY,
AT THE ALTAR OF SUCH A MERCIFUL LORD.

LENT IS THE PRAYER OF REPENTANCE,
A LOVE LETTER OF CONFESSION, AND A FORTY DAY VIGIL,
VIGILANT, HOPEFUL OF MERCY TO COME.

LENT IS SANCTIFICATION OF PRIORITIES,
THE RE-DEDICATION OF GOD'S TEMPLE,
THE REPENTANT ASSEMBLY OF THE COMMUNION,
THE RE-UNIFICATION OF THE BODY,
AND THE PRAYER OF THE FAITHFUL
IN THE FASTING OF FAITH
AND THE ALMSGIVING OF HOPE
IN THE PRAYERFUL LIFE
WHICH SPRINGS ETERNALLY STRONGER IN THE EUCHARISTIC LORD.

FOR LENT IS THE PREPARATION OF OUR HEARTS
AND THE ILLUMINATION OF OUR MINDS
FOR THE ARRIVAL OF THE CRUCIFIED SAVOIR OF OUR SOULS
IN THE NEW LIFE OF RESURRECTED CHARITY
FOUND IN THE EASTER SPIRIT
OF THE HEAD AND BODY OF THE RISEN AND VICTORIOUS CHRIST. +

+SINNER, SUSPECT IN TEMPTATION, SUSCEPTIBLE TO SIN IN HARD
TIMES, *AM I.*
SINNING *AM I,* IGNORING GRACE, FORGETTING PAST SALVATION
IN THE GREAT I AM.
BORN IN SIN, RAISED IN IMPERFECTION, AN ARTISAN OF AVARICE,
LANDLORD OF LUST, PURVEYOR OF PRIDE, *AM I.*
LOVE AS MERCY, ABUNDANT AND RELENTLESS IS THE GREAT I AM.
I AM, IN LOVE, TRANSFORMS *AM I* IN REPENTANCE, SANCTIFYING HIS
IMAGE AND LIKENESS, IN FAITH AND HOPE AND CHARITY RENEWED,
FOR THE SAKE OF THE LIFE OF THE BODY OF THE GREAT I AM.
OFFERING HIMSELF, PERFECTION, PERFECTLY IMMOLATED IN LOVE,
AM I CONSUMED IN THE CONSUMING OF HIS BODY AND BLOOD IN
FAITH. AND I BECOME PLEASING TO GOD, AS THE PERFECT BODY I
AM! +

+BAD MAN!
WIDE ROAD!
SELFISH ATTITUDE!
GOODNESS IS *THE OTHER WAY!*

GOOD MAN,
NARROW ROAD,
GOSPEL ATTITUDE!
CHRIST IS *THE ONLY SAFE WAY!*

THE WAY OF LIFE'S WATER.
THE WAY OF LIFE'S GRACE.
THE WAY OF LIVING BREAD.
JESUS IS THE WAY TO TRUTH,
AND WAY TO ETERNAL LIFE.

THE WAY OF THE WIDE AND SELFISH
IS THE VICE FILLED VOID OF DAMNATION;
BUT THE WAY OF THE NARROW AND THE SELFLESS
IS THE VIRTUE FILLED LIFE OF SALVATION! +

+TWO PATHS OF COVANENTAL PROMISE.
ONE OF LIFE AND BEATITUDE.
ONE OF DEATH AND ETERNAL DESPAIR.
ONE BORN IN FAITH, TRAVERSED IN HOPE,
AND EMPOWERED IN LOVE.
ANOTHER, A SELF IMPOSED BANISHMENT IN SIN,
A ROCKY TERRAIN IN DESPAIR AND DENIAL,
A BARREN WASTE LAND IN UNREPENTANT PRIDE.
FREE WILL IS WITHIN OUR POWER,
THE CHOICE IS OURS, GOD'S GRACE AWAITS!
LIFE AND LOVE
OR
DESTITUTION IN DEATH FROM SIN,
REPENT AND FOLLOW *THE WAY* OF THE SAVIOR!
FOLLOW THE NARROW TRAIL
OF THE BLOOD SHED OBEDIENTLY
FOR THE SALVATION OF ALL
WHO TRUST IN THE WORD,
THE FULFILLMENT OF ALL DIVINE PROMISES. +

+SIN REVEALED AND ACKNOWLEDGED
IS THE BEGINNING OF REPENTANT WISDOM.

REPENTANCE, TRULY CONTRITE,
THOUGH PAINFUL AND SEEMINGLY ISOLATED
IS THE JOY OF MERCY'S EYE.

FASTING AND PRAYER ARE SUBTLE ASSASSINS-
FOR THEY KILL OUR SIN AND OUR PRIDE-
IN THE STEALTH SPIRIT OF LOVE!

SINCERE WORSHIP,
THE TYPE OF DAILY CHARITY,
THIS MOVES GOD TO GRACE!

REND YOUR HEART,
POUR ASHES ON YOUR DESIRE,
PUT SACKCLOTH OVER YOUR PRIDE,
PRAISE GOD!

FREE THE SLAVE,
FORGIVE THE OPRESSOR,
SHARE GOD'S GIFTS...
THEN FAITH AND HOPE WILL SHINE IN LOVE! +

+**DROP** YOUR PRIDE, RAISE YOUR WEAKNESS,
TURN FROM THE WORLD, AND GLORY WILL SHINE FROM ON HIGH!
JUSTICE PRACTICED, MERCY DELIVERED,
COMPASSION ENFLESHED, TRUTH ENGENDERED,
THIS IS THE PATH TO JOY AND PEACE
AND PURPOSE AND INTEGRITY AND FULFILLMENT
AND EVERLASTING HAPPINESS.
GRACE WILL THEN DELIVER LIGHT FOR SIGHT,
DISCERNMENT IN DARKNESS, STRENGTH IN STRUGGLE,
AND LIVING WATER IN THE DESERT.
TEMPLES WILL BE REBUILT, BURNED BRIDGES REPAIRED, SOILED
SOULS SALVAGED!
GOD'S TIME WILL BE MANIFESTED, THE HOLY MASS REVERED,
THE BODY OF MERCY ILLUMINATED,
THE SPIRIT OF LOVE ENDEARED! +

EASTER

"GOD OUR FATHER,
TODAY IS THE DAY OF EASTER JOY.
THIS IS THE MORNING ON WHICH THE LORD
APPEARED TO MEN
WHO HAD BEGUN TO LOSE HOPE
AND OPENED THEIR EYES
TO WHAT THE SCRIPTURES FORETOLD:
THAT FIRST HE MUST DIE,
AND THEN HE WOULD RISE
AND ASCEND
INTO HIS FATHER'S GLORIOUS PRESENCE.
MAY THE RISEN LORD
BREATHE ON OUR MINDS
AND OPEN OUR EYES
THAT WE MAY KNOW HIM
IN THE BREAKING OF BREAD,
AND FOLLOW HIM
IN HIS RISEN LIFE.
GRANT THIS
THROUGH CHRIST OUR LORD.
AMEN.
EASTER SUNDAY/OPTIONAL OPENING PRAYER

"IN THE PSALMS IT SAYS, 'SING TO THE LORD A NEW SONG:
SING HIS PRAISE IN THE ASSEMBLY.' WE ARE URGED TO SING TO THE
LORD A NEW SONG. IT IS A NEW PERSON WHO KNOWS A NEW SONG.
BUT MAKE SURE THAT YOUR LIFE IS SINGING THE SAME TUNE AS
YOUR TONGUE. SING WITH YOUR VOICES, SING WITH YOUR HEARTS,
SING WITH YOUR LIPS, SING WITH YOUR LIVES...DO YOU WANT TO
SPEAK THE PRAISE OF GOD? THEN BE YOURSELVES WHAT YOU
SPEAK. IF YOU LEAD GOOD LIVES YOU ARE GOD'S PRAISES."
ST AUGUSTINE OF HIPPO

+I AM BOTH THE RICH MAN IN PURPLE,
AND LAZARUS!
-FESTERED WITH SORES, LICKED BY DOGS.

I AM BOTH TORMENTED IN COMFORT-
AND COMFORTED IN REJECTION AND DESOLATION.

AS I SIN THROUGH MY RICHES,
I REPENT IN THE SWEETNESS OF MY POVERTY.

FOR IN GAIN I FORGET THE DIVINE,
AS I DOUBT AND DESPAIR IN THE NATURAL.

BUT IN GRACE,
WITHIN MY LOSS, I HEAR A VOICE INSIDE,
A LOVING WHISPER,
AND I REMEMBER THE FACE OF MERCY.

AND IN FAITH AND HOPE,
BORN OF REPENTANCE GRACED,
ONCE AGAIN, THE SUPERNATURAL IS MINE! +

+OUR PRAYER AND OUR CHARITY
AND OUR ASCETICAL SACRIFICES
ARE NOT THE CROWN OF THORNS
TORMENTING THE BROW OF OUR BELOVED LORD.

THE THORN WHICH EVER PIERCES HIS SCALP,
DRAWING PRESCIOUS BLOOD,
-OF WHICH A DROP IS CAPABLE OF SAVING THE WORLD-
IS OUR PRIDE, AND OUR GREED, AND OUR RESISTANCE TO GRACE,
OUR VERY RELUCTANCE TO DESIRE *THY WILL BE DONE.*
THE CROSS AND THE TOMB WERE WILLINGLY ENDURED
IN UNFATHOMABLE LOVE FOR US!
AND THE RISEN LORD SEEKS
BUT FOR A PITTANCE OF FAITHFULNESS!
ALL HE DESIRES
-FROM OUR SMALL AND WEAK LITTLE HEART-
IS A LITTLE GIFT OF REPENTANCE AND THE PRAISE OF
THANKSGIVING. +

+THE PATH TO PARADISE
IS PAVED IN THE LIFE OF THE SAINT.

STUDY THEM WELL, IMMITATE THEM, AND LIVE!

THE ROAD WHICH LEADS TO REDEMPTION
IS FOUND SOLELY IN THE WAY OF THE CROSS!

STUDY IT WELL, ACCEPT IT, EMBRACE IT, AND LIVE!

FOR THE SAINT IS THE STUDENT OF THE CROSS,
AND THE LESSON LEARNED WELL
LEADS TO RESURRECTION AND ETERNAL LIFE
IN THE LOVING WISDOM OF GOD. +

+I AM RICH IN THE TREASURES OF THE MANY BLESSINGS
WHICH SURROUND ME, ENGULF ME, AND FORM ME,
IN SANCTIFYING GRACE,
AND FAITH, AND HOPE,
IN CHURCH AND SACRAMENT,
AND FAMILY AND HEALTH AND LIFE...
WHY WOULD I SEEK FOR A SIGN,
BUT IN WEAKNESS AND FEAR AND DOUBT AND SIN...
IN SEEKING FOR A SIGN, I WILL RECEIVE THE SIGN OF JONAH...
AND I WILL REPENT AND LIVE. +

+DEATH *WAS* THE ULTIMATE REASON FOR DESPAIR.
BUT CHRIST *LIVED* OUR EXPERIENCE!
TEMPTED, BUT WITHOUT SIN-SUFFERING, TO THE BITTER END-
DYING, PLACED IN A TOMB.
HAND IN HAND, COMPASSIONATELY,
THE GOD OF THE UNIVERSE, THE ALMIGHTY CREATOR,
ENTERED OUR FLESH AND WEAKNESS
AND WALKED OUR PATH-IN PERFECT LOVE-TO THE GRAVE...
AND BEYOND!
RISEN! HE HAS CONQUERED DEATH AND THE DEMONIC!
AND THE FATHER, IN THE SPIRIT,
HAS RE-CREATING MAN AND WOMAN
IN THE IMAGE OF THE RISEN LORD AND SAVIOR,
HIS BELOVED SON, JESUS OUR CHRIST. +

+THE FULLNESS OF THE MYSTERY OF GOD
BECOME MAN
IS THE LOVE WHICH GUSHED FORTH
FROM HIS PIERCED SIDE
OF THE CHRIST
IN LIVING WATER
AND SAVING BLOOD,
SEARING HIS BONES AS REFINING FIRE,
PURIFYING HUMAN NATURE
THROUGH HIS GLORIOUS PASSION,
PASSED ONTO HIS FAITHFUL DISCIPLES
-THROUGH FAITH AND HOPE IN GRACE-
ON LIFE'S PURGATIVE PASCHAL PATH,
WHICH LEADS TO LOVE
IN RESURRECTION AND ETERNAL LIFE. +

+PRAY TO THE EAST
FOR THE RISE OF THE SON,
FOR THE PURIFYING OF THE COSMOS,
AND THE VICTORY OF THE CROSS;
UNITED IN THE INCARNATION OF CREATOR
IN CREATION;
IN THE GOSPEL OF TRUTH AND LIFE,
IN THE PASSION OF MERCY IN FORGIVENESS,
IN THE RESURRECTION OF ETERNAL LOVE,
IN THE ASCENSION OF THE MEDIATOR OF ALL GRACE,
IN THE COMING OF THE PENTECOSTAL SPIRIT,
IN THE BIRTH OF HOLY MOTHER CHURCH,
IN THE PROMISE TO COME,
OF THE NEW HEAVEN AND THE NEW EARTH,
IN THE SPIRIT OF THE LOVE
BETWEEN THE FATHER AND THE RISEN SON. +

+WHAT GOD IN THE HISTORY OF GODS
HAS LAID DOWN HIS LIFE FOR A CREATURE?
IF THERE EVER WERE A GOD TO DO SO,
DID THIS GOD
RISE
LIKE THE PHOENIX,
ELEVATING THE CREATURE TO GOD...FOR LOVE? +

+JESUS INVITES US TO JOIN THE RANKS OF THE LIVING,
TO *CROSS-OVER TO LIFE.*

BUT THE CROSS-OVER, THE WAY TO *HIS* LIFE,
INVOLVES DENYING, DETACHING, DEFYING, AND ABANDONING
ALL THAT IS DETESTABLE AND DELECTABLE
IN THE PASSIONS AND THE PLEASURES OF *OUR* LIFE.

AND THIS DYING TO SELF, IN PASCHAL PASSION RENEWAL-
IS TRULY WON IN STORM AND TORMENT AND GRACE!

AND WHEN DARKNESS AND SUFFERING
HOVER OVER US IN FEAR AND DESPAIR,
WE MUST SEEK THE SIMPLE WHISPER OF THE SPIRIT WITHIN US.

CRYING FOR MERCY AND SALVATION,
IN THE SEA OF WAYWARD PILGRIMAGE,
WE WILL FIND CHRIST STRONG AMONG US!
AND HE WILL REBUKE OUR DOUBT AND OUR DESPAIR
IN THE CALMING GRACE OF FORGIVENESS,
AND OUR STORMS WILL WHIMPER IN THE FACE OF LOVE;
THUS BECOMING ACTIVE WAVES FOR OUR SALVATION. +

+**RISEN** JESUS,
RESCUE ME, SAVE ME IN YOUR SERENE SANITY,
FROM THE INSANITY OF MY WILD PASSIONS.
AND TRANQUIL IN HOPE,
SERENE IN FAITH, I WILL PROVE ROCK STEADY
ON THE ROCK OF YOUR LOVE
IN WITNESS TO MERCY AS THE BREATHE OF LIFE
AND THE WAY TO SALVATION.
UNCOVER ME FROM THE SHELTER OF MY COWARDICE,
REVEAL ME TO ME, IN THE LIGHT OF TRUTH.
TRANSFORM ME! TEACH ME! LET ME LIGHT YOUR WAY!
LET GOSPEL BECOME HERITAGE, SALVATION MY LANGUAGE,
CHRIST MY LIFE AND LOVE!
SALVATION MY CHRIST! MY WORSHIP THE CROSS!
MERCY MY FAITH AND HOPE!
AND LOVE, THIS IS YOU! LOVE DESCENDING TO ME.
LOVE, MY LORD, MY LOVER, MY LIFE, LOVE INCARNATE ME! +

+WHEN THE SPIRIT OF THE RISEN LORD ENTERS OUR TEMPLE,
THE INNER SANCTUARY OF OUR HEART,
WILL HE FIND TRUE DEVOTION,
OR WILL HE FIND GREED AND COVETOUSNESS AND DECEIT AND
ENVY AND SLAVERY AND ALL SORTS OF FLESHLY, TEMPORAL, AND
MATERIAL GOODS?

IF SO,
WILL WE REPENT UPON HIS MERCIFUL IMPULSE?
WILL WE NOT ALLOW THE CHRIST TO DRIVE OUT OUR BEASTS,
TURN OVER OUR TABLES,
WHIP OUR PRIDE,
AND TOSS OUR TREASURE ASIDE?

WILL WE NOT THEN *PRAISE* GOD
IN THE RAZING OF OUR TEMPLE
-AND AFTER THREE DAYS OF PASCHAL PURGATION-
IN THE RAISING-*ANEW*-OF CHRIST IN US? +

+SWEET DAY!
SWEET HOPE!
SWEET CHANCE!
ANOTHER OPPORTUNITY TO GRASP THE GIFT OF LIFE,
THE BEAUTY OF CREATION,
AND THE UNFATHOMABLE REALITY
OF GOD ALMIGHTY AS MY LOVING FATHER! +

+JESUS IS THE SON OF FULFILLMENT,
THE SON OF PROMISE.
JESUS IS THE SON OF DESERT FAITH,
THE SON OF STORM SURVIVED HOPE.
JESUS IS THE SON OF NOBLES AND BASTARDS AND SLAVES!
JESUS IS THE SON OF THE PERSEVERING,
THE SON OF THE VIGILANT,
THE SON OF THE *HUMBLE* HANDMAID!
JESUS IS THE SON OF REDEMPTION,
THE SON OF GOD, *THE SON OF MAN,* THE SON WHO ROSE,
AND RISES IN BREAD AND WINE,
RISING FROM THE EAST AS VICTORIOUS LORD,
CONQUERER OF SIN AND DEATH! +

+THE LOVE OF GOD IS NOT MERE SOFT SENTIMENT,
BUT UNBREAKABLE WILL!

AS MAN IS WEAK,
GOD IS STRONG!
AS MAN IS FORGETFUL,
GOD IS EVER FAITHFUL!
AS MAN IS PREDICTABLE,
GOD IS EVER SURPRISING...
AND WONDERFULLY UNFATHOMABLE!
AS MAN IS FALLEN,
CHRIST HAS RISEN!
FOR FAITH AND HOPE ARE GOD'S GIFT IN LOVE!
THE COMPASS *ON THE WAY!*
LED BY THE SPIRIT,
WE WILL FINALLY FIND *TRUE* HOME! +

+THE QUESTION OF THE RESURRECTION IS, RATHER,
A QUESTION OF WHETHER JESUS IS TRULY THE BREAD OF LIFE.

FOR JUDAS,
AND THE JUDAS OF OUR FALLEN NATURE,
THIS CLAIM, WHICH LIVES IN SPRIT AND FAITH,
TEMPTS AND TWISTS BETRAYAL FROM WITHIN.

YET FOR PETER, AND THE STRUGGLING PETER WITHIN,
THIS CLAIM IS FROM THE LIPS OF THE BELOVED,
"THE SON OF THE LIVING GOD."
THESE WORDS OF FAITH
ARE THE ONLY TRUE SOURCE OF HOPE
AND THE ONLY HEARTFELT PRESENCE OF SPIRIT AND LIFE.

FOR THE JUDAS IN US MUST DIE,
AND THE PETER IN US,
REPENTING IN GRACE,
MUST DAILY OPEN OURSELVES
TO THE SPIRIT OF WISDOM AND COURAGE,
NEVER DENYING THE TORCH OF THE TRUE LIGHT,
CARRYING THE BEAM OF BELOVED BEATITUDE
IN THE GREAT CROSS OF CHRIST. +

THE SAINTS

"THE POPULAR IDEA IS THAT A SAINT IS A PERSON WHO NEVER DOES ANYTHING WRONG, IS GOOD AND PURE TO THE CORE, AND LIVES THE PERFECT LIFE OF HOLINESS, IS NOT SUPPORTED BY REALITY. SAINTS ARE ENTIRELY HUMAN. WE PUT THEM IN STAINED GLASS WINDOWS, CARVE STATUES OF THEM, AND ERECT CHURCHES IN THEIR NAMES. WE HAVE SOUGHT EVERY WAY POSSIBLE TO ISOLATE THEM FROM OURSELVES AND MAKE THEM SOMETHING OTHER THAN WE ARE. WE SAY TO OURSELVES, 'THEY DID NOT KNOW THE PRESSURES WE KNOW OR EXPERIENCE THE STRESSES OF EVERYDAY LIFE. THEY ARE SIMPLY TOO DISTANT FROM OUR CONCERNS TO HAVE ANY KINSHIP WITH US.' WE PUSH THE SAINTS AS FAR FROM US AS WE CAN PLACE THEM. THAT WAY, WE DO NOT HAVE TO ASPIRE TO BE WHAT THEY ARE. WE PUSH THEIR EXAMPLE AWAY, PROTESTING, 'I'M NO SAINT,' BUT YET WE ARE TRAVELING THE SAME PATH...*ALBAN BUTLER* DECLARED, 'THE SAINTS ARE A CLOUD OF WITNESS OVER OUR HEAD, SHOWING US THAT A LIFE OF CHRISTIAN PERFECTION IS NOT IMPOSSIBLE.' THE PERFECTION THEY SHOW US IS FAR FROM BEING SPOTLESS OR INSULATED FROM REAL LIFE. WHEN WE REALIZE THIS, WE WILL SEE THE POSSIBILITIES FOR OURSELVES."
BERNARD BANGLEY
BUTLER'S LIVES OF THE SAINTS

"MARY BENEFITED FIRST OF ALL AND UNIQUELY FROM CHRIST'S VICTORY OVER SIN: SHE WAS PRESERVED FROM ALL STAIN OF ORIGINAL SIN AND BY A SPECIAL GRACE OF GOD COMMITTED NO SIN OF ANY KIND DURING HER WHOLE EARTHLY LIFE."
CATECHISM OF THE CATHOLIC CHURCH: 411

+SAINTS AND CHERUBS,
CHILDREN HELD IN LOVE
WITHIN THE MIGHTY ARMS OF MERCY,
WITNESS TO YOUR MYSTERIOUS WORKS OF JUSTICE
ON THE FACE OF THE EARTH.

FOR THEY VIEW THE STRUGGLES
AND THE SINS OF THEIR SIBLINGS,
AND THEY WITNESS THE GRACE AND THE POWER
OF THEIR FATHER,
IN THE SPIRIT WHICH RECONCILES GOD AND MAN
IN THE LOVE OF THE CHRIST ON THE CROSS,
IN THE TOMB,
AND IN HIS RISING!

FOR GOD BECAME MAN
SO THAT MAN MAY JOIN GOD
IN THE PERFECT LIFE OF LOVE. +

+THE DOUBT OF ST THOMAS
IS NOT FAR FROM THE DOUBTS OF OUR HEART.

FOR CHRIST SEEMS AS A GHOST
FOR VERY MANY OF US
IN TIMES OF TRIAL AND DRYNESS AND UNENDING PAIN.

SURELY WE WOULD OFFER A FISH
ONLY TO TOUCH HIS WOUNDS AND FEEL HIS PRESENCE.

THAT IS WHY WE MUST
REMAIN IN TOUCH WITH OUR SINFULNESS,
REMAIN IN TOUCH WITH OUR NEIGHBOR,
AND REMAIN IN TOUCH WITH THE SACRAMENTS,
FOR CHRIST HAS LEFT MERCY AND CHARITY AND GRACE,
SO THAT WE MAY ALSO TOUCH THE RISEN CRUCIFIED SAVIOR. +

+MARY,
PROPHETIC SOUL AND PRAISING SPIRIT, HUMBLE AND BLESSED,
WISE IN THE WAYS OF GOD, FULL OF LOVE AND GRACE,
PRAY FOR US SINNERS. +

+WHEN ST STEPHEN IS STONED
AND THE CHURCH BOLTS FOR SAFETY,
AN ALARM IS SET, IN THE SAINT AND MARTYR,
TO WITNESS!

PERSECUTION, AFTER ALL IS SAID AND DONE,
IS THE HEROIC TIME OF CHOICE,
WHERE ST PHILIP EVANGELIZES,
AND THE APOSTLES STAND THEIR GROUND,
AND THE BLOOD OF THE MARTYRS WORKS
AS THE "SEED" OF "THE NEW EVANGELIZATION"
IN THE SPIRIT OF THE RISEN CHRIST. +

+ST JOSEPH IS A MODEL OF FAITH,
A BEACON OF HOPE,
AND A CHANNEL OF LOVE FOR ALL HUSBANDS,
STRUGGLING IN ANONIMITY,
BATTLING TEMPTATION TO INFIDELITY,
AND FIGHTING FOR FAITH IN HOPE
AS FATHERS WHO LOVE THEIR CHILDREN
-SO INTENSELY-
AS TO MAKE THEIR LIFE WORK
THE GIFT OF THEIR FAITH, THEIR HOPE,
AND THEIR LOVE,
IMPLANTED IN THE HEARTS OF THEIR CHILDREN
UNTIL THE OFFERING OF THEIR LAST DYING BREATHE.

THIS IS THE DIVINE GIFT
OF THE SPIRIT IN ST JOSEPH THE WORKER. +

+MARY,
TEACH ME HUMILITY…
POWERFUL HUMILITY,
FAITHFUL HUMILITY,
HOPEFUL HUMILITY,
LOVING HUMILITY,
LIFE *GIVING* HUMILITY.

DEAR HANDMAID,
TEACH ME TO MAGNIFY THE LORD! +

+LIKE SAUL,
TRUE CONVERSION NEEDS THE SUPPORT AND WITNESS
OF A ST BARNABAS.

MANY A SINNER, STRUGGLING IN GRACE,
ON GOD'S TIME,
HAS TURNED THE CORNER,
RODE THE WIND OF THE VICTORIOUS SPIRIT,
IN NEW FOUND FAITH,
EXPRESSED IN SANCTITY,
ONLY TO MELT WITH THE DOUBT AND CRITICISM
OF THE VICTIMS OF THEIR PAST SIN.

GLORIOUS CONSEQUENCES! ALLELUIA!
HUMBLE REPARATIONS IN GRACE! ALLELUIA!
PRUNING PURGATION
IN THE DISCERNMENT OF THE CHURCH! ALLELUIA!

YET SET FREE IN THE MERCY OF THE LORD,
THE BODY MUST FOLLOW IN THE SPIRIT OF RECONCILIATION-
BETWEEN REPENTANT SINNER AND MERCIFUL SAVIOR. +

+ ST PAUL IS THE ZEALOUS FOOL OF THE LORD!

HAVING TAKEN AN ALMIGHTY RIGHT TO THE CHIN,
SO POWERFUL AS TO KNOCK HIM FAITHFUL,
HOW COULD THE WORLD BE SO FOOLISH
AS TO THINK THAT
STONING, FLOGGING, JAILING, ACCUSING, SHIPWRECKS, OPPOSITION,
PERSECUTION, DEPRIVATION,
AND THE SWORD OF BEHEADING
COULD THWART THE SPIRIT IN THIS HOLY REBEL?

MAY WE BE SO BLESSED AS TO GAIN THIS REBELLIOUS SPIRIT! +

+OH ST ELIZABETH,
WIFE OF ZECHARIAH,
MOTHER OF THE BAPTIST,
HOW WISE YOU WERE FOR PRAISING GOD'S WORK
IN THE PERFECT MOTHERHOOD OF MARY. +

+DEAR ST PAUL,

AT TIMES I WORSHIP AN UNKNOWN GOD. THIS UNKNOWING IS DUE
TO MY LACK OF LOVE AND, HENCE, MY LACK OF LOVE'S
UNDERSTANDING. MY WEAKNESS, FURTHERMORE, IS IN SITTING WITH
THE WORLD, WITH INTELLECTUALS AND PHILOSOPHERS, MOCKING
THE SUPERNATURAL OF GOD. MOCKING THE RESURRECTION! I
SUSPECT SOME OF THEM MOCK, NOT FROM INTELLECTUAL
ENLIGHTENMENT AND SCIENTIFIC AND PHILOSOPHICAL CONQUEST,
BUT RATHER, LIKE ME, FROM FEAR OF CONVICTION, FROM A
COWARDLY HEART WOUNDED IN SIN, AND A MENTAL DULLNESS
FROM A CONSCIENCE IN A COMA, AND A MIND SULLIED IN LIES. ST
PAUL, PLEASE *DO* COME AND SPEAK AGAIN OF THE RESURRECTION
OF THE CHRIST.
SINCERELY,
A MAN OF ATHENS +

+ ABRAHAM ENTERED THE FIRES
OF WHAT HE THOUGHT WAS HELL.

LEADING ISAAC TO HIS DEATH,
ABRAHAM WAS TRULY IN THE PURGATIVE FIRE OF GOD'S LOVE.

ONLY WITH TRUST,
AND FAITH FILLED COURAGE,
WAS ABRAHAM REWARDED WITH THE RAM IN THE THORNS.

AND WE, IN FAITH FILLED TRUST,
ARE SAVED BY THE LAMB WEARING THORNS! +

+JOHN PAUL THE GREAT, WITH A MESSAGE NEVER TOO LATE,
DECLARES TO ME, THAT ON THAT TREE,
CHRIST FULLY REALIZED
THAT UNIQUE GIFT OF LIFE THAT IS ME! +

+MARY, PERFECTED DAUGHTER OF THE FATHER,
MOTHER OF GOD THE SON, BRIDE OF THE HOLY SPIRIT,
TAKE ME, AS YOU TOOK ST JOHN AS YOUR SON...
ASSUMED-BE MY HEAVENLY MEDIATRIX,
MOTHER, BE MY HOPE! +

+MARY DID NOT DWELL ON THE CLOUDY SKY;
BUT TRUSTED IN THE SON BEHIND IT!
MARY COULD NOT FORSEE EVERY CURVE IN THE ROAD,
BUT WALKED IN HOPE,
TOWARD THE EASTERN SON-RISE!
MARY COULD NOT FULLY ENVELOPE HER THOUGHT
AND UNDERSTANDING
AROUND THE MIRACLE IN HER WOMB,
BUT ADORED THIS CHILD IN THE MYSTERY OF FAITH,
REVEALED IN GOD AMONG US! +

AS MARY WAS PROMISED THE INDWELLING CHRIST,
SO ARE WE.
AS MARY WAS THE HANDMAID OF THE LORD,
FAITHFUL TO THE CROSS AND BEYOND,
SO MUST WE.
AS MARY INTERCEDES AND AIDS THE ONE MEDIATOR
BETWEEN HUMANITY AND THE FATHER,
SO MUST WE.
AS MARY IS THE MOON OF HOPE,
WHO REFLECTS THE SON OF LOVE,
ON A DARK WORLD WITHOUT FAITH,
FAITHFULLY, SO MUST WE! +

+A SAINT IS FIRST AND FOREMOST A HUMAN BEING.
A SAINT IS SURELY AN ORIGINAL SINNER,
AND ONE WHO STRUGGLES WITH TEMPTATION
EACH AND EVERY DAY.
MANY SAINTS ARE ORDINARY,
UNSPECTACULAR BY HUMAN STANDARDS,
AND QUITE OFTEN OBSCURE
TO THE NAKED HUMAN JUDGMENT.
YET A SAINT IS A REPENTANT SOUL,
A HUMBLE AND OBEDIENT SPIRIT,
A MASTER OF ACQUIESCENCE
TO THE SPIRIT OF GOD'S WILL IN THEIR LIFE.
FINALLY, A SAINT BEARS THEIR CROSS,
DESCENDS IN DEATH TO SELF,
RISING IN DEVOUT INTIMACY
WITH THE LORD OF THEIR NEW FOUND LIFE. +

+FATHER ABRAHAM, FATHER ISAAC, FATHER JACOB,
PLEASE PRAY FOR MY FAMILY,
PRAY FOR THE CATHOLIC CHURCH,
PRAY FOR THE JEWISH PEOPLE,
FOR ALL TRULY FAITHFUL, SEARCHING FOR THE ONE TRUE GOD.

PRAY FOR GOD'S MERCY-THE WORK OF THE SPIRIT,
AND THE MISSION OF THE MESSIAH,
IN THE CHURCH,
FOR THE WORLD,
TODAY.
AMEN. +

+WE ARE ALL 'LEVI' AT ONE TIME OR ANOTHER.
SINNERS WE ARE!
BUT IN THE MIDST OF WHAT APPEARS TO BE
SECRET AND ISOLATED ACTIVITY,
CHRIST JESUS TAKES NOTICE.

AND IF WE OPEN OUR EYES, AND OUR HEART,
HE INVITES US TO *FOLLOW HIM.*

IN TURN, WE ARE TO INVITE SINNERS LIKE US
TO JOIN IN HIS PRESENCE IN MERCY AND LOVE. +

+ESTHER'S PRAYER
OF REPENTANCE,
CONTRITION,
AND SUPPLICATION
FOR FORTITUDE
AND VIRTUE,
HAS BEEN ECHOED THROUGH THE PROPHETS,
ENLIVENED AND DIVINIZED IN THE INCARNATION OF CHRIST,
EMBLAZENED IN THE PERFECT WORK OF GOD IN MARY,
AND EMBRACED BY CENTURIES OF SAINTS,
WHO CRY IN FAITH AND HOPE FOR THE LOVE OF GOD
TO REFORM AND TRANSFORM THE BELOVED BODY OF CHRIST
IN FAITHFUL LOVE FOR HER HEAD,
HER CHRIST,
AND HER LIFE. +

+AS BLESSED MOSES LIFTED THE PIERCED ONE IN THE DESERT,
SO TOO DID GOD LIFT THE PIERCED ONE ON THE CROSS.

FOR GOD HAS OFFERED US THE BEST OF HIS LOVE IN CHRIST
FOR OUR REDEMPTION
-IN LIVING FAITH-
TO ILLUMINATE GOODNESS
AND ROOT OUT THE DARKNESS
IN THE LIGHT OF THE LOVE,
WHICH BURNS IN GRACE,
AND FLOWS FROM GOD'S MOST SACRED HEART,
IN CHRIST JESUS OUR LORD. +

+THE GABRIEL OF GOD'S MERCY IS CALLING US,
HIS HIGHLY FAVORED, TO RECEIVE THE FULLNESS OF GOD'S GRACE,
IN ORDER TO BRING FORTH IN THE RICH AND PREGNANT FIAT
OF THE BLESSED VIRGIN MARY
THE BIRTH OF THE ANOINTED ONE WITHIN OUR LIVES.

GOD SO LOVES US
THAT HE HAS GIVEN HIS LIFE
SO THAT WE MIGHT DIE TO SIN
-DEFINITIVELY-
AND LIVE IN HIM THROUGH THE CROSS AND RESURRECTION
OF HIS SON
IN THE SPIRIT OF COMMUNION,
BROUGHT FORTH IN THE BAPTISM OF LIFE,
FLOWING FROM THE SIDE OF THE CRUCIFIED SAVIOR. +

+MARY OF MAGDALA,
SPARK OF SPECULATION,
MYSTERY AND UNCERTAINTY SHROUD YOUR REPUTATION,
BUT WHAT IS CERTAIN
-SOLID AS TRADITION,
TRUSTWORTHY AS SCRIPTURE-
IS SEVEN DEMONS GONE
AND A LIFE OF SERVICE TO THE LORD.
THAT IS WHY YOU, MARY, ARE ST MARY OF MAGDALA...
AND FROM YOUR HEAVENLY PERSPECTIVE,
NO ARROW OF ACCUSATION CAN HARM YOU. +

+ST PIO OF PIETRELCINA,
PLEASE PRAY FOR AN INCREASE OF CHARITY,
COMPASSION,
AND FORGIVENESS
IN MY HEART,
AND IN THE LIFE OF MY FAMILY,
AND IN ALL FAMILIES,
SO THAT ALL PEOPLE
MAY CATCH A GLIMPSE OF TRINITARIAN LOVE,
REFLECTED SO BEAUTIFULLY
IN THE LOVE OF THE NUCLEAR HUMAN FAMILY,
FATHER, MOTHER, AND CHILDREN.
AMEN. +

+MARTHA,
A HURRICANE,
A SPECTACLE IN MOTION,
MOVING TO AND FRO
IN PLAN AND VISION,
ENDING IN THE BITTER REALIZATION
OF FUTILITY IN HUMAN EFFORT ALONE.

MARY,
A GENTLE BREEZE,
SOFT AND SUBTLE,
REFRESHING AND DELIGHTFUL,
FOCUSED ON THE SON,
REAPING THE BENEFITS OF GRACE,
THROUGH EVAPORATION OF PRIDE
IN THE SPIRIT OF CONTEMPLATION. +

+SAINTS ARE BUTTERFLIES.
METAMORPHOSIS IS CHANGE IN GRACE.
THE LORD TOUCHES THE WORM IN SIN,
THE COCOON OF PRIDE IS RENT IN MERCY.
WINGS BORN OF REPENTANCE
GROW STRONG IN FAITH, HOPE AND LOVE.
SAINTS, REMEMBERING THEIR WORMY WEAKNESS,
RELY ON THE SPIRITED WIND
FOR FLIGHT IN THE LOVE WHICH NEVER ENDS. +

+LIKE ST PETER,
WE MAY SPEAK OF JESUS IN ONE BREATHE AS THE CHRIST,
AND IN THE NEXT BE SEDUCED TO SPEAK AS SATAN.

FOR WE ARE BUT FLESH AND BLOOD,
SOUL AND SPIRIT.
AND, MORE THAN WE WOULD LIKE TO ADMIT,
EVER SO RELIANT ON GRACE
FOR STRENGTH AND WISDOM
IN OUR PILGRIMAGE IN TRUTH.

YET, STUMBLE AS WE MAY,
THE WAY OF THE PASCHAL PILGRIM
IS ALREADY PAVED WITH VICTORY,
WON, IN THE FALLS AND THE RISING OF THE CHRIST. +

+SIMEON THE PROPHET KNEW WHO HE WAS...
THE HOLY SPIRIT KNEW WHO HE WAS...
JOHN THE BAPTIST KNEW WHO HE WAS...
THE DEMONS HE EXORCISED CERTAINLY KNEW WHO HE WAS...
AND GOD THE FATHER
GRACED ST PETER
WITH KNOWLEDGE TO PROCLAIM
JESUS AS THE CHRIST.

THIS SHOULD PUT TO REST
ALL CURRENT FOOLISH SPECULATION
CONCERNING THE CONFUSION OF THE CHRIST,
IN HIS STRUGGLE FOR SELF IDENTITY,
AS TO WHOM HE REALLY WAS. +

+THE BAPTIST WAS WILD AND POOR.
THE NAZARENE WAS NEVER THE CAESAR.
THE MARTYRS WERE TORN ASUNDER.
THE MAN OF ASSISI WORE ALL THAT HE OWNED.
THE PRIEST OF THE IMMACULATTA DIED A PRISON MARTYR.
THE GREAT ONE OF PIETRELCINA WITNESSED IN PIERCED PAIN.
WRINKLED MOTHER CALCUTTA WAS SMOOTH COMPASSION.
BENT AND WEAK, KAROL THE GREAT WITNESSED TO STRENGTH.
GOD'S MASTERPIECES ARE A PARADOX IN BEAUTY. +

+THE FAILURES OF ST PETER
AND THE PATIENCE OF THE LORD
-IN GRACE AND IN SPIRIT,
IN REPENTANCE AND PENTECOSTAL COURAGE,
IN THE TRANSFORMATION OF A BRASH FISHERMAN
INTO A COURAGEOUS DISCIPLE,
A DETERMINED FIRST POPE,
AND A WILLING MARTYR-
BRINGS CONSOLATION IN MY WEAKNESS,
AND HOPE IN THE LORD'S PATIENCE FOR ME,
IN FAITH THAT HIS LOVE WILL TRANSFORM ME
FROM BRASH MAN
TO COURAGEOUS DISCIPLE,
DETERMINED AND WILLING
TO FOLLOW THE WILL OF THE FATHER
IN THE SPIRIT OF SAINTLY GLORY
IN THE CHURCH OF ST PETER
ON THE WAY OF HIS LORD AND SAVIOR JESUS CHRIST. +

+DAVID
WAS THE TASTE OF RICHNESS,
AND SWEETNESS TO THE LORD.
HE WON FAVOR IN FIDELITY,
AND REGAINED IT IN ZEALOUS REPENTANCE.
SMALL IN STATURE,
LARGE IN FEAR OF GOD,
DAVID WAS THE BLESSED GIANT KILLER.
IN HUMBLE TRUST,
DAVID CONQUERED GOLIATH PRIDE!
FOR DAVID'S STRENGTH WAS ALWAYS GOD'S GOOD POWER.
VICTORY FOR DAVID
WAS VICTORY FOR GOD'S PEOPLE.
IF DAVID SLAYED TEN,
TENFOLD IN CREDIT WAS GIVEN TO HIM!
FOR FIERCE WAS THE HEART OF GOD'S WARRIOR!
AND MANY A FOE FELL.
FOR IN ALL THAT DAVID DID,
AND IN ALL THAT DAVID SAID,
HIS SONG, HIS PSALM, HIS HEART ALWAYS SANG:
PRAISE BE TO GOD! +

PURGATIVE LOVE

"'SHE IS IN GOD'S HANDS.' THAT GAINS A NEW ENERGY WHEN I THINK OF HER AS A SWORD. PERHAPS THE EARTHLY LIFE I SHARED WITH HER WAS ONLY PART OF THE TEMPERING. NOW PERHAPS HE GRASPS THE HILT; WEIGHTS THE NEW WEAPON; MAKES LIGHTNING WITH IT IN THE AIR. 'A RIGHT JERUSALEM BLADE.'"
C.S. LEWIS
A GRIEF OBSERVED

"ONLY ONE THING IN LIFE IS GUARANTEED: NOT HAPPINESS, NOT THE PURSUIT OF HAPPINESS, NOT LIBERTY, NOT EVEN LIFE. THE ONLY THING WE ARE ABSOLUTELY GUARANTEED IS THE ONLY THING WE ABSOLUTELY NEED: GOD. AND WISDOM CONSISTS ESSENTIALLY IN ABSOLUTELY WANTING THAT WHICH WE ABSOLUTELY NEED, IN CONFORMING OUR WANTS TO REALITY. JOB IS INCOMPARABLY WISER THAN ECCLESIASTES BECAUSE OF THAT. WE MUST IDENTIFY WITH JOB, NOT ECCLESIASTES, FOR ECCLESIASTES' VANITY IS THE PHILOSOPHY OF HELL, WHILE JOB'S SEARCH IS THE PHILOSOPHY OF PURGATORY, AND EVERYONE GRADUATES FROM THE UNIVERSITY OF PURGATORY WITH HONORS INTO HEAVEN."
PETER KREEFT
THREE PHILOSOPHIES OF LIFE

"JUST AS EASTER IS MEANINGLESS WITHOUT CALVARY, CALVARY IS INCOMPREHENSIBLE WITHOUT THE VICTORY OF THE EMPTY TOMB."
BENEDICT J. GROESCHEL, C.F.R.
ARISE FROM DARKNESS

+ASK FOR NOTHING BUT THE WISDOM TO CHOOSE
BETWEEN GOOD AND EVIL,
AND ALL TRUE PATHS OF SPIRITUAL PROSPERITY
WILL BE OPEN TO YOU.

FOR THE GIFT OF WISDOM
IS THE SIGHT OF TRUE FAITH,
AND THE STAMINA OF TRUE HOPE,
WHICH SEEKS TO DISCERN ALL PATHS
IN LIGHT OF THE GOOD NEWS OF CHRIST
ON *THE WAY* OF GOD'S UNCONDITIONAL LOVE.

AND TWO PATHS YOU *WILL* APPROACH.
THE WAY OF THE CROSS...AND THE WAY OF COMFORT.
THE FORMER WILL SCOURGE YOU IN PREPARATORY LIFE.
THE LATTER WILL STROKE
YOU IN SOOTHING AND SENSUOUS DEATH.

THE FORMER BUILDS IN VIRTUE AND CHARACTER.
THE LATTER DEFORMS IN VICE AND DECEPTION.
THE FORMER RESURRECTS IN THE IMAGE OF CHRIST.
THE LATTER CASTS DOWN IN THE SHAME OF FALLEN ANGELS. +

+PURITY IS FOUND IN CONSTANT CONTACT
    WITH ITS PURE AND SIMPLE SOURCE.
FIDELITY IS FOUND IN THE CONSTANT EXERCISE
OF *THE WAY* OF THE GIVER OF THE LAW.
OBEDIENCE IS FOUND IN CONSTANT PRAYER,
IN TOUCH WITH THE INDWELLING SPIRIT,
WHO PERSEVERES IN LOVE.
HOLY IS OUR GOD!
HOLINESS IS WHOLLY FOUND IN HIM!
AS THE WORD HAS SPOKEN HIS WORD,
SO MUST WE SPEAK HIS WORD
IN ACT AND WORD IN CHARITY.
JOY IS MY REWARD FOR SUFFERING IN FAITH,
AND HEALING IN HOPE,
AND SHARING IN LOVE,
WHICH PRECEDES ME.
FOR GOD IS MY ALL IN ALL! +

+VIRTUE MELTS AWAY ALL OBSTACLES
TO TRUE AND LASTING HAPPINESS.
FAITH PAVES NEW ROADS
TO PEACE AND JOY ETERNAL.

BUT DOUBT AND DESPAIR LEAD TO DEMONS WHO DEAL VICE,
AND ALL ROADS PAVED WITH OBSTACLES LEAD TO HELL!

FOR THE BALANCE OF THE CROSS,
SKYWARD IN WORSHIP AND GRACE,
OUTSTRETCHED IN CHARITY AND FORGIVENESS,
IS ALSO THE BALANCE OF JUSTICE AND MERCY,
WHERE VERTICALLY WE CHOOSE BETWEEN GOD AND SELF,
AND HORIZONTALLY WE ENACT *OUR CHOICE* ON OUR FAMILY. +

+THE GARMENT OF APPARENT WHOLENESS
OF WHICH I WEAR EACH DAY
IS MADE OF THE FLIMSY MATERIAL
OF VANITY AND SIN.

I PARADE AS RULER OF MY DOMAIN,
UNKNOWINGLY NOT IN CONTROL,
EVEN OF MY OWN LIFE.

AND I SIT ON THE THRONE
OF MY EARTHLY EFFORTS AND WORLDLY IDEALS,
ONLY TO HEAR OF MY FALL FROM AFAR.

FOR MY LOT HAS BEEN STRIPPED FROM MY HANDS.
THE GARMENT, YOU SEE, WAS NOT OF MY MAKING,
BUT A GIFT FROM GREATNESS ABOVE.
AND ALL THE TEARS IT HAS TAKEN
ARE ALL OF MY MAKING,
WHICH HAS LEFT ME TORN AND NAKED OF LOVE. +

+THE SCARS OF BATTLE OVER SELF,
-AGAINST PRIDE
AND VICE-
ARE THE PRICELESS MARKS OF BEAUTY,
WHICH RESEMBLE THE WOUNDS OF OUR SAVIOR. +

+*BLESSED* POVERTY IS JOY IN HEAVENLY RICHES.
BLESSED HUNGER IS *SOUL* SAIETY IN THE EUCHARISTIC BANQUET.
BLESSED WEEPING
IS ADORATION IN REPARATION FOR DISINTEREST IN LOVE DIVINE.
BLESSED PERSECUTION
IS SUFFERING FAITHFULLY AND CHARITABLY
IN THE FACE OF EVIL'S ENVY.
BLESSED ARE THOSE WHO SEEK NOT THE WORLD
AND THE WIDE WAYS OF PERDITION,
BUT LIVE TO KISS THE WOOD OF THE CROSS,
-DRINKING OF THE BLOOD, EATING OF THE BODY-
OF THE LORD OF THE HEAVENLY NARROW WAY. +

+FLEEING FROM AN AFFLUENT NEIGHBORHOOD,
AFTER TEARING DOWN THE PICKET FENCE,
AND DEMOLISHING THE PERFECT HOME,
AND FILLING IN THE LUXURIOUS POOL,
AND RAZING THE EXQUISITE GRASS,
AND CRUSHING THE TANTALIZING TOYS,
AND MELTING THE EXPERT TOOLS,
AND BURNING THE ALL CONSUMING BOOKS,
AND DISMISSING THE FASHIONABLE FRIENDS,
AND DESTROYING ALL MEANS WHICH SULLIED GOOD'S END...
I FOUND MYSELF, MY SOUL, MY MIND, AND MY HEART,
IN THE SIMPLICITY OF FAITH, HOPE, AND CHARITY,
BORN OF THE LORD WHO BLESSES ALL NECESSITIES. +

+**FAITH**, TRUE FAITH, SEEKS FOR THE GOOD OF ONES NEIGHBOR...
BUT FOR THE GLORY OF GOD...
CAMAFLOUGED FROM THE EYES OF EARTHLY GLORY
IN HUMBLE AND SINCERE OBEDIENCE.
FOR TRUE FAITH CONTEMPLATES THE WHISPERING WIND OF ELIJAH,
THE SILENT PONDERING OF MARIAN ANNUNCIATION,
AND THE GLORIFIED CHRIST YET TO LEAVE HIS TOMB,
AND REALIZES THE AWESOME POWER OF THE HOLY SPIRIT OF GOD.
PEIRCING THE HEART IN LOVE RECEIVED,
PENETRATING THE MIND IN THE WISDOM OF PRAYER,
THE SILENT SPIRIT SPURS THE SOUL TO STEALTH CHARITY...
ALL THIS IS GIVEN SO THAT THE WAY OF THE CROSS
MAY BECOME THE WAY OF ETERNAL JOY. +

+MY SINS HAVE LEFT SCARS,
BLESSED REMINDERS OF REDEMPTION!
FROM THE BAD THIEF ON THE LEFT,
TO THE GOOD THIEF TO YOUR RIGHT,
I HAVE BEEN TRANSFORMED IN GRACED REPENTANCE,
AND IN THE REDEMPTIVE EUCHARISTIC HOST.

SAVE ME! SAVIOR!
AND I, WEAK AND PRONE TO SIN,
WILL FOLLOW *YOUR WAY*,
FOR THE BENEFIT OF THE SALVATION OF SOULS.

GRACE THE CHURCH!
BUILD YOUR BODY!
LET THE EUCHARIST *REIGN*,
AS THE SOURCE AND SUMMIT OF YOUR LOVE! +

+HOLINESS PURSUES THE GLORY OF GOD
FROM A TRUE DENIAL OF SELF,
FROM A HEART AND A MIND AND A SOUL
DEEPLY IN LOVE WITH THE SELF OFFERING,
THE SELF DENYING,
EUCHARISTIC CHRIST
-WILLINGLY CAPTURED IN BREAD AND WINE AND TABERNACLE
FOR THE GLORY OF THE FATHER,
AND THE HOLINESS OF SO MANY BROTHERS AND SISTERS-
IN THE HOLY SPIRIT
WHO UNITES THE BODY TO HER HEAD
IN THE LOVE WHICH UNITES THE FATHER AND THE SON
AS HOLY TRINITY
IN THE ONE GOD-WHO IS LOVE. +

+**THE MASSES**: LET US GLOSS OVER INCONVENIENT TRUTH! LET US
SELECT CHARITY WHICH BEFITS *OUR* GLORY! LET US FORM RELIGION
FOR THE WORSHIP OF A GOD OF OUR OWN CHOOSING!
THE MEDIATOR:HEAR ME OH LORD, HEAR MY CRY FOR MERCY! I PRAY
AND PLEAD AND LAMENT, IN TEARS AND WORDS AND BLOOD, FOR
THEIR HOLINESS, THEIR HAPPINESS, AND THEIR SALVATION. YET,
THEY PREPARE MY DEATH. AN IGNOMINOUS DEATH! GIVE ME
STRENGTH! SHOW ME LOVE. SHOW THEM MERCY! +

+AS DISCIPLES OF CHRIST, GRACED IN SACRED SCRIPTURE,
NOURISHED IN THE MOST BLESSED SACRAMENT,
TUTORED BY HOLY MOTHER CHURCH,
WE ARE AMAZED AND ASHAMED AT THE HARDHEADED
AND HARD HEARTED STRUGGLE WITH PASCHAL TRUTH
IN WHICH WE SHARE WITH THE APOSTLES
AS THEY VENTURED TO JERUSALEM
IN THE GOOD AND PROPER TIME OF OUR REDEMPTION.

FOR THE GLORY OF GOD IS THE PERFECTION OF MAN,
AND THE PERFECTION OF MAN IS IN THE SERVANTHOOD
OF HOLY AND CHARITABLE SUFFERING.

FOR THE CROSS REDEEMS AND PERFECTS
IN THE WILLINGNESS TO BE CRUCIFIED
TO THE MERCIFUL WILL OF THE MOST LOVING FATHER. +

+I AM BOTH CURSED AND BLESSED.
I AM CURSED WITH THE DESIRE OF THE FLESH,
AND HOPE WHICH I PLACE IN THE FINITE.
WITH THE WORLD AS MY SOLE WONDER,
I AM POOR AND ARID AND LOST.
I AM CURSED BY MY OBSESSIONS.

I AM BLESSED IN HOMLINESS AND REJECTION AND LONELINESS!
-IN GRACED OBSCURITY-
FOR I AM RICH AND STRONG AND FOUND!
I AM BLESSED BY MY DESOLATIONS.

FOR A CURSE IS THE CHOICE OF THE WORLDLY.
AND A BLESSING THE GIFT OF THE REPENTANT POOR.
FOR THE RICH FIND SILVER AND GOLD AND FAME AND DEATH.
WHILE THE POOR SUFFER GRACE AND FORGIVENESS AND LOVE
AND RESURRECTION UNTO LIFE ETERNAL.

FOR THE HUMAN HEART, MISCHEVIOUS AND IMMATURE,
SEEKS BY THE SIGHT OF FLESH,
AND REAPS THE REWARDS OF ITS RUIN.
BUT SPIRIT AND GRACE SEEK FOR BUT ONE REPENTANT SEED.
AND FOUND, THE HEART IS RENEWED IN LOVE ETERNAL. +

THE UNIVERSAL CALL TO HOLINESS

"THE CLASSES AND DUTIES OF LIFE ARE MANY, BUT HOLINESS IS ONE-THAT SANCTITY WHICH IS CULTIVATED BY ALL WHO ARE MOVED BY THE SPIRIT OF GOD, AND WHO OBEY THE VOICE OF THE FATHER AND WORSHIP GOD THE FATHER IN SPIRIT AND TRUTH. THESE PEOPLE FOLLOW THE POOR CHRIST, THE HUMBLE AND CROSS-BEARING CHRIST IN ORDER TO BE WORTHY OF BEING SHARERS IN HIS GLORY. EVERY PERSON MUST WALK UNHESITANTLY ACCORDING TO HIS OWN PERSONAL GIFTS AND DUTIES IN THE PATH OF LIVING FAITH, WHICH AROUSES HOPE AND WORKS THROUGH CHARITY."

LUMEN GENTIUM 41
DOGMATIC CONSTITUTION ON THE CHURCH

+JESUS MY FOOD, MY DRINK,
MY BREAD AND MY WINE,
MY LIFE AND MY HOPE,
YOU ALONE ARE MY LORD, MY LOVE, AND MY SALVATION.

IN MY SIGHT AS WORD,
IN MY HEART AS SACRAMENT,
ON MY LIPS AS PRAYER,
YOU ARE EVER PRESENT AS SACRED HOST,
AS ECCLESIAL AND MYSTICAL BODY;
I AM NEVER OUTNUMBERED,
NEVER DEFEATED,
ALWAYS ALIVE,
IN FAITHFUL HOPE OF YOUR ETERNAL LOVE.

FOR IN LIFE OR IN DEATH, YOU HOLD ME NEAR!

AND ALL EXPERIENCES,
ALL TRIALS, ALL LOCATIONS, ALL TIMES,
-IN FAITH AND HOPE-
LEAD ME ON *YOUR WAY* TO ETERNAL BLISS
-IN UNFATHOMABLE INTIMACY-
BY YOUR SIDE, AMONG ANGELS AND SAINTS FOREVER. +

+IN PRAYER AND SACRAMENT AND SUFFERING AND SELF DENIAL,
THE HOLY TEMPLE OF THE LORD MUST BE RECONQUERED
-FOR TRUE DEVOTION IN PRAISE AND THANKSGIVING-
WITHIN THE PERFECT SACRIFICE OF THE CRUCIFIED CHRIST.

REDEDICATING IN REPENTANCE, CELEBRATING REDEMPTION,
AND REBUILDING IN THE UNION OF TRUE COMMUNION,
THE HUMBLE WARRIORS
OF THE ALMIGHTY KING OF LOVING MERCY
MUST COMMEMORATE THEIR EXODUS
FROM THE SLAVERY OF THEIR LOVE FOR THE PAGAN WORLD,
AND IN *FEAR AND TREMBLING*,
PERPETUATE THE REDEMPTIVE CELEBRATION
-IN ALL SEASONS, AND ALL PLACES, IN ALL CIRCUMSTANCES-
FOR THE GLORY OF THE SAVIOR,
AND THE SALVATION OF THE LOST TEMPLES OF THE LORD. +

+BORN IN ROYALTY.
BRED IN ANGER.
TRAINED IN DESTRUCTIVE ARTS.
KING AND CONQUERER.
LORD OF ARMIES.
DEVOURER OF LANDS.
SMITTEN BY GREED AND CRUELTY, FALLEN IN FAILURE,
"DYING OF MELANCHOLY IN A FOREIGN LAND."

THE REIGN OF THE TYRANT IS BUT A SEASON IN PASSING.
BUT THE REIGN OF THE MERCIFUL LIVES ON FOREVER. +

+UNLIKE A DESPOT,
A TYRANT,
A DICTATOR,
OR A UTILITARIAN OVERLORD,
OUR KING IS A KING OF LOVING EMPOWERMENT.

CHRIST THE KING
IS *NOT* A THREATENING
OR DEMEANING REALITY
FOR THE MANY SPIRITUAL
AND TEMPORAL PEASANTS AMONG US.

RATHER,
HIS KINGSHIP
IS OUR STRENGTH,
AND OUR HOPE,
AND OUR JOY,
AND OUR VOCATION,
AS CROSS BEARERS,
CARRYING BODILY THE PASCHAL PROMISE
OF RESURRECTION-
IN FAITH, HOPE AND CHARITY. +

+CHURCH MEN AND FAITH MEN ARE NOT ALWAYS THE SAME MEN. +

+A SINCERE PRIEST WITNESSES TO A SINCERE GOD. +

+FAITH IS TRULY MEASURED WHILE ENDURING SUFFERING. +

+STOKE THE FIRES OF TRUE DEVOTION,
IN THANKSGIVING FOR MERCY RECEIVED,
AND PRAISE FOR GRACED COURAGE IN LIFE'S PASSION.

DANCE AND DRINK IN MODERATION,
FRET NOT AFTER PRAYER;
FOR A SOBER MIND AND A TRANQUIL HEART
WILL BEAR TRUE AND CERTAIN WITNESS
TO THE RETURN OF OUR KING.

AWAKE WE MUST STAY,
ALERT WE MUST BE,
FOR LOVE DRAWS NEAR,
STEALTHILY, AMONG BURSTS OF CHAOS
-ONLY TO BE DISCERNED
BY A MIND OF FAITH,
A HEART OF HOPE,
AND A SOUL ANIMATED IN LOVE. +

+IN A SCREAMING WORLD,
WHICH COMPETES FOR OUR ATTENTION,
AND ADVERTISES COMFORT AND JOY,
CHRIST JESUS
IN THE SPIRIT,
-IMMANUEL-
IS THE TRIBULATION WHICH BRINGS TRUE COMFORT,
IN THE STORM OF DETACHMENT AND MORTIFICATION,
IN THE CROSS,
WHICH FREES US IN JOYFUL SUFFERING,
WHERE THE OLD MAN OF OUR SIN DIES,
AND THE INDWELLING SPIRIT BRINGS FORTH
-IN THE RE-CREATION OF THE HUMBLE DISCIPLE,
AN IMAGE OF CHRIST, A JOYFUL VICTIM, VICTORIOUS IN
RESURRECTION AND LIFE,
THROUGH THE GREATEST GIFT FROM GOD-
THE ANNHILATION AND REBIRTH OF ONESELF
IN THE GRACE AND THE WISDOM
OF THE ONE WHO HOLDS OUR PURPOSE
IN THE TRINITY
OF GOODNESS, TRUTH AND BEAUTY. +

+GO OUT IN THE COMPANY OF THE SPIRIT
IN THE FELLOWSHIP OF EVANGELISTS,
AND CARRY NOTHING SAVE THE WORD OF GOD,
THE TEACHING OF MOTHER CHURCH,
AND THE POVERTY OF SPIRIT, BLESSED IN BEATIFIC HOPE.

RELY NOT ON FANCY CLOTHES
-NOR MONEY BOUGHT MATERIALS-
TO IMPRESS THE LOST SOUL.

ENTER THEIR HOME
AS ENTERING THE CHAMBER
OF A KING AND A QUEEN.

RESPECT AND COMPASSION
MUST BE THE LANGUAGE AND THE DEMEANOR
FOR THE SUFFERING SERVANT OF THE MESSIAH-
HE WHO SEEKS FOR CONVERSION OF THE HEART.

OFFER ONLY THE GOODNESS
AND THE TRUTH
AND THE BEAUTY
OF THE CHRIST,
IN YOUR WORD AND YOUR DEED.

TEACH REPENTANCE AND CONVERSION...
IN THE WAY OF THE CROSS.

WITNESS IN HOPE, ENLIGHTEN IN FAITH,
HEAL IN LOVE, AND ILLUMINATE THE HEAVENLY HORIZON-
IN SUFFERING THE CROSS *NOW*,
BORN FAITHFULLY AND HOPEFULLY
IN THE RESURRECTION TO COME!

THEN WALK WHEREVER SENT, EXPECTING THE GRACE OF GOD
TO PROVIDE FOR THE NEEDS OF HIS MISSION.

AND REST ASSURED! YOUR REWARD IS WAITING IN HEAVEN.
UNFATHOMABLE TREASURES FORETASTED IN GRACE TODAY-
IN THE SPIRIT OF MERCIFUL LOVE. +

THE PROPHET

"THE TRUTH OF THE MATTER IS THAT THE PROPHETS OF ISRAEL DID NOT PREDICT THE FUTURE BECAUSE THEY WERE TOO BUSY GIVING EXPRESSION TO THE PRESENT. LIKE POETS OF ALL AGES, THEY SAW REALITY AT ITS DEEPEST LEVEL. THEY TOOK A LONG LOOK AT THAT REALITY AND EITHER SAW GOD OR THE ABSENCE OF GOD. FROM THAT DIVINE EPICENTER MOVED WAVES OF TENDERNESS OR ANGER AS YET UNEXPERIENCED BY THE MERCHANTS AND FARMERS OF ISRAEL OR JUDAH. PROPHETS KNEW THE VITALITY OF GOD AND SPOKE ACCORDINGLY. THEY SENSED THE FIRST STIRRINGS OF DIVINE ACTION. ONLY TO THAT EXTENT DID THEY PAINT THE FUTURE."
RICHARD J. SKLBA
PRE-EXILIC PROPHECY

"OUT OF THE DESPERATION OF EXILE, JEREMIAH ANNOUNCED A COMING TIME OF FULFILLMENT. AS HE FACED HIS OWN MOMENT OF DESPERATION, JESUS ANNOUNCED THAT *THAT* TIME HAD COME."
DIANNE BERGANT, CSA
PEOPLE OF THE COVENANT

"IN JESUS CHRIST, THE LOGOS IS NO LONGER THE REALM OF IDEAS, VALUES AND LAWS WHICH GOVERNS AND GIVES MEANING TO HISTORY, BUT IS HIMSELF HISTORY. IN THE LIFE OF CHRIST THE FACTUAL AND THE NORMATIVE COINCIDE NOT ONLY IN *FACT* BUT *NECESSARILY*, BECAUSE THE FACT IS BOTH THE MANIFESTATION OF GOD AND THE DIVINE-HUMAN PATTERN OF TRUE HUMANITY IN GOD'S EYES."
HANS URS VON BALTHASAR
A THEOLOGY OF HISTORY

+WE DIG FOR TRUTH,
AND PLUMMET TO THE DEPTHS OF THE SEA FOR ANSWERS.
WE SEARCH THE SKIES,
AND PROBE THE GALAXY FOR KNOWLEDGE.
WE DIVIDE THE CELL
AND SPLICE THE GENE,
IN HOPE OF FINDING LIFE'S SECRETS.
WE RE-READ HISTORY'S WORKS,
REDEFINING WHAT WAS,
WHILE PREDICTING WHAT WILL BE.
YET, WE SPEND PRECIOUS LITTLE TIME
ON WHO WE ARE,
AND WHY WE ARE HERE,
AND WHERE WE ARE GO TO…
AND WHAT WE ARE MEANT TO BE.

FOR IN FINDING FACTS,
WE SEARCH FOR THE WHAT AND FORGET THE WHO…
AND IN NEVER SURVEYING THE CANVAS FOR ITS MESSAGE,
BUT RATHER THE PARTICULARS OF ITS MATTER,
WE MISS THE ARTIST OF ALL WE SEE. +

+SPOKEN ONCE IN THE LOVE OF THE SPIRIT,
THE WORD OF GOD IS THE FATHER'S ETERNAL PLAN *ALIVE!*

YET THE WORD IS MORE THAN WORDS.
THE WORD IS LOVE AND TRUTH AND MERCY
AND LIFE-PERFECTED-
IN THE COMMUNION
OF THE DIVINE AND THE INCARNATE NATURE,
OF THE SAVIOR OF ALL CREATION.
PERFECTED
IN SUFFERING AND SACRIFICE,
PRESENT IN SACRAMENT AND SPIRITED COMMUNION,
EVER WILLING AND ABLE TO TRANSFORM OUR HEARTS
FROM DEATH TO LIFE,
EVER BREATHING ETERNAL LIFE, MEDIATING GRACE,
PREPARING OUR ABODE IN HEAVEN,
EVER PROTECTING, EVER FORGIVING, EVER SUSTAINING,
EVER LOVING, ALWAYS OUR LORD AND SAVIOR. +

+PATIENCE WILL BEAR SEED,
AND VIGILANCE WILL WITNESS FULL BLOOM,
IN THE GARDEN OF GRACED CONVERSION,
WHERE TRANSFORMATION
OF MIND AND HEART AND SOUL AND SPIRIT
WILL BEAR WITNESS TO THE LOVE OF THE FATHER
IN THE PASSION AND DEATH OF HIS BELOVED SON,
OUR LORD AND SAVIOR,
RISEN IN THE SPIRIT
OF THE COMMUNION
OF THE RECONCILIATION OF GOD AND MAN
MADE POSSIBLE IN THE FIRST DROP OF JESUS' PRECIOUS BLOOD
WHICH HIT THE EARTH AND RENEWED CREATION
FOR EVER MORE-
IN THE LOVE OF THE FATHER AND THE SON
IN THE MOST HOLY SPIRIT. +

+IF GOD IS THE ROCK OF MY SALVATION,
WHY DO I DROWN IN MEDIOCRITY,
AND LIVE IN THE EVER PRESENT FEAR
OF PERMANENT FAILURE?

IF YAHWEH WERE *TRULY* MY LIGHT AND MY FORTRESS,
I WOULD BE ILLUMINATED IN HIS BRILLIANCE,
AND ENCOURAGED ETERNALLY IN THE SUCCESS OF HIS RISEN SON!

FOR LIFE IS A SERIES OF CHOICES,
A BOUT WITH THE DEMON WITHIN.
LIFE, HOWEVER, IS ALSO A CHANCE FOR GRACE,
AN OFFERING OF THE INDWELLING, FORGIVING,
AND SANCTIFYING SPIRIT.

LIFE IS SHORT. DEATH IS DEFINITIVE.
AND WHAT LIES BEYOND THE GRAVE
IS OF *OUR* CHOOSING.

YET GOD IS EVER PRESENT
TO GRACE US WITH OUR CHOSEN DESTINY.

THEREFORE, *TRUST, BELIEVE, AND CHOOSE LIFE!* +

THE PRIEST

"THIS IS THE MISSION OF THE CHURCH, CATHOLIC AND APOSTOLIC, TO REUNITE MEN WHOM SELFISHNESS AND DISILLUSIONMENT MIGHT KEEP APART, TO SHOW THEM HOW TO PRAY, TO BRING THEM TO CONTRITION FOR THEIR SINS AND TO FORGIVENESS, TO FEED THEM WITH THE EUCHARISTIC BREAD, AND TO BIND THEM TOGETHER WITH THE BONDS OF CHARITY."
POPE JOHN XXIII
IN MY OWN WORDS

"YOU PRIESTS MUST BE MEN OF GOD, HIS CLOSE FRIENDS. YOU MUST DEVELOP DAILY PATTERNS OF PRAYER, AND PENANCE MUST BE A REGULAR PART OF YOUR LIFE. PRAYER AND PENANCE WILL HELP YOU TO APPRECIATE MORE DEEPLY THAT THE STRENGTH OF YOUR MINISTRY IS FOUND IN THE LORD AND NOT IN HUMAN RESOURCES. YOU MUST TRY TO DEEPEN EVERY DAY YOUR FRIENDSHIP WITH CHRIST.
YOU MUST ALSO LEARN TO SHARE THE HOPES AND THE JOYS, THE SORROWS AND THE FRUSTRATIONS OF THE PEOPLE ENTRUSTED TO YOUR CARE. BRING TO THEM CHRIST'S SAVING MESSAGE OF RECONCILIATION...
THROUGH YOU, CHRIST JESUS WANTS TO ENKINDLE HOPE ANEW...THROUGH YOU IN YOUR HEART, JESUS CHRIST WANTS TO LOVE THOSE OF WHOM HE DIED...
WHEN YOU CELEBRATE THE SACRAMENTS AT THE DECISIVE MOMENTS OF THEIR LIVES, HELP THEM TO TRUST IN CHRIST'S PROMISED MERCY AND COMPASSION. WHEN YOU OFFER THE REDEEMING SACRIFICE OF THE EUCHARIST, HELP THEM TO UNDERSTAND THE NEED FOR TRANSFORMING THIS GREAT LOVE INTO WORKS OF CHARITY...
MY BROTHERS, BE AWARE OF THE *EFFECT ON OTHERS OF THE WITNESS OF LIVES.*
POPE JOHN PAUL II
PRAYERS AND DEVOTIONS

+WE CANNOT ERECT OUR OWN TEMPLE,
SHAPE OUR OWN ALTAR,
SCULPT OUR OWN CHALICE,
DEFINE OUR OWN LITURGY,
APPOINT OUR OWN FEASTS,
DEFINE OUR OWN DOGMA,
AND ERECT STATUES TO THE GOD OF OUR OWN MAKING,
WITHOUT COMMITTING THE SIN OF JEROBOAM
IN DECEIVING THE PEOPLE
INTO FALSE AND PERVERSE WORSHIP
IN MAN MADE RELIGION
FOR PERSONAL GAIN
AND PERSONAL GLORY,
WHICH ONLY LEADS TO APOSTACY
AND THE RUIN OF MANY A SOUL
IN THE DEPRAVITY OF ONE MAN
WHO FOLLOWS THE PATH
NOT OF THE SECOND,
BUT THE FIRST ADAM
IN SELF-ABSORBED DISTINCTION FROM HIS GOD. +

+THE WORLD IS FULL OF HUNGRY PEOPLE!
THE BREAD WE BEAR IN OUR HEARTS WILL ONLY FEED
IN THE FULLNESS OF OUR FAITH.

FOR THE BREAD WHICH FEEDS THE WORLD
IS HARVESTED SOLELY IN FAITH
WHICH TRUSTS IN DIVINE PROVIDENCE.

FOR SEVEN LOAVES IN FAITH AND CHARITY AND FORGIVENESS
BECOME AN ABUNDANT STOREHOUSE OF GRACE FILLED BREAD
IN THE HUMBLE GIFT OF FOOD
FOR THE POOR CHRIST
IN BREAD FOR THE BELLY
AND TRUTH FOR THE MIND
AND RESPECT FOR THE SOUL
IN THE FEEDING OF THE MANY
IN THE SEVEN LOAVES OF FAITH
IN THE LIVING BREAD OF SALVATION,
JESUS CHRIST AND LORD. +

+TO SEEK SALVATION IN ONES FELLOW
IS TO SEEK FOR LIGHT IN A DARK SHAFT
IN THE MIDDLE OF THE NIGHT.

IN THE PITCH BLACK,
SQUATTING IN CONFUSION,
THE SEEKER OF LIGHT IN THE DARKNESS OF MAN
SETTLES DOWN IN THE ABYSS OF NOTHINGNESS.

TO SEEK FOR SALVATION
IN THE UNSEEN GOD,
THE GOD IN BREAD AND WINE,
IS TO SEEK FOR LIGHT
IN THE DAWN OF TRUST
AND THE DAYLIGHT OF FAITHFUL WITNESS.

IN THE LIGHT OF FAITH,
AND THE GLIMMER OF HOPE,
THE SEEKER OF LIGHT
IN THE UNSEEN GOD,
THE GOD IN BREAD AND WINE,
SETTLES DOWN IN THE WARMTH
OF THE SON
THAT HAS RISEN. +

+*THE SERVANT* OF GOD
SERVES THROUGH THE SUFFERING AND VICTORIOUS SERVANT.
THE TEACHER OF THE FAITH
TEACHES THROUGH THE TRUTH, THE LORD JESUS CHRIST.
THE PRIEST
OF THE MOST BLESSED SACRAMENT
STANDS IN THE PERSON OF CHRIST.
THE CHILD OF GOD
LIVES THROUGH THE LIFE OF THE HOLY SPIRIT
IN AND THROUGH THE MERITS
OF THE CRUCIFIED AND RISEN SON.
THE CHURCH IS ALIVE,
SOLELY,
IN THE BREATHE OF THE SPIRIT OF GOD.
HE WHO IS LOVE! +

+FOR THE SINS OF MY ANCESTORS,
LORD HAVE MERCY.

FOR THE CRIMES IN MY LIFE,
CHRIST HAVE MERCY.

FOR THE WRONGS OF MY CHILD,
LORD HAVE MERCY.

SAVE US OH LORD!
MY MOTHER AND MY FATHER, SINNERS SO FRAIL,
LORD HAVE MERCY.

MY LIFE, SUCH SIN!
CHRIST HAVE MERCY.

MY SPOUSE, MY CHILD, MY FRIEND, MY NEIGHBOR...MY ENEMY,
VULNERABLE TO A FAULT,
LORD HAVE MERCY.

PURGATION PREVAIL, I PRAY! LOST BE FOUND, I BESEECH!

I THANK YOU LORD
IN FAITH OF YOUR MERCY
IN HOPE OF YOUR FORGIVENESS
AND IN LOVE WITH YOUR CROSS...
THE ONLY WAY
TO THE EMPTY TOMB. +

+WITH THE APOSTLES IN OUR MIDST, LET US CLIMB FAITH'S
MOUNTAIN AND PRAY.
AND THE LORD, IN OUR HUMILITY, AND OUR SINCERITY, AND OUR
HUNGER, WILL APPEAR IN SPLENDOR,
IN A VEIL OF BREAD AND WINE,
PERFECT IN HUMILITY, IN SINCERITY, READY TO FEED OUR HUNGER,
IN BLOOD AND BODY DIVINE.
AND IN INTIMATE SILENCE, HE WILL SPEAK TO OUR HEART,
BECOMING ONE WITH US, CONSUMING US IN THE FIRE OF HIS LOVE,
ASSUMING US IN HIS SPIRIT, AS ACCEPTABLE SACRIFICE
TO THE HEAVENLY FATHER ABOVE. +

+FORGIVENESS IS THE ROPE THAT SAVES FALLEN MAN
FROM THE PRECIPICE OF SIN.
THE ONE WHO FALLS
IS SAVED BY THE ONE WHO TOSSES THE ROPE.
THE ONE WHO TOSSES THE ROPE
IS SAVED IN SAVING THE FALLEN...
FOR THE ROPE HAS A KNOT ON BOTH ENDS...
FOR PULLING AND BEING PULLED.
LIFE, FULL OF SLIPPERY SLOPES,
INVITES MAN TO TOSS AND RECEIVE.
YET, THE VIEW FROM HEAVEN
IS QUITE DIFFERENT,
AND THE PRECIPICE SHIFTS LIKE A PENDULUM
AND GOD'S HAND IS ALWAYS PULLING UPWARD. +

+THE NATIVITY SHEPHERDS WITNESSED CHRIST!
NOW, DETACHED FROM URBAN GLITTER,
AND SHEPHERDING A FLOCK, LOOSED FROM SPECTACLE,
GUIDING IN CARE, CHRIST RE-EMERGES. +

+TRUST IN THE POWER AND THE FAITHFULNESS
OF THE GOOD SHEPHERD.
HE IS THE ONE YOU MEET IN SACRAMENT AND CELEBRANT;
AND PERFECT, HE WILL NOT FAIL! +

+THE GOOD SHEPHERD SENDS SHEPHERDS
TO PASTOR HIS SHEEP.
WHEN A SHEPHERD INJURES HIS SHEEP
HE INJURES THE SHEEP'S TRUST IN THE GOOD SHEPHERD. +

+GOOD THEOLOGY
IS ETERNAL WISDOM TURNED EXISTENTIAL NOURISHMENT. +

+HOLY BISHOP, HOLY PRIEST, HOLY DEACON,
SISTER AND BROTHER RELIGIOUS,
THOUGH FALLIBLE YOU ARE-A WRETCH LIKE ME-
I SHALL RESPECT THE GARMENTS YOU WEAR
FOR THE SAKE OF THE HOLY ONE WHOM YOU REPRESENT.
DISSENSION COMPOUNDS SIN! UNITY HEALS ALL WOUNDS!
SEMPER FIDELIS! GRACE! SEMPER FIDELIS! +

THE SERVANT KING

"EARTHLY HONORS COUNT FOR NOTHING, AND MONEY AND WEALTH COUNT EVEN LESS AND ARE EXTREMELY DANGEROUS, BUT HOLINESS AND THE EFFORT TO MAKE OTHERS HOLY IS THE HEIGHT OF HUMAN HAPPINESS; THIS IS OF THE GREATEST IMPORTANCE FOR OUR PRESENT LIFE AND THE LIFE TO COME."

POPE JOHN XXIII
IN MY OWN WORDS

+GIVING WITHOUT COUNTING THE COST
IS NOT NATURAL FOR THE WALKING WOUNDED LIKE ME.

MY NORMAL MODE OF OPERATION
IS TO SEEK FOR WHAT I CAN GET,
WHILE RETREIVING PREVIOUS LOSSES.

BUT, TRUTH BE TOLD,
I WILL NEVER RECAPTURE THE BANDITS OF MY PAST.
FOR THEY ARE VAPOROUS,
AND LIE SOLELY IN THE WOUNDS
WHICH I PROTECT FROM HEALING.

FUNNY, BUT WHAT I FEAR TO DO THE MOST,
IS WHAT I FULLY NEED FOR HEALING...
GIVING, WITHOUT COUNTING THE COST. +

+COMMUNION IS NOT COMPETITION;
COMPASSION IS NOT CONCEIT.
THE CHURCH IS NOT A CONGLOMERATION OF BODIES;
CHRIST IS NOT THE SUGGESTOR OF WAYS.

RATHER, COMMUNION IS OF ONE MIND,
COMPASSION IS *AGAPE,*
THE CHURCH IS ONE BODY,
AND CHRIST LEADS ONE WAY!

ONE FAITH, ONE LORD, ONE BEATITUDE! +

+LORD, CUT THE CORD
THAT TIES MY DESIRE TO GLORY AND FAME.
GROUND ME IN REALITY, YOUR WILL AND MY PATH.
GIVE ME PEACE ONLY IN PRAYER,
GIVE ME MOTHER MARY AND MOTHER CHURCH,
GIVE ME BROTHER JESUS AND THE EUCHARIST...
AND CARRY ME EVERY DAY, EVERY MOMENT,
LIKE A BABE IN ARMS,
IN YOUR SPIRIT,
TO THE ONLY PLACE OF PEACE AND REST,
YOUR MOST SACRED HEART. +

+MARTY,
I TRUST IN YOU MORE THAN ANY OTHER MAN.
YOUR SCARS, YOUR PAIN, YOUR WEAKNESS,
HAVE MADE YOU A MAN OF INTEGRITY-
CHRIST LIKE. +

+BECOME CHRIST IN THOUGHT AND DESIRE...
LIVE VICARIOUSLY IN CHRIST...
SEEK RELEVANCE THROUGH SERVITUDE...
DIE A THOUSAND DEATHS TO PRIDE...
LIVE FOR ONE THOUSAND RESURRECTIONS IN GRACE...
REST DAILY ON BENDED KNEE...
AND EVANGELIZE CHRIST IN ACT AND WORD
"TO THE GLORY OF GOD THE FATHER." +

+I AM BOTH RICH IN GLORY AND POOR IN NEED;
GRACED AND FALLEN.
TWISTED IN ADAM,
REMODELED IN CHRIST,
I AM CALLED TO BOLD HUMILITY!

CHARITY FROM GIFTEDNESS-
REPENTANCE FROM EMPTINESS,
ARE MY DAILY CALLING.

VOCATION IS THE BALANCE OF REALITY;
CHRIST FOR SANCTITY,
CHRIST FOR FORGIVENESS,
CHRIST FOR SALVATION,
CHRIST FOR GLORY...
THE GLORY OF GOD! +

+MARIA LOURDES, IS A MOM AND A WIFE AND A DAUGHTER AND A
SISTER AND A NEIGHBOR AND A FELLOW WORKER WITH A MIND
OPEN TO TRUTH, A HEART EVER SEEKING LOVE'S EXPRESSION, AND
AN EYE FOR THE BEAUTY OF LIFE IN EVERY ENCOUNTER; GENTLE,
COMPASSIONATE, WILLING TO SERVE, EAGER TO SHARE, A TRUE
FRANCISCAN IN NATURE AND SPIRIT, A BEAUTIFUL CREATURE OF
GOD, GENTLE SISTER OF CHRIST, MOTHER OF MARISSA, WIFE OF AN
UNDESERVING MAN. +

GRACE

"WERE WE ONLY TO CORRESPOND TO GOD'S GRACES, CONTINUALLY BEING SHOWERED DOWN ON EVERONE OF US, WE WOULD BE ABLE TO PASS FROM BEING SINNERS ONE DAY TO BEING GREAT SAINTS THE NEXT. WE ARE CONTINUALLY IMMERSED IN GOD'S MERCIFUL GRACE LIKE THE AIR THAT PERMEATES US."
FATHER SOLANUS CASEY O.F.M. CAP.
FATHER SOLANUS

"MOST MERCIFUL JESUS, FROM THE TREASURY OF YOUR MERCY, YOU IMPART YOUR GRACES IN GREAT ABUNDANCE TO EACH AND ALL. RECEIVE US INTO THE ABODE OF YOUR MOST COMPASSIONATE HEART AND NEVER LET US ESCAPE FROM IT...
THIRD DAY PRAYER
DIVINE MERCY NOVENA AND CHAPLET

+NAME ME ONE SAVIOR WHO SAVES
LIKE OUR SAVIOR AND LORD,
SWEET JESUS.

SHOW ME ONE ROCK WHO SHELTERS
LIKE THE ROCK OF TRUE FAITH,
CHRIST THE LORD!

SHOW ME JUSTICE,
EARTHLY JUSTICE,
AS JUST AS THE SOURCE OF JUSTICE,
THE JUST ONE, JESUS.

SHOW ME MERCY, WORLDLY MERCY,
AS MERCIFUL AS THE CRUCIFIED AND RISEN MESSIAH.

SHOW ME SALVATION,WORLDLY SALVATION,
AS SALVIFIC AS THE SPIRITOF THE ETERNAL ONE.
SEEK! AND WHEN YOU TIRE,
COME AND TASTE THE GOODNESS OF THE LORD.   +

+FAITH IN THE FESTIVAL OF LIGHT,
OF BIRTH AND BAPTISM AND RECONCILIATION AND EUCHARIST,
IS FAITH FOSTERED IN THE VISIBLE TOUCH OF LOVE.

BUT FAITH IN THE CRISIS OF DARKNESS
IN DEATH AND DYING, IN SUFFERING AND INSECURITY,
THIS IS THE FAITH WHICH SEEKS FOR THE INVISIBLE TOUCH OF LOVE.

FOR FAITH IN LIGHT IS NOT TESTED THROUGH HOPE,
BUT WITNESSES TO LOVE MANIFEST.
BUT FAITH IN DARKNESS,
RELIES HEAVILY ON THE RESERVES OF HOPE,
TO PERSEVERE THROUGH TEMPTATION
IN DOUBT AND DESPAIR-
SO AS TO WITNESS TO LOVE'S LIGHT BREAKING THROUGH.

SO NIGHT LEADS TO DAY
AS FAITH BUILDS UPON HOPE,
AS THE SPIRIT IN THE DARKNESS CARRIES US THROUGH. +

+WE HAVE BUILT YOU A TEMPLE
OF WOOD AND STONE.
YOU HAVE PREFERRED TO REMAIN
IN THE DARK CLOUD OF HEAVENLY FREEDOM AND MYSTERY.
WE HAVE BUILT YOU A THRONE
OF IVORY AND MARBLE.
YOU HAVE PREFERRED TO EMBRACE
THE POVERTY AND HUMILITY OF THE CROSS-
IN THE DARK CLOUD OF YOUR PASSION AND OUR REDEMPTION.
WE HAVE BUILT YOU EXTERNAL LIVES
OF PIOUS AND CHARITABLE ACTIVITY.
YOU HAVE PREFERRED TO ENTER THE TEMPLE OF YOUR CREATION
IN OUR VERY HEART AND OUR VERY MIND,
WITHIN THE DARK CLOUD OF CONSCIENCE AND TRUTH. +

+THE FRINGE OF CHRIST'S CLOAK
HAS THE HEALING POWER OF MERCY FOR LIFE.

FOR THE FRINGE VERSE
OF THE *OUR FATHER*
CONDITIONS OUR FORGIVENESS
ON THE FORGIVENESS OF OUR BROTHER.

AND THE FRINGE TOUCH
OF OUR PRAYER FOR ANOTHER,
TOUCHES THE VERY HEART OF OUR FATHER,
AND SELFLESS SPIRITUALITY
LEADS TO THE SAVING SPIRIT IN GRACE,
FOR THE PRAYER,
AS THE PRAYED FOR.

FOR GRACE
WHICH INSPIRES FRINGE ACTIVITY
IN FORGIVENESS AND CHARITY,
WITNESSES IN FAITH AND HOPE
TO THE HEALING POWER OF GOD'S LOVE.

I AM BUT A FRINGE!
I AM BUT ONE DISCIPLE!
YET A FRINGE AND A DISCIPLE SO VITAL. +

SCRIPTURE, TRADITION, AND MAGISTERIUM

""THE APOSTLES ENTRUSTED THE 'SACRED DEPOSIT' OF THE FAITH (THE DEPOSITUM FIDEI), CONTAINED IN SACRED SCRIPTURES AND TRADITION, TO THE WHOLE OF THE CHURCH. 'BY ADHERING TO THIS HERATIGE THE ENTIRE HOLY PEOPLE, UNITED TO ITS PASTOR, REMAINS ALWAYS FAITHFUL TO THE TEACHING OF THE APOSTLES, TO THE BROTHERHOOD, TO THE BREAKING OF THE BREAD AND THE PRAYERS. SO, IN MAINTAINING, PRACTICING, AND PROFESSING THE FAITH THAT HAS BEEN HANDED ON, THERE SHOULD BE A REMARKABLE HARMONY BETWEEN BISHOPS AND THE FAITHFUL...

"THE TASK OF GIVING AN AUTHENTIC INTERPRETATION OF THE WORD OF GOD, WHETHER IN ITS WRITTEN FORM OR IN THE FORM OF TRADITION, HAS BEEN ENTRUSTED TO THE LIVING, TEACHING OFFICE OF THE CHURCH ALONE. ITS AUTHORITY IN THIS MATTER IS EXERCISED IN THE NAME OF JESUS CHRIST...

"YET THIS MAGISTERIUM IS NOT SUPERIOR TO THE WORD OF GOD, BUT IS ITS SERVANT..."
CATECHISM OF THE CATHOLIC CHURCH 84-86

+AS A YOUNGER MAN,
I FOLLOWED EVERY WHIM, AND EVERY NEW BREEZE,
IN SEARCH OF MEANING, IDENTITY AND PURPOSE.

AND NOW,
OLDER AND GRAY-ER,
WISER IN HUMILITY,
-EARNED IN FALLING OFTEN-
I FOLLOW EVERY PRECEPT
AND EVERY SPIRIT FILLED WHISPER
IN SEARCH OF MEANING, IDENTITY AND PURPOSE
IN CHRIST JESUS.
OLDER,
WISER,
I PRAISE HIM FOR MY PAIN!
FOR IN EVERY FALL,
MY GRIP ON THE WORLD LOOSENED.
AND IN MOVING FORWARD,
WITH EMPTY HANDS,
I AM BETTER ABLE TO CARRY THE CROSS OF MY SALVATION.
THE CROSS OF CHRIST'S COMFORT
IN HOPE OF THE THIRD DAY OF MY RISING. +

+GOD OFFERS HIS WORD FREELY,
AS A GIFT OF LOVE.
YET MANY CHOOSE TO LIVE ON THE PERIPHERY OF TRUTH,
EASILY LOSING THE WORD
TO THE MANY VOICES OF THE WORLD.
SOME LISTEN,
BUT DON'T PERCEIVE,
TAKING THE WORD AS OBLIGATION, BUT NEVER AS TRUE LIFE.
OTHERS UNDERSTAND WITH THEIR MIND,
BUT NEVER EMBRACE THE WORD
WITH THEIR HEARTS AND THEIR LIVES.
AND THEN THERE ARE THE POOR!
THOSE TOO HUMBLE TO DENY THE KING.
THEY REPENT AND THEY ARE SAVED.
THEY SEE AND BELIEVE.
THEY HEAR AND HOPE.
THEY ARE LOVED...AND THEY LOVE IN RETURN. +

+IN A FRACTURED CHURCH
WHERE ORTHODOXY AND HETERODOXY
BUMP HEADS...
THE HARDENED PHARISEE AND THE LISCENTIOUS PAGAN
OF SCRIPTURE
REVEAL THEMSELVES TO ME
IN THE FRACTURED FAITH STRUGGLE
WITHIN MY BROTHER-
AND ALSO WITHIN ME. +

+I PRAY THE PROMISING WORDS OF SCRIPTURE...
AND I WONDER,
'WILL THERE BE ANYONE
(IN THIS FAITHLESS GENERATION)
TO READ AND PRAY THIS FAITH-TRUTH
CENTURIES FROM NOW?'

AND I REALIZE THAT OUR CATHOLIC TRADITION
IS CENTURIES BLESSED
WITH PRAYERFUL DISCIPLES
WONDERING THE SAME THING.

THEN GRACE HITS ME. *GOD IS IN CONTROL!* +

+BEWARE OF THE DANGER OF THE BRAND NEW CHRIST,
THE BRAND NEW SPIRIT, THE BRAND NEW RELIGION,
AND THE BRAND NEW FAITH.

MORE THAN LIKELY,
IT IS JUST THE RESURFACING OF VERY OLD LIES!

FOR THERE IS BUT ONE CHRIST, IN ONE CHURCH, *ALIVE* IN ONE SPIRIT,
EXPRESSED IN THE TRUE RELIGION, OF THE ONE TRUE FAITH,
BORN IN, AND SUSTAINED BY, THE BODY OF CHRIST,
IN LOVING SUBMISSION TO HER SPOUSE AND HEAD.

SHE IS NONE OTHER THAN THE BODY AND BRIDE OF CHRIST,
SHE IS THE FAITHFUL, BAPTIZED, ALIVE IN THE EUCHARIST.
SHE IS OUR MOTHER, THE CHURCH UNIVERSAL,
THE CATHOLIC CHURCH. +

+CRY IN POVERTY AND WEAKNESS,
FOR THIS IS THE CRY WHICH REACHES OUR GOD!

LET GO! SOFTEN YOUR HEART.
FOR DOCILE FAITH AND OBEDIENT HOPE
ATTRACT THE LOVE OF THE LORD.

GO TO YOUR MOTHER! MARY AND THE CHURCH!
SHE WILL *TEACH* THE HUMBLE WAY OF SALVATION!

CRY IN POVERTY AND HOPE,
FOR THIS IS THE CRY WHICH REACHES TO HEAVEN. +

+AMERICAN FREEDOM IS A BLESSING
WHICH FLOWS FROM A DECLARATION
AND A CONSTITUTION
WHICH RESPECTS THE SOVERIEGNTY OF GOD,
THE UNIVERSALITY OF TRUTH,
THE DIGNITY OF THE HUMAN PERSON,
AND THE FREEDOM WITHIN SOUND LAW
TO *PURSUE* HAPPINESS.

LIKEWISE, THE CATHOLIC IS BLESSED
WITH A TWOFOLD REVELATION
IN SCRIPTURE AND TRADITION,
WHICH RESPECTS THE SOVERIEGNTY OF GOD AMONG US,
THE UNIVERSALITY OF CHRIST'S TRUTH,
THE DIGNITY OF EVERY HUMAN PERSON,
AND THE FREEDOM WITHIN GOD'S LAW
TO PURSUE SALVATION AND ETERNAL BEATITUDE.

MAY THE LORD BLESS THE AMERICAN CATHOLIC! +

+THE MORE YOU LOVE, THE MORE YOU UNDERSTAND SCRIPTURE,
BECAUSE THE MORE YOU SEE CHRIST! +

+FOUR FACES, FOUR WINGS, FOUR GLORIOUS CREATURES.
HOLY MESSANGERS: ANGEL, LION, BULL AND EAGLE.
ANNOUNCING THE COMING OF FIERY TRUTH; PROCEEDING FROM THE
FURNACE OF THE FATHER'S BURNING LOVE. +

+AS CHRIST COMMISSIONED THE APOSTLES,
HE WARNED OF THE DIRE CONSEQUENCES
FOR THOSE WHO DID NOT HEED THEIR WORDS.

TODAY,
MANY A CATHOLIC
-TO INCLUDE THOSE IN POWER, POLITICAL AND ECONOMIC-
DO NOT HEED THE WORDS OF THE SUCCESSORS TO THE APOSTLES,
FOUND IN THE BISHOPS OF THE ROMAN CATHOLIC CHURCH.

THE LORD WARNED
OF A FATE WORSE THAN SODOM AND GOMORRAH.

SURELY, THE DOUBTING CATHOLIC TAKES THIS LIGHTLY.
BUT PRAY THE CATHOLIC BISHOP
HEEDS-SERIOUSLY-THE LORDS WORD,
AND HOLDS THEM TO THE TEST! +

+DOES ANYONE *FULLY* GRASP
THE WORDS OF SACRED SCRIPTURE?
DOES ANYONE *FULLY* GRASP
THE TRADITION OF THE LORD?
DOES ANYONE KNOW THE DIRECTION
OF THE SPIRIT IN THE FOUR WINDS?
CAN ANYONE CHALLENGE
THE UNPARALLELED BREADTH AND DEPTH OF MEANING
FOUND IN LAYER UPON LAYER OF SPIRIT INSPIRED WORD?
NOT I! YET I TRUST IN THE LORD'S CHURCH
TO KEEP HIS WORD AND HIS TRADITION, WHICH LASTS FOREVER. +

+PULL AWAY FROM THE PUNDITS, POLLSTERS, AND
PROGNOSTICATORS OF THE WORLD.
TURN FROM THE SNAKE OIL SALESMEN,
THE SEDUCERS, AND THE CYNICS.
RETURN TO THE SCRIPTURES, THE TRADITION, THE SACRAMENTS,
AND THE SAINTS OF THE CHURCH.
REJUVENATE THE MIND, THE HEART, THE SOUL, THE SPIRIT,
AND THE CONSCIENCE,
IN THE STANDARD OF THE SPIRIT OF TRUTH.
THEN...BECOME 'THE HERALD OF GOOD NEWS.' +

THE CREED AND THE CATHOLIC CHURCH

"AS A MOTHER WHO TEACHES HER CHILDREN TO SPEAK AND SO TO UNDERSTAND AND COMMUNICATE, THE CHURCH OUR MOTHER TEACHES US THE LANGUAGE OF FAITH IN ORDER TO INTRODUCE US TO THE UNDERSTANDING AND THE LIFE OF FAITH."
CATECHISM OF THE CATHOLIC CHURCH 171

+AS A BABY I NURSED AT MY MOTHER'S BREAST,
CONTENT IN HER ARMS,
NOURISHED BY THE MILK SHE PROVIDED,
COMFORTED BY HER VOICE ALONE.

NOW FULLY GROWN,
IN SEEMING MANHOOD,
I SEEK CONTENTMENT
IN THE ARMS OF PRECARIOUS CHOICE,
FORRAGING FOR MY OWN MILK
AT THE BREAST OF SEDUCTION,
SEARCHING FOR COMFORT
IN STRANGE AND VARIED VOICES.

AND LIKE A BABE,
TIRED, HUNGRY AND SOILED,
I YEARN FOR THAT TRUE MOTHERLY EMBRACE.

AND GOD UNDERSTANDS!
FOR GOD AS FATHER
UNDERSTANDS OUR MATERNAL DESIRE,
AND HE GRACES US TIMES THREE
IN THE GIFT OF OUR EARTHLY MOTHER,
IN THE GRACE OF OUR PILGRIM MOTHER CHURCH,
AND IN THE MOTHER OF OUR BEATITUDE,
THEOTOKOS,
MARY, OUR HEAVENLY MOTHER. +

+TWELVE APOSTLES, ONE LORD.
TWELVE APOSTLES, ONE SPIRIT.
TWELVE APOSTLES, ONE FAITH.
TWELVE APOSTLES, ONE HOPE.
TWELVE APOSTLES, ONE BAPTISM.
TWELVE APOSTLES, ONE BREAD, ONE BODY.
TWELVE APOSTLES, ONE CUP, ONE MISSION.
TWELVE APOSTLES, ONE APOSTOLATE.
TWELVE APOSTLES, LARGE HARVEST, SO FEW WORKERS.
TWELVE APOSTLES, ONE COMMANDMENT, ABUNDANT GRACE!
TWELVE APOSTLES, ONE CHURCH, ONE LIFE TO CHOOSE!
TWELVE APOSTLES, ONE CROSS...ONE RESURRECTION. +

+THE SIGN OF THE CROSS
REMINDS US OF OUR NEW LIFE IN CHRIST,
FOUND IN OUR BAPTISMAL PLUNGE,
INTO HIS VERY DEATH, AND OUR DEATH TO SIN,
AND OUR NEW LIFE IN SPIRIT AND GRACE.

THE SIGN OF THE CROSS
REMINDS US OF OUR APOSTOLIC MISSION
TO BAPTIZE ALL NATIONS
IN THE MERCY AND GRACES OF THE FATHER,
THE SON, AND THE HOLY SPIRIT.
TO WITNESS IN HOLINESS AND EVANGELIZE IN TRUTH.

THE SIGN OF THE CROSS
REMINDS US OF OUR FAITH
AND OUR HOPE
-THROUGH ALL PASSIONS, ON ALL CROSSES-
OF GOD'S FAITHFULNESS IN RESURRECTION
AND HIS PROMISE OF LIFE TO COME
IN THE VERY PRESENCE OF HIS COUNTENANCE
WITHIN THE SACRED HEART OF HIS LOVE. +

+ON THE ROAD TO EMMAUS,
CHRIST POINTED OUT THE STORIES
THAT POINTED RIGHT BACK TO HIM.
THEIR HEARTS WERE BURNING BECAUSE THE GARDEN, ABRAHAMS
JOURNEY, THE FALL AND THE RISE OF JOSEPH, THE RED SEA MIRACLE,
THE WANDERINGS IN THE DESERT, THE GOLDEN CALF, THE MANNA,
THE ROCK OF LIVING WATER, THE SERPANT ON THE STANDARD, THE
JUDGES, THE PROPHETS, THE KINGS, THE EXILE, AND THE MACCABEAN
STRUGGLES...
ALL POINTED TO GOD'S PROVIDENTIAL MERCY,
CULMINATING IN THE CROSS AND THE EMPTY TOMB
OF THE CRUCIFIED AND RISEN CHRIST.

THIS IS WHERE SALVATION HISTORY,
PRIOR TO AND FLOWING FROM,
DRAWS ALL MEANING: "GOD IS LOVE"
LOVE, INDEED, THAT DIES...
YET, *RISES* FOR A FRIEND. +

+AWESOME IS THE TREE
THAT SPREADS SO HIGH AND WIDE.
AWESOME IS ITS TRUNK,
STRONG TO THE CORE,
AND REACHING DEEP INTO THE EARTH.
AWESOME IS ITS FOLIAGE,
COLORFUL AND CREATIVE,
AS IT DANCES IN THE SPIRIT WIND.
AWESOME IS ITS STEADFAST PRESENCE,
ALWAYS THERE, GIVING AIR FOR OUR BREATHE,
ALWAYS LISTENING.
AWESOME IS THE TREE,
FOR IT PORTRAYS-IN SACRAMENTAL WAYS-
THE GREATNESS OF HER LOVING CREATOR. +

+OPEN THE PAGES OF THE OLD TESTAMENT, ANEW!
READ THE WORDS OF THE *FIRST* TESTAMENT
WITH THE WORD OF GOD
IN YOUR HEART
AND YOUR MIND.
SEE CHRIST
IN CREATION
AND EXODUS
AND PATRIARCHS
AND PROPHETS
AND PRIESTS
AND SACRIFICES
AND KINGS
AND EXILES
AND SUFFERINGS
AND PROMISE
AND SILENCE
AND THE DARK NIGHT...
WITH THE STAR SO BRIGHT! +

+THE CRUCIFIXION IS NOT A PHILOSOPHY!
IT IS LIFE,
BLOOD,
AND PASSION;
MEETING IN LOVE! +

HEAVEN, HELL AND PURGATORY

"LOOKED AT IN THIS WAY, IT IS NOT THE BATTLE BETWEEN THE TWO CITIES OF JERUSALEM AND BABYLON THAT FORMS THE THEOLOGICAL HEART OF HISTORY, BUT A DEEPER, MORE HARD FOUGHT, MORE CRUCIAL STRUGGLE. IT IS THE 'BABYLON WITHIN US' WHICH WE MUST THROW TO THE GROUND AT WHATEVER COST.
HANS URS VON BALTHASAR
A THEOLOGY OF HISTORY

"UNITED WITH CHRIST BY BAPTISM, BELIEVERS ALREADY TRULY PARTICIPATE IN THE **HEAVENLY** LIFE OF THE RISEN CHRIST."
CATECHISM OF THE CATHOLIC CHURCH 1003

"WE CAN RECEIVE THE HEAVENLY BLESSINGS OF SEEING GOD "FACE TO FACE" ONLY WHEN OUR HEARTS ARE WHOLLY **PURIFIED**."
CHRISTOPH CARDINAL SCHONBORN
LIVING THE CATECHISM OF THE CATHOLIC CHURCH

"THE GATES OF HELL ARE LOCKED ON THE INSIDE...IN HEAVEN MAN SAYS TO GOD, 'THY WILL BE DONE;' IN HELL GOD SAYS THIS TO MAN."
C.S. LEWIS
QUOTE ONE: PROBLEMS OF PAIN
QUOTE TWO: THE GREAT DIVORCE

+HEAVENLY MATTERS FIRST:
MATTER DIES! SPIRIT ALWAYS LIVES!
ALL BUT FAITH AND HOPE ARE MERE CLAY OF THE EARTH.
ALL BUT FAITH AND HOPE COME TO DEATH.
FAITH AND HOPE ARE FROM THE BREATH OF GOD,
WHICH IS LOVE.
IN THE END ONLY LOVE REMAINS!

FOR GOD IS LOVE
AND LOVE DESIRES TO LOVE
AND SAINTS ARE LOVE'S DESIRE;
BELOVED IN THE LOVE OF THE LOVER,
EVER BECOMING WILLING LOVERS IN LOVE FIRST RECEIVED.
IN THE END, ONLY LOVERS REMAIN! +

+PURGATION PREPARES FOR PERPETUAL PEACE:
SUFFERING IS: THE CONSEQUENCE OF SIN, OF SINS,
OF OTHER'S SIN, AND OF NATURAL ENCOUNTER.
SUFFERING CAN BE: A SOURCE OF PURITY,
ENLIGHTENMENT, AND STRENGTH.
IN THE TOUGHEST BATTLE WE FACE, AND CHRIST FACED BEFORE US,
-WHICH HE WON IN BITTER SUFFERING-
WE CAN CHOOSE THE PATH OF DESPAIR…
VIEWING SUFFERING AS FROM A VINDICTIVE GOD-
OR WE CAN VIEW SUFFERING
WITH THE GLORIOUS CROSS AS THE BACKDROP
OF HOPE AND LOVE
IN GOD,
WHO IS *ALWAYS* WITH US! +

+HELL IS FREELY CHOSEN!
TO SPURN GOD IS TO GO TO HELL.
FOR THE *GIFT* OF PURGATION
IS FOR THE HEAVEN BOUND PILGRIM ONLY.
FACE AWAY AND SEE NOTHING!
TURN BACK TO GOD AND SEE HEAVEN…
THROUGH THE BEAUTIFUL PATH
OF THE CRUCIFIED! +

+WHAT YOU PLANT NOW, BLOOMS LATER!   +

THE HOLY MASS

"HOW OFTEN I REGRET THAT DAILY HOLY COMMUNION WAS NOT RECOMMENDED WHEN WE WERE YOUNG. I FEEL NOW THAT WE MISSED SO MUCH THAT WOULD HAVE STRENGTHENED US AGAINST THE DANGERS AND TEMPTATIONS OF YOUTH."
FATHER SOLANUS CASEY O.F.M. CAP.
FATHER SOLANUS

"FROM HERE TEILHARD (DE CHARDIN) WENT ON TO GIVE A NEW MEANING TO CHRISTIAN WORSHIP: THE TRANSUBSTANTIATED HOST IS THE ANTICIPATION OF THE TRANSFORMATION AND DIVINIZATION OF MATTER IN THE CHRISTOLOGICAL 'FULLNESS.' IN HIS VIEW, THE EUCHARIST PROVIDES THE MOVEMENT OF THE COSMOS WITH ITS DIRECTION; IT ANTICIPATES ITS GOAL AND AT THE SAME TIME URGES IT ON."
POPE BENEDICT XVI
THE SPIRIT OF THE LITURGY

"AFTER SO MUCH THAT'S SO HEAVY DUTY, THE MASS SEEMS TO END TOO ABRUPTLY-WITH A BLESSING AND 'THE MASS HAS ENDED. GO IN PEACE.' IT SEEMS STRANGE THAT THE WORD 'MASS' SHOULD COME FROM THESE HASTY FINAL WORDS: 'ITE, MISSA EST (LITERALLY, 'GO, IT IS SENT).' BUT THE ANCIENTS UNDERSTOOD THAT THE MASS WAS A SENDING FORTH. THAT LAST LINE IS NOT SO MUCH A DISMISSAL AS A COM*MISS*IONING."
SCOTT HAHN
THE LAMB'S SUPPER

+COME TO THE ALTAR WHERE LIVING WATER FLOWS.
FACING EAST,
EVER VIGILANT FOR THE RISING SON,
THIS ALTAR FLOWS WITH GIFTS OF PRAISE AND THANKSGIVING,
WHICH IN SPIRIT,
BEAR FRUIT IN THE HEALING POWER OF LOVE,
IN CHRIST ETERNAL. +

+ALL
  MEN
  EMBRACING
  NEW LIFE IN CHRIST +

+MERCY
  ENTERS
  REAL
  COMPASSIONATE
  YEARNINGS +

+THE THREE FACES OF CHRIST
IN THE WORD, THE POOR AND THE EUCHARIST,
REVEAL THE THREE FACETS OF GOD
IN GOODNESS, BEAUTY AND TRUTH,
IN THE THREE PERSONS
OF THE FATHER, THE SON AND THE HOLY SPIRIT
IN ONE ESSENCE WHICH IS LOVE,
MOST INTIMATELY EXPERIENCED
AS MERCY.

AND THE FACES
AND THE FACETS
IN THE PERSONS
OF THE TRINITY
BECOME OBSCURED IN SIN AND WOUNDEDNESS AND THE WORLD.

BUT THE CRY OF THE INDWELLING SPIRIT,
AND THE GOSPEL JESUS
BRING US BACK IN BODY AND BLOOD
TO TRUE KNOWLEDGE
OF OUR LOVING FATHER. +

+FIVE LOAVES AND TWO FISH
FED FIVE THOUSAND
WITH TWELVE BASKETS OF SCRAPS COLLECTED.

GOD HAS FULFILLED HIS PROMISES
TO THE TWELVE TRIBES OF ISRAEL
THROUGH JESUS CHRIST
IN THE MINISTRY OF THE TWELVE DISCIPLES.

SEVEN LOAVES FED FOUR THOUSAND
WITH SEVEN BASKETS OF SCRAPS COLLECTED.

GOD FEEDS THE FAITHFUL,
IN THE SEVEN OF ETERNAL FULLNESS,
IN THE APOSTOLIC MINISTRY OF THE TWELVE,
PERPETUATED IN APOSTOLIC SUCCESSION
IN THE PERPETUAL SACRIFICE OF CHRIST ON HIS CROSS
WITHIN THE HOLY MASS
IN THE BODY AND BLOOD OF THE EUCHARISTIC LORD. +

+IN THE WOMB OF THE MOTHER,
IN THE SHADOW OF THE CROSS,
FAITH IN THE LORD, AND HOPE IN SALVATION IS BORN.

IN THE WOMB AND UNDER THE CROSS, DEMONS FLEE,
AND THE WORLD IS TORN ASUNDER!

IN OUR MOTHER, AT THE FOOT OF THE SON,
ANGELS ROAM TOO AND FRO,
PROTECTING GOD'S CHILDREN.

FOR FIRE AND STORM AND BEAST
WILL NEVER OVERTAKE
THE SAFE INHABITANTS OF CHRIST'S CHURCH AND CROSS.

FOR THE BRIDE AND THE GROOM AND THE CROSS
BRING FORTH HIS BLOOD
FOR THE LIFE AND THE LOVE,
WHICH OUTLAST THE ACCUSER,
TIL ETERNITY COME. +

+ENSLAVED,
AND BARREN,
IN A HARSH
AND FOREIGN LAND,
I HAVE BEEN RESCUED
IN GRACE, IN FORGIVENESS
IN LIFE,
TO NEWNESS IN SANCTITY
AND COMMUNION
IN THE BODY AND BLOOD OF FAITH
IN SALVATION
AND HOPE IN HEAVENLY BLISS
TO TASTE
AND TO SEE
THE MERCIFUL FACE OF GOD
IN THE LOVE OF SELF
-IN HOLINESS-
AND THE LOVE OF NEIGHBOR
-IN FORGIVENESS-
AND THE LOVE OF GOD
IN OBEDIENCE AND HUMILITY,
PROTECTED IN REPENTANCE,
AND FED IN CHRIST,
IN THE BODY AND BLOOD,
WHICH MANIFESTS THE CHARITY
OF TOTUS CHRISTUS. +

+**THE** TASTE OF EUCHARTISTIC COMMUNION
IS A FORETASTE OF HEAVEN TO COME.
THE FORETASTE OF HEAVEN TO COME
IS COMMUNION WITH THE DEARLY DEPARTED,
RESTING JOYFULLY AND PEACEFULLY IN THE ARMS OF GOD.
IT IS ALSO A FORETASTE OF TODAY'S SOLIDARITY
IN THE TOIL AND SUFFERING OF A PILGRIM CHURCH.
A FORETASTE OF TOMORROW'S REUNION
IN THE GLORIOUS RETURN OF THE CHRIST,
IN THE PAROUSIA OF THE KING OF THE NEW JERUSALEM.
A FORETASTE OF CHRIST'S CROSS IN SUFFERING GLORY,
IN DEATH'S RELINQUISHMENT OF POWER,
AND IN THE PROMISE OF RESURRECTION TO COME. +

THE WIT AND WISDOM OF MARISSA (12Y/O)

BORN SHE WAS FROM THE WOMB OF MY WIFE.
THE MOST PRECIOUS OF BEAUTY TO ENTER MY LIFE.
WHO IS THIS GIRL
WHOM I HOLD IN MY ARMS,
SO FULL OF LIFE
BLESSED OF THESE ANGELIC CHARMS?
WHO WILL SHE BE,
WHAT WILL SHE DO,
WHAT MUST I BE
TO FATHER HER TRUE?
MY FEAR RUNS SO WILD
WHEN MY DREAMS OF HER UNFOLD,
AS LOVE GROWS FOR THIS CHILD
SO MUST MY FAITH IN GOD BE BOLD!
FOR FATHERHOOD IS MY VOCATION
AND THE SPIRIT IS MY GUIDE,
ALL LIFE MY PREPARATION
WITH CONFIDENCE IN GOD BY MY SIDE!

TIME TO TURN TO MARISSA:

TO RISE ABOVE

WHEN THE DARKNESS CONQUERS ALL-

THE WORLD WILL FALL/

LOVE AND WAR/
WILL BE NO MORE/

LIGHT AND DARK/
NO LONGER APART/

AND EMPTY WORDS FALL/
WITH NO HOPE AT ALL/

CHAINS WILL HANG
FROM EVERY WOMAN
AND EVERY MAN/

OCEANS RED FROM BRAVE WHO BLED/

BUT GOD'S LOVE
WILL HELP US RISE ABOVE/

THE LIGHT WILL WIN
AND CONQUER SIN...

CHECK OUT "HOPE FOR DRY BONES"

BUILDING RELATIONSHIPS
WITH GOD

BY THOMAS V. YANOTI MTS

TO ORDER,
VISIT
WWW.FIGHT4TRUTH.ORG

Made in the USA
Middletown, DE
04 August 2022

70518621R00152